D0302914

Green Infrastructure for Landscape Planning

Green infrastructure integrates human and natural systems through a network of corridors and spaces in mixed-use and urban settings. Gary Austin takes a broad look at green infrastructure concepts, research and case studies to provide the student and professional with processes, criteria and data to support planning, design and implementation.

Key topics of the book include:

- the benefit of green infrastructure as a conservation and planning tool;
- requirements of ecosystem health;
- green infrastructure ecosystem services that contribute to human physical and psychological health;
- planning processes leading to robust green infrastructure networks;
- design of green infrastructure elements for multiple uses.

The concept of ecosystem services is extensively developed in this book, including biological treatment of stormwater and wastewater, opportunities for recreation, urban agriculture and emersion in a naturalistic setting. It defines planning and design processes as well as the political and economic facets of envisioning, funding and implementing green infrastructure networks.

The book differs from others on the market by presenting the technical issues, requirements and performance of green infrastructure elements, along with the more traditional recreation and wildlife needs associated with greenway planning, providing information derived from environmental engineering to guide planners and landscape architects.

Gary Austin is a landscape architect who studied under John Lyle and taught at the California State Polytechnic University, Pomona. He has practiced in the public and private sector and has taught landscape architecture at the University of Washington and the University of Idaho. His teaching and research focus on community revitalization, urban biological diversity and treatment of wastewater and stormwater for water quality improvement.

Green Infrastructure for Landscape Planning

Integrating human and
natural systems

Gary Austin

Routledge
Taylor & Francis Group

LONDON AND NEW YORK

First published 2014
by Routledge
2 Park Square, Milton Park, Abingdon, Oxon OX14 4RN

and by Routledge
711 Third Avenue, New York, NY 10017

Routledge is an imprint of the Taylor & Francis Group, an informa business

© 2014 Gary Austin

The right of Gary Austin to be identified as author of this work has been asserted by him in accordance with sections 77 and 78 of the Copyright, Designs and Patents Act 1988.

Every effort has been made to contact and acknowledge copyright owners. If any material has been included without permission, the publishers offer their apologies. The publishers would be pleased to have any errors or omissions brought to their attention so that corrections may be published at a later printing.

All rights reserved. No part of this book may be reprinted or reproduced or utilized in any form or by any electronic, mechanical, or other means, now known or hereafter invented, including photocopying and recording, or in any information storage or retrieval system, without permission in writing from the publishers.

Trademark notice: Product or corporate names may be trademarks or registered trademarks, and are used only for identification and explanation without intent to infringe.

British Library Cataloguing in Publication Data
A catalogue record for this book is available from the British Library

Library of Congress Cataloging in Publication Data
Austin, Gary (Gary D.)
   Green infrastructure for landscape planning/Gary Austin.
   pages cm
   Includes bibliographical references and index.
   1. Urban ecology (Sociology) 2. City planning – Environmental aspects.
   3. Environmental engineering. 4. Municipal engineering. 5. Ecological
   landscape design. 6. Sustainable urban development. I. Title.
   HT241.A97 2014
   307.76 – dc23
   2013022990

ISBN: 978–0–415–84353–9 (hbk)
ISBN: 978–1–315–85678–0 (ebk)

Typeset in Humanist 777
by Florence Production Ltd, Stoodleigh, Devon, UK

UNIVERSITY
OF SHEFFIELD
LIBRARY

Contents

Acknowledgements

I'd like to thank my colleagues and students at the University of Idaho for the interactions and atmosphere that fostered concepts in this book. The university and the Landscape Architecture Program provided valuable support in the form of a sabbatical, the Paul G. Windley award and support for travel to visit case study projects. Stephen Drown, the program chair, is a continuing inspiration and provided more support than he knows. My wife, Leslie, is an always patient and encouraging collaborator. Thank you. The reviewers, editors and staff at Routledge improved the book through their suggestions and careful work. I thank the many individuals who have shared the wonderful images that illustrate the text. I apologize to my friends and family for the scarcity of interaction during the year of research and writing.

CHAPTER ONE

Introduction

Most planners, landscape architects, architects and engineers have an environmental ethic as well as an eagerness to improve the wellbeing of people. The contradiction of advancing ecologically focused (ecocentric) and anthropocentric values simultaneously may explain the gap between philosophy and what we have built over the last five decades. This ethical dualism arises because the professions are heterogeneous in practice types and application scales. Therefore, many design professionals may focus on the parcel scale and not see the cumulative impact of their work. Also, for many professionals the absence of opportunity and the lack of knowledge might explain ineffective or insufficient application of sustainable urban design. Consideration of environmental values and anthropocentric practice is clouded by a veneer of sustainability rhetoric and a focus on the site scale rather than on the larger, more important issues impacting local ecosystems. The small population of professionals engaged in the planning and design of the built environment may also dampen the expectation that individuals, or even the whole profession, can make meaningful stewardship contributions toward solving the worldwide problems of poor human health, habitat loss, species extinctions, global warming, etc.

Value systems

Ecocentric values

The ecocentric perspective posits that every species should have an equal survival opportunity.[1] An estimated 21–36 percent of the world's mammal species, 13 percent of birds, 30–56 percent of amphibians and 30 percent of conifers are threatened with extinction. The number of threatened species has increased in every category since 1996. In 1996, for example, 3,314 species were in the threatened, endangered and critically endangered categories, compared to 7,108 in 2011.[2]

Fossil records provide us with a normal extinction rate, with the exception of the few mass extinction events, for the earth's history. Today the species extinction rate is 600–6,000 times the normal rate indicated by the fossil record.[3] The primary cause of extinctions and biological diversity (biodiversity) reductions is habitat loss.[4] The rapid growth of the human population and the conversion of land to human use is the reason that the survival of so many species is threatened. Clearly, the ecocentric ethic does not guide enough human decisions to secure the survival of thousands of other species. Is it immorality, ignorance, impotence, unrecognized cumulative impact or intractable problems that result in such destructive behavior by governments, professions and individuals? Have the seven billion humans simply exceeded the carrying capacity of the planet? These are troubling questions and the planning and design professions can begin to address only a few of them. However, there are many opportunities for the design professions to positively impact the lives of people and their relationship to the survival of other species. This book explores the values, concepts, knowledge areas, planning processes and detailed design techniques that lead to positive human and ecosystem outcomes.

Anthropocentric values

Urban design professionals are anthropocentric in their processes and outcomes.[1] The anthropocentric perspective gives humans an elevated status based on philosophical or religious foundations, or simply through overwhelming self-interest. It also expresses man's relationship to the environment in terms of resource management, husbandry of some species or ecosystems instead of others, or conversion of the natural world for the economic and cultural benefit of humans (Figure 1.1).

When involved in community planning or master planning of large developments, landscape architects use participatory and strategic planning processes to resolve conflicts among competing interests. In a deliberative democracy, decisions about land and resource use are social decisions that, ideally, involve the clear communication of information, goals, interests and power relationships. Unfortunately, economic self-interest, political philosophies and social prejudices are all involved in this process, with the possible effect of subverting or corrupting the democratic process. From the perspective of power relationships, the strongest interests and values in the planning process will determine the character of the outcome. Human, and especially economic, interests dominate planning and design solutions since the process itself is anthropocentric.[1] The empirical expression of this is the relentless expansion of

Figure 1.1
Sprawling low-density residential development at the edges of all American cities is represented in this view of Tucson, Arizona. The energy, climate, habitat and other impacts of this growth are well understood and better models have been demonstrated. Photo 32°12′43.87″ N 110°51′23.93″ W by Google Earth.

suburbs. At the current rate of suburban growth we can expect more that 60 million acres of land in the US to be converted within a few decades.

Green infrastructure

Human population growth leads to the loss of biodiversity. The world population is expected to grow from 7 billion to 9.1 billion,[5] while in the US the change from 309 million to 439 million is expected by 2050.[6] The twin impacts of population growth and low-density residential housing are causing more damage than the environment can sustain. Either reductions in population growth or new strategies for high-quality and higher-density residential living are necessary.

Using information emerging from urban ecology and ecosystem research, planners and designers can fashion a set of policies and practices that embed both ecocentric and anthropocentric values into green infrastructure systems at various scales. As a systematic, holistic approach, involving transdisciplinary cooperation, green infrastructure addresses pollution, habitat, recreation, open space and urban form (Figure 1.2).

In addition to the erosion of habitat and subsequent loss of biodiversity, municipal governments are increasingly unable to provide the amenities and services sought by citizens within the political and budget constraints of single-use solutions. We must also adapt to changes in the global climate that will disrupt our food and energy systems and impact natural ecosystems in unpredictable ways.

We need effective and efficient solutions to these problems and others. Furthermore, the solutions should not generate other future problems. In fact, we want solutions that improve the quality of our lives, through better living, working and recreation environments.

Figure 1.2
Restoration of creeks, the creation of constructed wetlands for pollution reduction and high-density mixed-use development can be combined, as at Thornton Creek in Seattle, Washington.

The need to address many problems simultaneously is what makes green infrastructure cost-effective and efficient. A comprehensive network of linear parks, open spaces and habitat patches can structure our neighborhoods and save threatened species. It can remove the pollutants from road runoff and feature inspiring trails through naturalistic landscapes. It can conceal our electrical and data lines below urban agriculture. It can assure the purity of our drinking water, serve as educational resources for our schools and entice new business and residents to locate in our towns and cities.

This book challenges municipalities to reformulate their policies for trails, parkland, stormwater management, wildlife habitat and other green infrastructure components. Green infrastructure won't significantly mitigate greenhouse gas emissions, but it can help us adapt to the changes we can no longer avoid.

Definitions and themes

"Green infrastructure" is a term that is evolving in its meaning. We are familiar with the infrastructure of transportation (highways, bridges, traffic signals, automobiles, petroleum refineries, etc.), potable water (wells, reservoirs, water mains, etc.), sewage treatment, communications (telephone, data, television, radio, internet) and energy generation (hydroelectric dams, transmission lines, transformers, etc.). These foundational systems of urban life are sometimes called gray infrastructure. Even a quick consideration reveals that these systems are important to human health and wellbeing, particularly if the regional food system is also considered to have infrastructure components. This book defines infrastructure as a system of components connected by a network, just as are the transport, communication and electric networks.

There are, of course, networks in nature. Rivers, streams, lakes and oceans compose a natural infrastructure that supports ecological functions. For many plants and animals access to this infrastructure is necessary for survival. It is easy to construct other spatial, energy, material and movement networks, in our imagination, when considering the needs of plants and animals.

As a continuous network of corridors and spaces, planned and managed to sustain healthy ecosystem functions, green infrastructure generates pollution mitigation, recreation, economic value, urban structure, scenic and other human benefits. The context of green infrastructure is suburban and urban, but optimally connects to wild nature and fully functioning ecosystems.

Green infrastructure is a phrase sometimes used to mean the conversion of a gray infrastructure element to a more renewable or sustainable one. For example, photovoltaic generation of electricity is sometimes suggested as a green infrastructure option since it reduces the need for finite fossil fuel. However, that definition is far too narrow to capture the concept advanced by this book. Site scale elements, however environmentally beneficial, are not considered part of the green infrastructure if they are geographically isolated from a network of open-space corridors and spaces. This distinction emphasizes that connectivity between spaces large enough to support ecosystem functions and human use is a critical characteristic. Multiple functions are other key aspects of the definition. Single-purpose solutions, such as stormwater detention ponds, are impoverished green infrastructure components even if they were connected to the network, unless additional benefits of recreation, habitat, water quality improvement and aesthetics are added to them. These secondary benefits increase cost-effectiveness and efficiency through multiple use and compact organization.

In summary, this book will develop the following themes:

- the benefits of green infrastructure as a planning and conservation tool;
- the requirements of ecosystem health and the provision of ecosystem services by healthy ecosystems;
- green infrastructure ecosystem services that contribute to human physical and psychological health;
- planning processes leading to robust green infrastructure networks;
- design of green infrastructure elements for multiple uses.

Green infrastructure model

A model of green infrastructure is presented here as the interaction of three systems. They are, first, ecosystem services (see Figure 1.5), second, ecosystem health (see Figure 1.6) and, third, human physical and psychological health (see Figure 1.3).[7] A healthy ecosystem within the green infrastructure, through the provision of ecosystem services, benefits human health.

Chapter 2 reviews human health and the influence of physical exercise, pollution and the physical environment. Evidence that the indicators optimal for physical and psychological health (Figure 1.3) are improved by the proximity of green infrastructure to living and working environments is discussed.

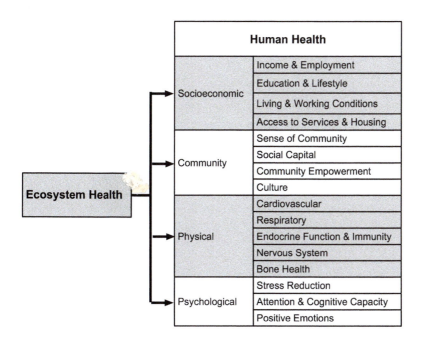

Figure 1.3
Ecosystem health is related to human health. Human wellbeing has four aspects, each composed of contributing parts. Healthy ecosystems sustain human wellbeing in direct and indirect ways. Adapted from Tzoulas, 2007.[7]

Figure 1.3 identifies four categories of human health, at the community and individual scale, which are influenced by the capacity of the ecosystem to deliver services to people. This book will discuss the indices of human health, and the contributions that the ecosystem offers to foster health.

Human conditions and activities also affect every category of ecosystem health (see Figure 1.6). A declining economy often leads to calls for the abandonment or weakening of environmental protections in order to boost economic output. This is a common scenario in the energy, agriculture and forestry sectors. Chapter 3 explores the characteristics of ecosystem health before Chapter 4 addresses the goods, services and intangible benefits provided to humans by a healthy ecosystem.

Green infrastructure components

Figure 1.4 identifies many of the components that could be assembled to form a green infrastructure. Each component is a corridor, place or setting that could contribute to, or detract from, ecosystem health and human wellbeing. Optimally, each element in Figure 1.4 interacts with other components. A green infrastructure might include biological treatment of stormwater and wastewater, as well as opportunities for recreation, urban agriculture and emersion in a naturalistic setting with opportunities for wildlife viewing and diverse habitats for plants and animals. Chapter 5 explores how multidisciplinary teams of planners, landscape architects and engineers with the participation of citizens and city government should organize these interactions to devise a comprehensive green infrastructure. Chapters 6 through 11 provide detailed planning and technical information derived primarily from ecology and environmental engineering to guide planners, landscape architects and engineers in the design of elements that should be included in the system of open spaces and corridors. These elements, such as open-space systems, ecological corridors, stormwater and wastewater treatment facilities and green roofs, can provide significant economic and environmental improvements over current practices. The holistic design of community open space is the topic of Chapter 7, while Chapters 8 and 9 take up the related issues of stormwater management and green roofs, and their contribution to green infrastructure. Community agriculture (Chapter 10) is a topic of increasing interest as planning for greater food security and local economic development is implemented. The technology, spatial requirements and multiple functions of wastewater treatment landscapes are the topics of Chapter 11.

Ecosystem services

Consider the ecosystem functions and services that can be furnished by a green infrastructure (Figure 1.5). The spatial and environmental settings that the many green infrastructure components represent generate outcomes through natural processes that are benefits to the ecosystem and to humans. For example, trees in urban parks reduce air pollution by capturing particulates, improving human health. Similarly, insects and microorganisms decompose fallen leaves and return nutrients to the soil, which benefits plants directly and animals indirectly. The eight ecosystem services identified in Figure 1.5 have either an economic or an intangible value. However,

Green Infrastructure				
Corridors	Ecological	Dispersal	Networks	
		Migration		
		Commuting		
		Urban		
	Streams & Rivers	Wild	Orders	
		Urban		
	Swales	Natural	Orders	
		Stormwater		
	Bike/Pedestrian Paths	Recreation	Networks	
		Commuting		
	Boulevards			
	Utility Infrastructure		Networks	
Spaces	Habitat Preserves		Linked	
	Habitat Fragments		Networks	
	Constructed Wetlands	Stormwater	Linked	
		Wastewater	Linked	
	Parks	Regional	Linked	
		City		
		Neighborhood		
	Yards		Linked	
	Community Gardens		Linked	
	Green Roofs		Linked	
	Plazas	Civic	Linked	
		Commercial		
		Residential		

Figure 1.4
An effective green infrastructure is a network of corridors and spaces assembled from ecocentric, anthropocentric and mixed components. The components can be organized to reinforce each other and lead to land use efficiencies. Ideally, the components are arranged in networks of spaces and corridors. Adapted from Tzoulas, 2007.[7]

these values and the capacity of the ecosystem or green infrastructure to deliver these services are dependent on the health of the ecosystem. Chapters 4 and 5 introduce the processes involved and provide examples of their provision by green infrastructure elements. The point of the chapters is that the ecosystems services are of great value, but can only be provided if ecosystem health is maintained.

Ecosystem health

Figure 1.6 suggests six indicators of ecosystem health. Clearly, if soils in the green infrastructure are compacted, then this will reduce the capacity of the land to provide water purification, nutrient cycling, vegetation and other services or benefits. There

Figure 1.5
Ecosystem services and
products are provided
through green
infrastructure to
humans. The services
flow to human society
only when the viability
of the ecosystem is
maintained. In every
case, the components
listed here are not
independent; instead
they are embedded and
interact within an
ecosystem. Adapted
from Tzoulas, 2007.[7]

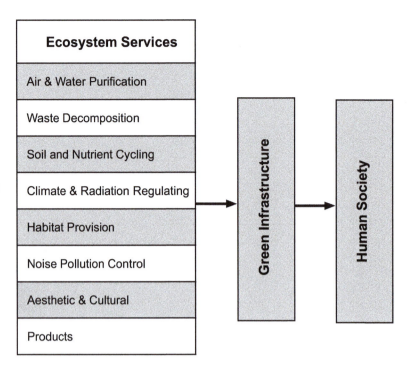

is a clear link between the health of the ecosystem within the green infrastructure and its ability to deliver ecosystem services. Again, there is a great degree of interaction between the various elements contributing to ecosystem health. For example, poor air quality can result in diminished water quality. Each measure of ecosystem health can be improved through a focus on landscape ecology. The spatial and other standards required for planning to achieve ecosystem health in rural and urban settings will be explored. The issue of global warming and the impact that it will have on planning for changes to natural ecosystems are discussed.

Locating and sizing habitat remnants and the ecological corridors that connect them are important contributions to urban ecosystems. The planning and technical issues involved in providing this network to serve both urban ecosystem health and human amenities are the topic of Chapter 6.

Human benefits

This book develops each of the human health topics to discover positive impacts of green infrastructure. Figure 1.3 illustrates that green infrastructure, through healthy ecosystems, makes positive contributions to the individual and the community. Human health, economic and social facets of society are all beneficiaries of landscape infrastructure networks. Careful planning in the location of green infrastructure components is necessary to impact living and working conditions.

The social and cultural dimensions of green infrastructure are topics of Chapters 4 and 7. These chapters advocate for, and provide case study examples of, community health benefits obtained when a compelling green infrastructure generates place

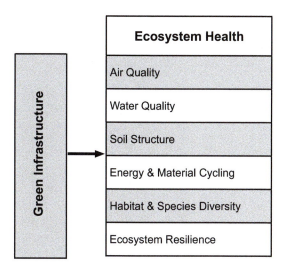

Figure 1.6
Green infrastructure
contributes to
ecosystem health as
defined by six
parameters. Ecosystem
functions create or
maintain the attributes
shown unless impacted
by human or natural
catastrophes. Adapted
from Tzoulas, 2007.[7]

attachment. Citizens are motivated to participate in the improvement and maintenance of civic landscapes when they contribute to the quality of life of the residents. Attention to the configuration, extent and content of the green infrastructure is required to achieve the community benefits. In particular, Chapter 7 emphasizes the planning and public participation processes that lead to the most robust community health system, including the integration of the green infrastructure into residential and urban matrices.

Chapter 5 builds on the principles and concepts of ecosystem health and human benefits to define planning and design processes, as well as the political and economic facets of envisioning, funding and implementing green infrastructure networks. Included is the opportunity for green infrastructure to join new urbanism or smart growth approaches to provide structure and amenities for new development and infrastructure renewal of older urban areas. Green infrastructure planning and design requires an integrated and holistic approach that addresses the full range of possible green infrastructure components at various scales.

A brief history of green infrastructure

Beginning in 1857 Fredrick Law Olmsted, the father of landscape architecture in America, began the design and implementation of enormous, pastoral parks in urban centers in the northeast. Central Park in New York was the first of these, followed by Prospect Park (1859) in Brooklyn and finally Franklin Park (1878) in Boston. However, Olmsted pursued the opportunity to link Franklin Park and a number of other public open spaces in Boston with a stream corridor and even a boulevard. This network of corridors and open spaces of over 1,000 acres, called the Emerald Necklace, was the first municipal-scale open-space planning project in the US. Olmsted believed that naturalistic settings were physically and psychologically restorative and a necessary palliative to the stress created by crowding, air and water pollution, and the long work hours of the emerging industrial economy. The Emerald Necklace was multifunctional, offering many passive recreation opportunities, flood control and wildlife habitat. Olmsted's thinking evolved during his career and despite the success of the large urban parks he said, "No single park, no matter how large and how well designed, would provide the citizens with the beneficial influences of nature." Instead, parks need "to be linked to one another and to surrounding residential neighborhoods."[8] Olmsted's associate, Charles Elliot, added significantly to the Emerald Necklace to create the Metropolitan Boston Park System (1899).

Comprehensive open space and urban design in the United Kingdom was demonstrated according to the theories of Ebenezer Howard when the towns of Letchworth (1904) and Welwyn (1920) were developed along rail lines leading to London. These towns are surrounded by green belts of agriculture and parkland to provide recreation and a limit to growth. Parks are linked to the town center with corridors (Figure 1.7), although these are not naturalistic. The British Garden City concepts were best applied in the US to Radburn, New Jersey in 1928. Here, super-blocks accommodate automobiles in service courts (Figure 1.8) while the residences face public open space that allows access to schools and shopping without crossing roads. While the Great Depression stopped the full development of Radburn, three new towns, Greenbelt, Maryland, Greenhills, Ohio and Greendale, Wisconsin were developed using a similar model, which was abandoned in post-World War II America, unfortunately.

A statewide effort to plan for ecological, recreation and cultural resources was first undertaken by Philip Lewis, a landscape architect working in Wisconsin. He noted that 90 percent of the 220 natural and cultural resources that he mapped occurred along what he called ecological corridors. Lewis articulated two important principles as the result of his study and the formulation of the Wisconsin Heritage Trail Plan (1962). First, preserving the ecological corridors could efficiently provide a wide range of public and natural amenities. Second, the interests of diverse constituent groups were adjacent, coincidental or overlapping within the 190 miles (300 km) of corridors.[8]

Figure 1.7
Letchworth, England. Promenade connecting the city park and train station.

The work of Philip Lewis anticipated the modern challenge of creating even more inclusive green infrastructure networks.

Water and air pollution, as well as toxic waste disasters caused by mining and manufacturing sectors, reached a height in the 1960s that was beyond the mitigation or restoration capacities of local governments. This led to the creation of the US Environmental Protection Agency (1970), National Environmental Policy Act (1970), Water Pollution Control Act (Clean Water Act) of 1972, the Safe Drinking Water Act (1974) and other federal laws and funding to protect the health of Americans. State and municipal governments followed the lead of the federal government in regulating pollution discharges and the protection of threatened and endangered species.

Corridor planning was expanded in the 1970s due to federal legislation to protect the environment and address the problems of water pollution. However, it was during the Lyndon Johnson administration that green infrastructure became a national goal. In 1987 the President's Commission on Americans Outdoors in the USA advocated green networks "to provide people with access to open spaces close to where they live, and to link together the rural and urban spaces in the American landscape threading through cities and countrysides like a giant circulation system."[9]

At this time green infrastructure was defined as a linear landscape (greenway) shared by recreationists and wildlife that was often associated with abandoned rights-of-way and undevelopable land. In 1990 *Greenways for America*[10] by Charles Little inspired the planning and implementation of greenways that established natural or landscaped linear corridors for use as pedestrian and bicycle routes in cities across

Figure 1.8
The residences at Radburn faced the open-space system while the rear of the residence contained the automobile and service functions.

Figure 1.9
Riverside bike and
pedestrian path,
Minneapolis.

the US (Figure 1.9). Despite considerable success, the constituency for greenways was too small to generate the planning, funding and implementation for extensive systems.

In the US greenways emerged from the impulse to provide people with access to the American countryside, while in Europe linear landscapes were initiated to protect wildlife species. Today the American and European counterparts have evolved to express largely the same forms and functions.[11] Over the last two decades the concept of green infrastructure matured from a linear landscape (greenway) to embrace wide-ranging uses. Emerging concern for human health and research demonstrating the benefits or services provided to people by a healthy and proximate green infrastructure has added to the impetus for community-wide networks. Similarly, the startling expansion of cities as low-density metropolitan regions dependent on the automobile, at a time when the production of fossil fuel had passed its peak, inspired New Urbanism and Transit Oriented Design organizations to generate new urban planning concepts intended to make living and working environments more humane and to preserve farm and forest land. Landscape ecologists supported this goal since loss of biodiversity and the rate of species extinction are accelerating. The habitat requirements of plants, animals and birds in the face of increasing urban and suburban expansion were increasingly unmet. The accumulation of evidence that the global climate is being altered by human activities added weight to the desire for more sustainable cities and buildings.

Case studies

This book offers many examples of implemented green structure elements and dedicates Chapter 12 to a case study of Stockholm and Hammarby Sjöstad, Sweden. The second extensive case study is the Stapleton redevelopment project on the east side of Denver, Colorado (Figure 1.10). Discussion and examples from this case study are distributed throughout the book rather than concentrated in a dedicated chapter. This approach links theory, research and implementation within the topically presented chapters.

Stapleton is the largest brownfield infill project in the US. It is located five miles east of downtown Denver, near the junction of Interstate 70 and Interstate 270 and Quebec Street. It was the site of the 345-acre Denver Municipal Airport established in 1929. Eventually the airport grew to 4,700 acres and its agricultural fringe was replaced by the suburban development facilitated by the construction of Interstate 70. Design problems, traffic, limited expansion opportunities and noise complaints caused the city to seek a new location for the airport. In 1989, Adams County and the City of Denver annexed over 35,000 acres for construction of a new international airport.[12] This freed the Stapleton property, which is located only ten minutes from downtown Denver, for redevelopment.

Although some phases are yet to be implemented, the community will occupy 4,700 acres (1,902 hectares) and house more than 30,000 residents and 35,000 workers. It will provide 8,000 homes, 4,000 rental apartments, and contribute a

Figure 1.10
The 29th Avenue Neighborhood Center in Stapleton.

huge amount of office (10 million ft^2/929,000 m^2) and retail space (3 million ft^2/278,700 m^2).[13] Of particular interest is the open-space system of urban plazas, formal parkland and restored habitat.

References

1   K. Nilsson, "Ecological Scientific Knowledge in Urban and Land-Use Planning," in *Ecology of Cities and Towns: A Comparative Approach*, Cambridge: Cambridge University Press, 2009.

2   International Union for Conservation of Nature and Natural Resources, "Summary Statistics," 2011. [Online]. Available: www.iucnredlist.org/about/summary-statistics# Tables_1_2 (accessed 11 April 2013).

3   F. He, "Species–Area Relationships Always Overestimate Extinction Rates from Habitat Loss," *Nature*, vol. 473, pp. 368–371, 2011.

4   R. M. Hassan, S. R. Carpenter, K. Chopra, D. Capistrano and Millennium Ecosystem Assessment, *Ecosystems and Human Well-being*. Washington, DC: Island Press, 2005.

5   US Census Bureau, "International Programs," *International Programs, World Population Summary*, 28 August 2012. [Online]. Available: www.census.gov/population/international/data/idb/worldpopinfo.php (accessed 11 April 2013).

6   US Census Bureau, "The Next Four Decades," 2010. [Online]. Available: www.census.gov/prod/(2010)pubs/p25–1138.pdf (accessed 11 April 2013).

7   K. Tzoulas, K. Korpela, S. Venn, V. Yli-Pelkonen, A. Kaźmierczak, J. Niemela and P. James, "Promoting Ecosystem and Human Health in Urban Areas Using Green Infrastructure: A Literature Review," *Landscape and Urban Planning*, vol. 81, no. 3, pp. 167–178, 2007.

8   R. Ahern, "Greenways in the USA: Theories, Trends and Prospects," in *Ecological Networks and Greenways*, Cambridge: Cambridge University Press, 2004.

9   US Government, *Americans Outdoors: The Legacy, the Challenge*. Washington, DC: US Government Printing Office, 1987.

10 C. Little, *Greenways for America*. Baltimore, MD: Johns Hopkins University Press, 1990.

11 R. H. Jongman and G. Pungetti, *Ecological Networks and Greenways: Concept, Design, Implementation*. Cambridge and New York: Cambridge University Press, 2004.

12 B. Palmberg, "Planning for Large Scale Urban Infill: The Case of the Stapleton Redevelopment," Masters Project, University of North Carolina, Chapel Hill, 2006.

13 Urban Land Institute, "Stapleton," *ULI-Development Case Studies*, vol. 34, no. 4, 2004.

Physical and psychological health

Introduction

Chapter 1 identified the aspects of human physical and psychological health that will be explored in this chapter. Green infrastructure contributes to positive health through opportunities for physical activity and stress reduction. For those in good health, physical activity prevents a wide range of diseases and helps people achieve robust health and even social wellbeing. For those in poor health pursuing physical activity can attenuate chronic, non-communicable disease. Outdoor activity settings require the planning, design and implementation of green infrastructure. This is a rich opportunity for planners, landscape architects and health care professionals to collaborate and achieve significant benefits for people of all ages. This chapter reviews the health status of people living in the US and UK and the relationship of health, physical activity and the environment.

Improved diet and physical activity are inexpensive and effective measures that the individual can take to prevent or reduce the effects of heart disease, stroke, cancer, chronic respiratory diseases and diabetes. These are the five major non-communicable diseases in the world. This kind of disease is responsible for 60 percent of deaths in the world. This percentage is expected to increase by 17 percent over ten years unless people and their governments take measures to reduce the risk factors for these diseases. The elimination of tobacco use, a healthier diet and physical activity would prevent 80 percent of premature heart disease, an equal percentage of strokes and type 2 diabetes and 40 percent of cancer.[1]

Environmental factors, such as exposure to pollutants and extreme temperatures, also impact human health, especially that of the already frail. According to the Center for Disease Control, which collects health and disease data in the US, those at risk for fair to poor health varies widely between cities. The percentage of people at risk can be more than double, depending on the city.

Physical activity

There are many contributors to robust physical health, including good nutrition, exercise and the absence of toxic substances. Maintaining an optimum weight supports positive health, but in the US the percentage of adults 20 years of age and older who are obese increased from 22 percent to 34 percent between 1988 and

Figure 2.1
Fewer than half of the children in the US meet recommended daily activity levels.

2008.[2] Data from the UK reflects a similarly alarming trend.[3] A combination of diet and exercise is necessary to avoid high risks of poor health for those who are obese or overweight.

The US Department of Health and Human Services established physical activity guidelines for Americans in various age groups in 2008, based on premature mortality and other research. Engaging in physical activity for as little as seven hours per week reduces the risk of premature death by 40 percent. The guidelines indicate that children and adolescents should engage in moderate to vigorous activity for at least an hour each day, but only 42 percent of children and 8 percent of adolescents meet this activity level (Figure 2.1). Greater health benefit is associated with more time and more vigorous activity than suggested in this minimum recommendation. There is strong evidence that sufficient physical activity among children and adolescents leads to improved cardio-respiratory and muscular fitness, bone health, cardiovascular and metabolic health, favorable body composition and probably reduces symptoms of depression.[4]

For adults, five hours of moderate or 2.5 hours of vigorous activity per week is recommended, with additional benefits from additional activity time. The exercise is effective in several long sessions or many shorter sessions. At least twice each week adults should engage in muscle-strengthening activity. Only about 23 percent and 17 percent of adults 18–44 years old and 45–65 years old, respectively, meet the recommendations for both aerobic activity and muscle strengthening. Older adults should follow the recommendations for adults, but moderate them based on the presence of any chronic health issues, and focus some activity on maintaining balance. Only about 10 percent of adults older than 65 meet the physical activity recommendations.[2] The data on levels of weekly activity is based on surveys. It is clear, based on direct measures of activity using devices such as accelerometers or pedometers, that self-reported levels are inaccurate. In a study in the UK, collection of data directly from a subset of those surveyed indicated that fewer than one-quarter of the respondents who reported meeting the activity standards actually did.[3]

Scientific evidence supports a long list of health benefits from regular physical activity for adults and the elderly. In the area of disease control, exercise reduces the risk of coronary heart disease, stroke, high blood pressure, adverse cholesterol conditions, type 2 diabetes, metabolic syndrome and colon and breast cancer. Similarly, exercise prevents weight gain, improves cardio-respiratory and muscular fitness, prevents falls, reduces depression and supports cognitive function in older adults. Additional research indicates probable risk reduction for other cancers, bone density loss and better sleep quality.[4] Given the remarkable health benefits that an active lifestyle provides, environmental designers and health care professionals need to be advocates for all measures that foster physical activity.

Cardiovascular health

The cardiovascular system involves the heart, arteries, veins and capillaries. Cardiovascular problems are responsible for most of the premature disease and death in the world. Since these systems are metabolic in nature, they respond rapidly to physical activity. Moderate activity levels reduce the risk of cardiovascular disease by 30 percent, and higher activity levels reduce risk by as much as 40 percent (Figure 2.2). Increasing fitness is measured by the ability to extend exercise duration, which reduces cardiovascular risk by 8 percent for each minute that the activity can be extended. Improvements in cardio-respiratory fitness are the result of exercise sessions as short as ten minutes each, while maintaining the total number of minutes of activity consistent with daily exercise recommendations. This is true for healthy individuals as well as those struggling with several types of cancer and cardiovascular disease, peripheral arterial disease, adverse cholesterol and triglycerides profile, type 2 diabetes, metabolic syndrome and hypertension.[4] Since the proportion of Americans that engage in active lifestyles is abysmally low among all age groups and because of the great impact of non-communicable diseases, attention to physical activity promotion is an urgent public issue as well as a concern for individuals.

Aerobic activity for 40 minutes, three to five times per week, is effective at reducing blood pressure. Blood pressure fluctuates between a maximum (systolic) and minimum (diastolic) amount. Normal blood pressure is 112 mmHg systolic pressure and 64 mmHg diastolic pressure, although there is great variability between individuals (mmHg is a measure of pressure exerted at the base of a column of Mercury 1 mm high). As little as a 2 mmHg drop in resting systolic blood pressure reduces the chance of death from heart disease and stroke and a 5 mmHg decrease in systolic pressure reduces mortality from heart disease and stroke by 9 percent and 14 percent, respectively (this is equivalent to 27,600 lives in the US). Chronically high blood

Figure 2.2
Less than 30 percent of high-school students get at least 60 minutes of physical activity every day. Pedestrian and bicycle paths, separated from roads, provide attractive exercise opportunities and less polluted air.

pressure (hypertension) is an indicator of heart disease and stroke risk. For hypertensive people, aerobic exercise is especially effective in reducing blood pressure (about a 7 mmHg drop).[4]

Stiffening of the arteries responds positively to regular exercise, but best results come from undertaking an exercise program while health is good. LDL (bad) cholesterol is a dietary or genetic problem and is not affected by physical exercise, but HDL (good) cholesterol and triglycerides are positively affected by regular exercise.[4]

Respiratory fitness

Maximum VO^2 is a measure of the greatest amount of oxygen a person's body can consume in one minute and is an indication of respiratory fitness. Sedentary people can increase their maximum VO^2 by about 17 percent by gradually increasing the frequency and intensity of aerobic activity until they can walk briskly, or jog for 200 minutes per week. This represents about 12 miles of walking or jogging per week, but any equivalent aerobic activity will achieve the same respiratory benefit, although variety in exercise frequency and intensity seems to enhance positive outcomes. Several exercise sessions per week are more beneficial than infrequent, long sessions.[4]

Green infrastructure for aerobic activity

With the understanding that adults need 2.5–5.0 hours of activity, depending on how vigorous it is, and that, of this activity, 40 minutes should involve aerobic activity five times per week, then what should the green infrastructure provide to encourage participation? It is immediately clear that there are spatial, temporal, physical and social factors involved in the definition of our hypothetical activity area. Beginning with the physical and spatial elements, assume a neighborhood park occupying a typical 300′ × 250′ block. This is 1.7 acres (0.69 ha) with a perimeter of only 0.15 miles (0.24 km). If a person walks at four miles per hour (mph) then they would need to make 17 circuits around the park to satisfy a single 40-minute activity requirement. Regardless of how beautiful the landscape, no one would find satisfaction doing this day after day. So the typical neighborhood park is too small. Conversely, a single, 40-minute circuit around a park would require 278 acres, which is unlikely to be available in the neighborhood. Unless the neighborhood park contains stationary exercise equipment, or aerobic classes (see Figure 2.6), it is not suitable for walking or jogging for exercise. Of course, one could walk around the neighborhood, but there are a surprisingly large number of barriers to walking in neighborhoods. Sidewalks are absent or in poor repair, traffic noise, fumes and hazards, steep terrain, lack of trees for shade, dogs, the absence of benches and sometimes a crime risk make the neighborhood unsuitable. Therefore, the first green infrastructure requirement for the support of daily physical activity is neighborhood walkability. However, a better solution is a nearby path separated from the road that is designed explicitly for a great walking or biking experience.

Air pollution

Especially those living in dense urban areas are impacted by poor air quality and worry that exercising outdoors could harm their respiratory health. Although the atmosphere contains particles from natural sources, such as dust and particles from forest fires, this amount is multiplied by human activities. Some of the added particles, such as plasticizers, are exclusively human in origin. Characterizing air quality – to guide citizens in their individual actions and to guide agencies charged with protecting public health – is complex since many substances are involved. The US Environmental Protection Agency collects data on six pollutants that are regulated by the Clean Air Act since they are known to cause human or environmental damage. Carbon monoxide, lead, nitrogen dioxide, ozone, particulate matter of different size fractions and sulfur dioxide are the six pollutants, but they are joined by another set of 188 air toxins known to cause cancer or other serious diseases.

Carbon monoxide and lead are almost entirely from human sources, principally vehicle emissions, but these have dropped 75 percent since 1980 for carbon monoxide and virtually eliminated for lead. Similarly, nitrogen oxides are almost all the result of the combustion of fuels. These gases are highly reactive and contribute to the production of ozone and acid deposition, which have significant negative human and ecosystem health impacts. The amount of nitrogen oxide emission varies significantly by region and is related to fossil fuel combustion for generation of electricity.

In the northeast and north-central portions of the US acid rain and acidification of water bodies is a significant problem. However, compared to the 1992 levels, the ambient level of nitrogen dioxide is well below the national air quality standard, and nationally the emission of nitrogen oxides decreased by 17 percent between 1990 and 2002.

Nitrogen oxides react with volatile organic compounds and sunlight to produce ozone. Human sources of these compounds are industrial processes, chemical manufacturing and combustion of fossil fuels in power production. However, forest trees and other natural sources produce most (72 percent) of the volatile organic compounds in the atmosphere. Vehicles cause less than half of the anthropogenic volatile organic compounds. These gases are important because they react to form ozone. Some, like benzene, are very harmful to human health. Human-caused emissions of volatile organic compounds dropped 25 percent between 1990 and 2002.[4]

At ground level breathing high levels of ozone creates many respiratory problems and exacerbates others, such as asthma and lung diseases (Figure 2.3). Ozone is probably responsible for premature death of some patients with existing respiratory diseases. Although ozone levels have been gradually dropping in the US for 25 years, in most regions they remain above the national air quality standard. Ozone is the most pressing air pollution problem in the nation.[4] Shading of the street by trees or other objects reduces the formulation of ozone. Ozone levels drop markedly with increasing distance from the edge of busy streets.

Mercury and benzene are air toxics of principle concern. Benzene is found in gasoline. In fact, a large proportion of the hazardous air pollutants is associated

Figure 2.3
Sometimes emissions, meteorology and topography conspire to create unhealthy air in cities around the world. Pollution, as overwhelming as shown in this image of Kuala Lumpur, creates short-term health crises for those suffering from chronic respiratory disease and unhealthy conditions for everyone.

with vehicles. The largest proportion of toxic air emissions is related to stationary sources like factories, refineries and power generators. Other sources of toxic air pollutants are dry-cleaning facilities (perchloroethylene), industrial solvents (methylene chloride) and indoor sources such as cleaning solvents and construction materials. Only a small proportion of toxic emissions come from natural sources such as volcanoes and forest fires. It is heartening to report that in the US the emission of toxic air pollutants decreased from more that seven million tons to about 4.6 million tons per year between 1990 and 2002.[5]

The control of air pollutants, such as sulfur dioxides and particulates, has been improved by regulations adopted across the world. Pollution from combustion of fossil fuel is linked to a range of detrimental health effects ranging from cardiovascular to infections disease.[6] One measure of air quality is the amount of solid and liquid particulates in the air. Particles less that 10 micrometers (PM10) can enter the lungs and cause respiratory disease, bronchitis, impaired lung function, lung cancer and other problems.[7] Humans, through fossil fuel combustion for electrical power generation, petroleum production and other industrial processes, produce 14 percent of particulates (PM10). In the US, the anthropogenic PM10 dropped 27 percent between 1990 and 2002, although it increased in two regions of the country. A major source (60 percent) of particulates is road dust.[5] Airborne particulates collect on plant leaves and bark where they are held until they are washed away by precipitation.

Despite the negative health impact of poor air quality, the cardiovascular and respiratory benefit of frequent and vigorous exercise substantially outweighs the impact of a sedentary lifestyle except in the most polluted cities. Nevertheless, attention to air pollution advisories is prudent, especially for those with respiratory problems. During periods of high air pollution, exercising indoors where there is an advanced air filtration system makes sense.

Green infrastructure and air quality

The negative impact of air pollution and its heightened level at the road edge and in very dense urban centers is a disincentive for physical activity. The exposure to pollutants is highest within the traffic lane, but diminishes rapidly as one moves to the road edge and beyond. More roadside planting, especially along gravel roads, provides a distinct health benefit. As with the earlier walking-in-the-park hypothesis, planting the street edge is a remedial response that is sorely needed, but to encourage physical activity removing the bicyclist and pedestrian from the road edge to a dedicated path is more likely to encourage regular physical activity, especially if the path is well vegetated (Figure 2.4).

Green infrastructure should provide paths and connect to sport facilities that are also separated from heavily trafficked roads to avoid significant exposure to air pollution from vehicles. In addition, progressively increasing the limits on the emission of particulate and other air pollution is important to improve human health. A lifelong reduction in lung function is associated with childhood life in cities with high air pollution. Air polluted with particulates, nitrogen oxides, ozone and sulfur dioxide is estimated to annually cause two million deaths worldwide.[6] These health hazards need urgent consideration by policy makers, planners and designers.

Figure 2.4
A landscape setting can
be planned to avoid the
highest levels of
pollution from vehicles
and to capture
particulates.

Endocrine functions and immunity

Good metabolic health is maintained by a healthy weight (body mass index of 18.5–25 or a body fat percentage of 21–24 for women and 14–17 for men), regular exercise, not smoking and eating a diet rich in fiber, such as whole grains, beans, fruits and vegetables. Poor metabolic health is characterized by increased blood pressure, a high blood sugar level, excess body fat or abnormal cholesterol levels (Figure 2.5). These conditions can lead to metabolic syndrome and diabetes. In the US, 47 million people have metabolic syndrome and 20.8 million Americans suffer from type 1 or type 2 diabetes. About 90 percent of those with diabetes have type 2. Type 1 is a chronic disease affecting children and adolescents and is increasing around the world at about 2–3 percent per year. There is also a startling increase in the number of children and adolescents who have type 2 diabetes. Those with diabetes have three times the risk of cardiovascular disease and premature death.[4]

A sedentary lifestyle, characterized by several hours per day watching television or at a computer, doubles the risk of metabolic syndrome. Conversely, moderate-intensity physical activity for about 2.5 hours per week has been shown to reduce this syndrome and to prevent type 2 diabetes. In one study, people with metabolic syndrome engaged in aerobic exercise for 20 weeks. This eliminated the syndrome in 30.5 percent of those who engaged in the physical activity, compared to a control group. Increasing muscular fitness also reduces the risk of metabolic syndrome.

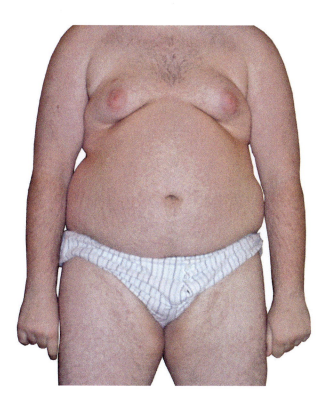

Figure 2.5
Obesity is a problem in many developed countries. Perhaps most alarming is the increase in obesity among children. In 2008 nearly one in five children over the age of five was obese.[2]

Bone health

Bone is living tissue where cells are gained and lost throughout life. However, there is more gain than loss in bone mass and strength until about 35 years of age. Older adults lose more bone strength than they generate. Osteoporosis, an age-related disease that affects 44 million Americans, is characterized by increased porosity of the bones due to losses in protein and minerals, especially calcium. When the mass of the bones diminishes it leads to bone fractures, especially fractures of the hip, spine and wrist. Hip and spine fractures often require major surgery, putting the elderly patient at risk. Women are five times more likely than men to develop osteoporosis after menopause due to reduced estrogen production.

Drugs are available to treat osteoporosis, but diet and exercise are important for all adults to maintain high levels of bone density. In fact, the development of peak bone density as a young person improves bone health later in life. Using X-ray and ultrasound technologies, in a study of over 700 young men, researchers measured bone mineral density, bone microarchitecture and bone geometry. They discovered that greater amounts of weight-bearing physical activity led to better bone shape and to higher peak bone density.[8] In youth and middle age, activities such as aerobics, dancing, jogging, tennis, walking and lifting weights build healthy bones. Elderly people may require gentler weight-bearing exercise, but it cannot be omitted from a healthy lifestyle.

Exercises as simple as five exercise sets of ten vertical and twisting hops are an effective weight-bearing program to increase bone density. The hops apply a force of about 2.5 times body weight on the femur and hip, common osteoporosis fracture points. This physical activity builds bone density and reduces the risk of fractures. Engaging in the exercise every day over a six-month period increases bone mass density about 2 percent compared to a small loss in those with no exercise activity. Engaging in the activity four days per week reduces the gain to about 1 percent. Animal studies suggest that even small percentage gains in bone density significantly increase the amount of stress that bones can bear before fracture.[9]

In summary, the physical health of Americans seems to be deteriorating due to weight gain and the lack of sufficient physical activity. While there are certainly adverse health impacts from exposure to environmental pollution, this burden on physical health is less than in previous decades. Planning and design have a role to play in the continued reduction in exposure to environmental pollutants and in the provision of landscapes that foster physical activity. Satisfying the need for muscle-strengthening and weight-bearing activities is easier in neighborhood parks since the spatial requirements are small. Nevertheless, deliberate attention to the settings and equipment needed for this activity is necessary. Creating programs or classes at parks and targeting various age groups to teach safe exercise practices, build social support networks and introduce a variety of activities may be as important for encouraging daily physical exercise as providing the space and facilities (Figure 2.6).

Figure 2.6
Programming activities in parks encourages regular physical activity and teaches safe techniques. Fred Fusilier leads a fitness aerobics class during the Health and Wellness Department Fitness Expo in 2009.

Psychological health

Recovery from stress

The restorative effect of activities in a naturalistic setting was a central tenant in the philosophy of landscape architect Fredrick Law Olmsted, who contributed to the design of Central, Prospect and Franklin Parks in the second half of the nineteenth century. Most people have had experiences in nature through hiking, camping, boating, bicycling or many other pursuits where they felt the wonder of nature. The majesty of soaring mountains, precipitous canyons or towering trees creates a sense of awe. The complexity and variety of plants and insects is mysterious and astounding. Emersion in exquisite environments like those protected in national parks provides these satisfying emotions for the millions of people who visit these special places each year.

While not as sublime, nature in urban parks, and natural areas near our neighborhoods, also provide humans with satisfying experiences (Figure 2.7). In fact, the daily opportunity for contact with nature may be more important to our personal wellbeing than the thrilling excursions in our national parks. While nearly everyone has personal experience of the benefit of naturalistic spaces, researchers have still tried to isolate the factors that seem to resonate in people. It turns out to be a rather difficult phenomenon to objectively research because there are so many variables at play. One factor is simply that the urban context is stressful.

Figure 2.7
A spring day draws office workers together for lunch, socializing and sunbathing.

Urban areas are noisy, filled with visual stimuli and more polluted. There is traffic and perhaps threats from crime to be constantly aware of. We know that stress over long periods has harmful effects on psychological and physical health. Research shows that regular walks in the woods lead to a reduction in the secretion of cortisol, a stress hormone. Compared to those walking in the suburban environment, the forest walkers reported less anxiety and a much-improved mood. Of course, urban areas also provide social opportunities and the positive stimulation of great architecture, products and other man-made wonders, but occasionally the stimulation presented by our urban environment, jobs and personal relationships feel burdensome. More than one study suggests that urban living is stressful enough to become evident in surveys of psychological health.

A study, using the data collected by the Center for Disease Control from over 60,000 respondents from 94 counties within 24 states in the US, analyzed self-reported information on the level of psychological distress. People living in urban counties were found to be at 17 percent higher risk for both mild to moderate, and serious psychological stress compared to those living in rural counties.[10] Perhaps provision of naturalistic parks within urban centers, as shown in the example from London (Figure 2.8), is more necessary as an opportunity for stress relief and exercise than we previously imagined.

Attention capacity, cognitive capacity and sleep

Perhaps we are evolutionarily predisposed toward natural scenes. This might explain why a walk in a lightly forested area produces positive emotions, while a similar walk in a medium-density urban setting elicits the opposite.[11] Perhaps people process stimuli in natural settings differently than in urban settings. This concept is supported by studies on attention and, more concerning, attention deficit hyperactivity disorder (ADHD), which afflicts two million children in the US.

A study of 16 children with ADHD, 7–12 years old, reported the effect of 20-minute walks in three different environments on the ability of the children to perform tasks requiring attention and concentration. The walking environments were in an urban park, a suburban neighborhood and a downtown area. All of the walking environments were chosen to offer similar characteristics. They were well maintained, flat, quiet and had minimal levels of pedestrian traffic. The walks were conducted after sessions of puzzle-solving activities intended to create attention fatigue. The park walks resulted in restoration of attention and significant improvement in the ability to concentrate compared to walking in the other environments. The park walk had an effect similar to the peak effectiveness of two drugs commonly used to treat ADHD.[12] This result supports other studies demonstrating the benefit of natural areas for relief from stress and has important implications for the design of schools and neighborhood open space. If people with ADHD are surrounded by nature, at their home for example, there are long-term benefits, but even short-term exposure to a natural setting provides short-term benefit. There is research evidence of stress and depression reduction from outdoor activities.

Research clearly demonstrates that time spent in a natural setting has a positive effect on the psychological health of humans. Being physically active also has

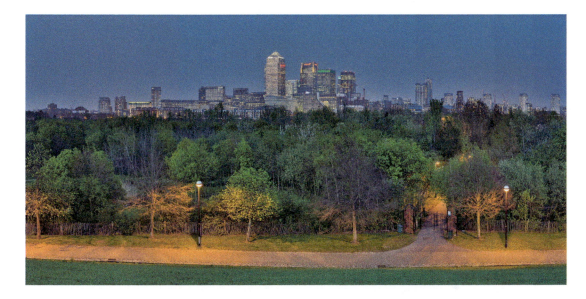

psychological benefits. Aspects of cognitive function are improved, and engaging in regular physical activity reduces some symptoms of dementia. This activity can delay the onset of dementia.[4]

Regular, restorative sleep is an important aspect of human health. Unfortunately, sleep deprivation, arising from 70 sleep disorders, affects 50–70 million Americans each year. Physical activity programs can significantly improve sleep quality. One study demonstrated that those engaged in regular physical activity were 40 percent less likely to have insomnia than those who were sedentary. The impact of sleep disorders on the economy is similarly high. An estimated $50 billion is the cost to business due to reduced productivity of employees suffering from sleep disorders and daytime sleepiness.[4]

Figure 2.8
Natural or naturalistic landscapes adjacent to high-density urban environments provide people with opportunities to disengage from the stress of urban life or personal problems.

Positive emotions

Self-esteem is an indicator of psychological adjustment. Physical activity seems to have some effect on self-esteem and certainly increases among adults as their physical fitness increases. In fact, physical activity ameliorates serious mental health conditions. The effect is strongest for depression and cognitive decline and dementia associated with aging. Activity also improves problems of poor sleep, anxiety and fatigue.[4]

Depression is a condition that affects 4 percent of men and 8 percent of women in the US, and costs the nation about $83 billion per year. The core symptoms of depression are low motivation, fatigue and reduced pleasure. Mild to moderate depression is common and harms physical health and job performance and leads to inactivity and social irritability.[13] In the US, active people are 30 percent less likely to have symptoms of depression than inactive people. Studies in other countries have found that activity reduces the risk of having depression by 45 percent.[4] Anti-depressant drugs are no longer recommended for treatment of mild to moderate

Figure 2.9
Social benefits are other
important aspects of
green infrastructure and
group sport
opportunities.

depression. Their effectiveness is limited and their side-effects outweigh their benefits. Instead, counseling and physical exercise, such as guided and structured physical activity for 45 minutes, three times per week over ten weeks, are often recommended.[14]

Vigorous physical activity has been shown to reduce depression symptoms, but walking regimens are also effective according to a review of eight excellent research trials. Almost all participants in the trials were diagnosed with moderate depression, with the exception of a small group who were not depressed but overweight. The participants were adults over 18 years old (most of the studies focused on adults older that 50) and selected primarily from primary care settings in psychiatric hospital inpatient or outpatient programs. The participants did not include those with bipolar disorders, mental illness or those suffering from diseases such as cancer.[14]

Depression was significantly reduced in six of eight trials by exercise, but the exact mechanism is not confirmed. Activity intensity, duration and context are probably responsible for reduced depression, but energy expenditure is not directly related to its reduction. There was also a lack of correlation between physical fitness and reduction in depression. Research is needed on the impact of walking frequency, activity intensity, duration and type, such as indoor, outdoor, individual or group situations.[14]

Physical infrastructure for promotion of health

The first part of this chapter established the undeniable physical and psychological health benefit of physical activity. Chapters 5 and 7 will address specific measures to consider in the planning and design of landscapes focused on recreation and physical activity. Time in natural settings reduces stress and improves our outlook, while physical activity, fostered by those landscapes, promotes human health. Therefore, these twin benefits should be promoted by the collaborative efforts of those shaping the built environment and health care professionals. Research indicates that the design of the physical environment does not induce physical activity, but it does afford the opportunity for physical pursuits and emotional satisfaction. This may seem a semantic distinction, but it points out that there are many personal and social factors that influence whether people engage in physical activity. Activity programming and education can encourage people to be more active and secure the physical and psychological benefits it offers. However, the public landscape must be available for activity. The planning and design of that landscape needs to focus on removing obstacles to use and then on creation of supportive and satisfying environments that sustain use and interest.[15]

There are at least 12 environmental attributes that can be modified by planning and design to contribute to the amount of physical activity people participate in daily. The access, density and the proximity of parks and other recreation facilities support activity. Similarly, research shows that the density of residential dwellings

Figure 2.10
Beautiful landscape opportunities to walk, bicycle and explore encourage physical activity. Even places to rest improve human health.

and the distribution of retail shops, schools and other destinations can be organized to foster more daily walking. Walking needs an infrastructure and its character, especially in an automobile-dominated setting, is critical to the amount and enjoyment of walking for pleasure or transportation. The control of traffic speed and volume is particularly important in safe routes to schools for children, but also for healthy walking opportunities for adults. This is also true for promotion of bicycling where in-street lanes and preferably dedicated paths and connectivity throughout the community lead to increased activity. No single factor listed above is consistently associated with increased physical activity. This suggests that removing as many impediments to the use of the outdoor environment and creating or improving as many incentives to use as possible may create landscapes that best promote physical activity.[16]

A study of older adults seems to contradict the general evidence that the design of the urban environment does not lead directly to an increase in physical activity. Proximity to green space did lead to greater physical activity in people of 60 years or more,[17] and vigorous physical activity by young adults.[16] For older adults, social support by friends and family and good neighborhood safety lead to greater physical activity.[17]

One study used life span as an indicator, since it is one of the many dimensions of human physical health. The study demonstrated that the presence of walkable green spaces, including tree-lined streets, in urban residential districts (Figure 2.11) increased longevity in senior citizens. The five-year study in Tokyo of over 3,000 ambulatory residents ranging in age from 74 to 91 years old at the initiation of the study showed that those with nearby green space lived longer. This result was not changed by variables of socio-economic status, age, gender or marital status. The physical attributes of the environment, including the amount of sunlight reaching the residence, nearby parks, walkable green streets and reduced noise from auto-mobiles and factories, predicted longer life spans. Accessible green space was the most important of these factors. The implication of these results is that planning and design of green space within dense urban areas where residents have no access to private open space will result in better health of senior citizens.[18]

Similarly, for children several factors contribute to greater physical activity. A positive pedestrian environment with low traffic volumes and speed, access to nearby recreation facilities, a mixture of residential densities and, finally, a mixture of residential and commercial and open space are associated with greater physical activity of pre-adolescent children. For adolescents, mixed land use and residential density are the factors contributing most to increased physical activity.[16]

People use outdoor spaces for stress reduction.[19] A person's level of stress seems to be related to their preference for certain outdoors activities and the sensory content of various landscape types. A Swedish study of 953 participants assessed their levels of stress and concluded that those more likely to experience high stress were younger adults, particularly women, those who more often took sick-leave, those with small children, those dissatisfied with their home environment and those with poorer access to green space, but wishing to use public green spaces more often. Participants in the study identified activity preferences from a list of 70 options. The 70 activities were grouped into 17 activity types. The most stressed participants

Figure 2.11
Pedestrian amenities
such as paving, seating,
plenty of space to
socialize and
opportunities to eat
and shop encourage
walking even on a cool
winter day.

preferred restful activities, animal activities and walking activities. Playing with small animals or watching and studying pets or exotic animals characterize the type of animal activities. Rest activities include enjoying the weather and fresh air, viewing wild plants, resting in a green, open space and being in a place to experience quiet and reduced activity. Walking for recreation and to enjoy natural or ornamental vegetation and to enjoy the seasons and fresh air are in the walking activities group.[20]

The landscape attributes preferred by those with high levels of stress are places offering a sense of refuge and those that seem completely natural.

People can readily classify spaces based on sensory information that they perceive (Figure 2.12). A classification of landscape types has evolved based on research beginning in 1980. Eight landscape types include serene, spacious, natural, rich in species, and those offering cultural and social opportunities and those offering refuge and prospective vantage points.[19] Landscapes offering refuge are characterized by a sense of safety, enclosure and opportunities to watch active adults and children. The natural category is characterized by a wild or seemingly untouched landscape.

In the Swedish study, the preferred sensory characteristics of the landscape were paired to the preferred activities to find if there were significant correlations for highly stressed people. The most highly ranked activity and sensory pair for people with high stress was animal activities associated with natural sensory elements. The next highest-ranking pairs of activity and sensory type were animal activities/refuge and rest activities/nature. The third-ranking pairs were animal activities/rich in species, and rest activities/nature.[20] This research is significant because it illustrates that

Figure 2.12
People experiencing high levels of stress prefer certain landscape characteristics. This image expresses a sense of refuge, high species presence, the prospect of seeing wildlife and a sense of undisturbed nature.

planning and design can respond to the needs of various population groups. Effective pairing of activities and the spatial or sensory characteristics of spaces lead to better user satisfaction. It also suggests that the public landscape needs to be heterogeneous to respond to the expectations and desires of a diverse population.

The following chapters accept the evidence that Americans, Britons and others in developed countries have diminished physical activity profiles that increase their risk for a host of non-communicable diseases. The change to more sedentary work and leisure activities is certainly a factor, but the planning and design of the physical environment, and especially the green infrastructure network, will lead to better health and wellbeing. The details of how to plan and implement this network are the subjects of the following chapters.

References

1   World Health Organization, "Interventions on Diet and Physical Activity: What Works – Summary Report," 2009.
2   US National Center for Health Statistics, "Health, United States, 2010: With Special Feature on Death and Dying," 2011.
3   Health and Social Care Information Centre, Lifestyles Statistics, "Statistics on Obesity, Physical Activity and Diet: England, 2013," 2013.
4   US Department of Health and Human Services, "2008 Physical Activity Guidelines for Americans," 2008.
5   US Environmental Protection Agency (EPA), "EPA's 2008 Report on the Environment," National Technical Information Service, Washington, DC, Environmental Assessment EPA/600/R-07/045F, 2008.

6   J. Thornes, "Atmospheric Services," in *Ecosystem Services*, vol. 30, 2010, pp. 70–103.
7   R. M. Hassan, S. R. Carpenter, K. Chopra, D. Capistrano and Millennium Ecosystem Assessment, *Ecosystems and Human Well-Being*. Washington, DC: Island Press, 2005.
8   K. I. Eleftheriou, J. S. Rawal, L. E. James, J. R. Payne, M. Loosemore, D. J. Pennell, M. World, F. Drenos, F. S. Haddad, S. E. Humphries, J. Sanders and H. E. Montgomery, "Bone Structure and Geometry in Young Men: The Influence of Smoking, Alcohol Intake and Physical Activity," *Bone*, vol. 52, no. 1, pp. 17–26, 2013.
9   C. A. Bailey and K. Brooke-Wavell, "Optimum Frequency of Exercise for Bone Health: Randomised Controlled Trial of a High-Impact Unilateral Intervention," *Bone*, vol. 46, no. 4, pp. 1043–1049, 2010.
10 S. S. Dhingra, T. W. Strine, J. B. Holt, J. T. Berry and A. H. Mokdad, "Rural–Urban Variations in Psychological Distress: Findings from the Behavioral Risk Factor Surveillance System, 2007," *International Journal of Public Health*, vol. 54, no. S1, pp. 16–22, 2009.
11 T. Hartig, G. W. Evans, L. D. Jamner, D. S. Davis and T. Gärling, "Tracking Restoration in Natural and Urban Field Settings," *Journal of Environmental Psychology*, vol. 23, no. 2, pp. 109–123, 2003.
12 A. Faber Taylor and F. E. Kuo, "Children With Attention Deficits Concentrate Better After Walk in the Park," *Journal of Attention Disorders*, vol. 12, no. 5, pp. 402–409, 2009.
13 F. D. Legrand and C. R. Mille, "The Effects of 60 Minutes of Supervised Weekly Walking (in a Single vs. 3–5 Session Format) on Depressive Symptoms among Older Women: Findings from a Pilot Randomized Trial," *Mental Health and Physical Activity*, vol. 2, no. 2, pp. 71–75, 2009.
14 R. Robertson, A. Robertson, R. Jepson and M. Maxwell, "Walking for Depression or Depressive Symptoms: A Systematic Review and Meta-Analysis," *Mental Health and Physical Activity*, vol. 5, no. 1, pp. 66–75, 2012.
15 C. Ward Thompson, "Activity, Exercise and the Planning and Design of Outdoor Spaces," *Journal of Environmental Psychology*, vol. 34, pp. 79–96, 2013.
16 D. Ding, J. F. Sallis, J. Kerr, S. Lee and D. E. Rosenberg, "Neighborhood Environment and Physical Activity Among Youth," *American Journal of Preventive Medicine*, vol. 41, no. 4, pp. 442–455, 2011.
17 M. L. Booth, N. Owen, A. Bauman, O. Clavisi and E. Leslie, "Social-Cognitive and Perceived Environment Influences Associated with Physical Activity in Older Australians," *Preventive Medicine*, vol. 31, no. 1, pp. 15–22, 2000.
18 T. Takano, "Urban Residential Environments and Senior Citizens' Longevity in Mega-City Areas: The Importance of Walkable Green Space," *Journal of Epidemiology and Community Health*, vol. 56, no. 12, pp. 913–918, 2002.
19 U. K. Stigsdotter, O. Ekholm, J. Schipperijn, M. Toftager, F. Kamper-Jorgensen and T. B. Randrup, "Health Promoting Outdoor Environments: Associations between Green Space, and Health, Health-Related Quality of Life and Stress Based on a Danish National Representative Survey," *Scandinavian Journal of Public Health*, vol. 38, no. 4, pp. 411–417, 2010.
20 U. K. Stigsdotter and P. Grahn, "Stressed Individuals' Preferences for Activities and Environmental Characteristics in Green Spaces," *Urban Forestry & Urban Greening*, vol. 10, no. 4, pp. 295–304, 2011.

CHAPTER THREE

Ecosystem functions and health

Introduction

This chapter identifies components, structures and processes that are indicators of ecosystem health. This inquiry, like the review of human health status in the previous chapter, is necessary to understand how to define healthy and viable ecosystems before we can begin planning how they might be co-located with human settlement. Once we know more about how to support and measure ecosystem health, we can establish goals for green infrastructure at the regional and urban scale.

Within ecosystems, the interactions of abiotic and biotic systems motivated by agents, such as photosynthesis or tidal action, establish ecosystem structure and processes. The results of these processes are termed "ecosystem functions." Ecosystem functions are the physical, chemical and biological processes that sustain the ecosystem, such as primary production, water purification, nutrient cycling, carbon sequestration, decomposition, carbon cycling, etc. When ecosystems directly or indirectly contribute to human wellbeing, these contributions are defined as ecosystem benefits to humans.[1] Ecosystem services and benefits to humans are presented in the next chapter.

Six measures of ecosystem health were identified in the introductory chapter as: air quality, soil structure, energy and material cycling, water quality, habitat and species diversity, and ecosystem resilience. These factors are grouped under biophysical, chemical and biological diversity headings in the discussion below.

Biophysical

Ecology is the study of organisms interacting with each other and their environment. Therefore, an ecosystem is an assembly of organisms and processes within a spatial context. Although ecosystems are dynamic, geographically distributed ecosystem types arise locally or regionally due to precipitation, temperature, soil and other characteristics (Figure 3.1). The salient characteristics or dominating species are often used to name ecosystems and to map their extent. Knowing the geographic area of each ecosystem and monitoring its expansion or reduction over time gives us a crude measure of ecosystem health.

With the exception of organisms linked to human society, such as domesticated plants and animals, most species populations have been reduced because of human

activity. One of the primary reasons for reduced populations and extinctions is habitat loss.[2] This loss can come from biological and chemical changes, as discussed below, or from the conversion of habitat to human uses virtually devoid of ecological values. In extreme cases, the physical removal of vegetation, water, soil and other elements results in the death, not simply displacement, of almost all organisms originally resident. The amount of habitat loss leading to species extinction is larger than previously thought, and the rate is hundreds to thousands of times higher than fossil records indicate as typical.[3]

Huge metropolitan regions and commodity agriculture eliminate almost all native species in favor of plants hybridized by humans, domestic pets and exotic and invasive species. Plants require space, light, nutrients and water. Animals share these requirement, but also require territory for acquisition of food and water, breeding, migration and distribution of offspring. Furthermore, a minimum number of individuals within each species are required to achieve a viable, sustainable population. This includes sufficient genetic variety and contact with other populations of the same species to allow for long-term health. Mapping the extent of the prehuman or preindustrial ecosystems or species habitat is of academic, and perhaps restoration, interest, but is less useful with the prospect of burgeoning human population and the expansion of human settlements. The elimination of habitat due to human settlement is

Figure 3.1
A number of habitat types are discernable in this image. They respond to differences in soil moisture, soil type and depth, as well as many other factors.

exacerbated by the water supply, agriculture, mining, commercial forestry and other resources and activities needed to support them. Instead, determining the minimum viable populations of species and the habitat sizes required to sustain them is the approach that we must take in the face of diminishing ecological values almost everywhere.

Mapping the extent of habitat areas

State, national and international agencies have taken the first steps in defining the distribution of habitat by collecting geographic information about vegetation, soils, topography, etc. This data is then often assembled, interpreted and analyzed by other agencies or teams of scientists and planners to define the geographic extent of remaining habitat, especially habitat that supports a rich diversity of species or many endangered and threatened species. For example, a 1992 study used US federal data collected by satellite for each 300 × 300 m block of the upper midwest region (Illinois, Indiana, Michigan, Minnesota, Ohio and Wisconsin). Other scientists then analyzed the data to identify undeveloped land (any area not classified as urban, industrial, residential or agricultural). They then assessed the undeveloped land according to three criteria: (1) level of biological diversity (species, communities and ecosystems); (2) sustainability (the potential for the system to persist without external management); and (3) rarity of land cover, species and genus. The study scored each of the three criteria (diversity, sustainability and rarity) on a scale of 0 to 100. Most of the undeveloped land in the region scored between 20 and 80 on the diversity indicator. This indicates moderate ecosystem and species variety. Ninety percent of the undeveloped land was scored 50 or above for sustainability. Fragmentation, as well as physical, chemical and biological agents, reduced the ecological sustainability of the landscapes in the region. The northern part of the region was more diverse and more sustainable than the central and southern portions. In contrast to the sustainability measure, very little of the region scored above 50 on the rarity indicator. This means rare ecosystems or species occupy only a small area within the region. The results of this ecological condition study will serve as the baseline to which subsequent assessments of the same area can be compared.[4] In this way, the success of conservation programs and the impacts of urban growth can be monitored.

Initially, ground-based surveys of physical, vegetation and other biological information were used to create maps. Although accurate, these surveys are time-consuming and expensive to execute and repeat periodically. Especially for large areas, such as national or global ecosystem mapping, remote-sensing data from sensors on satellites are used to determine the extent of various ecosystems. For smaller areas, sensors mounted on aircraft can provide more detail. Periodic collection of data and comparison with previously collected information allows for temporal and spatial monitoring to identify changes in ecosystem size, fragmentation and health.

Improved resolution of various sensors now allows for the detection of large species, such as mature trees, within ecosystems and even measurements of the primary productivity in dry grasslands.[5] Nevertheless, the detailed imagery is often augmented by census counts of large mammals using aircraft. Although cost efficient for mapping large areas, detailed information is often added to the remotely sensed

information through the use of ground-based surveys, of at least portions, of the mapped ecosystems. Ground-based surveys also are used to verify and assess the accuracy of imagery derived from satellite data.

Mapping the diversity of ecosystems is possible at increasingly high accuracy (Figure 3.2), but species numbers and species diversity is estimated in large-scale planning by using indicator species, refined habitat definitions or primary productivity.

Geographic information systems (GISs) are used to map and analyze survey data. Significantly, the geographic extent and continuity of habitat can be presented

Figure 3.2
This image is derived from high-resolution NASA light detection and ranging (LIDAR) combined with other map data. This map distinguishes 19 land and vegetation classes.

graphically, which is important information for urban and conservation planners. The vertical structure and other attributes of ecosystems can increasingly be linked to GIS maps that can be queried (searched). The attribute data increases with new scientific studies of habitats and species and as sensors and computer applications improve. Thematic maps, such as vegetation and hydrology, can be compiled to identify locations where factors interact.

GISs also facilitate modeling human activity impacts on ecosystems by using population density, road network density, air pollution data and many other data collections. Similarly, alternative future scenarios can be explored by making sets of development or resource use assumptions. More detail about the tools and processes used in planning for urban growth, habitat and ecological corridors is presented in Chapter 5.

Forest ecosystems

Comparing ecosystem maps over time establishes trends and influences management decisions. For example, tracking the land area occupied by various forest types is important since forest ecosystems are large components of both temperate and tropical climate zones. Coarse-resolution mapping of forest cover types in the US has a long history that allows trends to become apparent. The size of forest ecosystems in the US has generally increased over the last 50 years, with a few exceptions. However, this recent increase recovered only about one-third of the forest area lost due to activities during the 1800s. There was a small increase in forested land between 1907 and 1938, but between 1938 and 1977 more than 16 million acres of forestland was lost. During the next three decades forestland increased by 5.3 million acres. Contrary to the recent trend is the twentieth century loss of 22 million acres and 12 million acres in the south-central region and southwest region, respectively. In the mid-Atlantic region and upper midwest region forestland cover increased by 13 million and 10 million acres, respectively. Some forest types made particularly large gains. For example, maple–beech–birch forests and oak–hickory forests gained 27.5 and 23 million acres, respectively, since 1953.[4]

Fir-spruce and western hardwood forests each increased about 11.5 million acres, while hemlock–Sitka spruce, pinyon–juniper and ponderosa–Jeffrey pine forest types decreased by about 13.6 million, 8.8 million and 8.7 million acres, respectively. Of concern is the loss of western white pine forest, since the 5.3 million acre decrease equals about 96 percent of its 1953 acreage (Figure 3.3).[4]

The total area occupied by ecosystems is one indicator of viability, but the configuration of the area is also important. Natural events and, especially, human activities fragment ecosystems. Most of the mammal, reptile, bird and amphibian species found in forest ecosystems are negatively impacted by fragmentation of habitat which implies some loss of total habitat area as well. This is because fragmentation increases the proportion of edge conditions, reduces the amount of interior habitat and makes access to other fragments difficult. The number of interior species will decline or disappear as interior habitat is reduced, while edge and open field species will generally increase.[6]

Figure 3.3
Most forest types in the
US have recovered
some area following a
decrease in the
nineteenth and portions
of the twentieth
century. Western white
pine forest, shown
here, is one type whose
acreage declined.

Fragmentation

Fragmentation is the splitting apart of habitat. By itself this has a relatively small impact on species variety or abundance. However, the spitting agent, such as a road, might have an impact larger than its area suggests. The damage caused by roads is due to wildlife mortality and a wide zone of ecological disturbance on either side of the road due to noise, pollution, invasive species and other factors.

The term "fragmentation" is really meant to imply four outcomes. First, habitat is divided, resulting in more fragments or patches. Second, there is an increase of edge condition and reduction of interior habitat. Third, fragmentation decreases the total area of habitat. Fourth, fragmentation increases the isolation of the patches (Figure 3.4).[6] The last two characteristics are particularly problematic. When large areas of habitat are converted to other land uses, such as residential or agricultural,

Figure 3.4
In this landscape a substantial amount of the original forest ecosystem has been replaced with agriculture and urban uses. The remaining forest habitat is fragmented, but the degree of fragmentation varies. The patches are not widely isolated and there is fairly good connectivity to the largest patch.

it is the loss of habitat that is most damaging to biodiversity. The habitat fragments might still be of value to native species if they are not too small and they are close together (Figure 3.5). The combination of habitat loss and widely isolated patches is most detrimental. In the study discussed below, the "patchy" category best matches the isolation characteristic of fragmentation.

The US Forest Service developed a model to measure the amount of fragmentation evident in forests within the contiguous 48 states. Four categories of forest area (core, interior, connected and patchy) were established. The categories differed according to the percentage of forest surrounding each 30 × 30 m forest land-cover unit. The core (unfragmented) category equaled 26 percent of the total forest area. The interior category was defined as being surrounded by 90–100 percent forest. The connected category (surrounded by 60–90 percent forest) and patchy category (surrounded by less than 60 percent forest) comprise a large proportion of the forest ecosystem. The connected and patchy categories represent almost 50 percent of the total forest area, although in the midwest these account for almost 70 percent of the forest condition. This study illustrates that the forest ecosystems in the US are highly fragmented. This is especially true near cities and in agricultural regions. This assessment was based on 2001 data and there has not been a new assessment to establish a trend, but this baseline will be important for future comparisons.[4] The negative impact of fragmentation can be mitigated somewhat if habitat fragments are linked. If fragments are close to each other they may function as if they were connected for some species.

As suggested above, the planning and design of a green infrastructure at the municipal and county level is key to mitigating the loss of habitat and biodiversity. Chapter 6 provides research and develops recommendations for the dimensions of ecological corridors and habitat fragments within the two contexts.

Figure 3.5
This poorly planned expansion of suburban development has eliminated much of the original forest and unnecessarily isolated many of the remaining habitat fragments. Continuation of the suburban pattern will eventually eliminate almost all of the native species in the area. Better planning in advance of development could have established a much better system of habitat patches and corridors while allowing for residential development, although its configuration and density could also be improved. Photo 48°15′15.21″ N, 122°19′31.34″ W by Google Earth (accessed 15 May 2013).

Connectivity

Although habitat loss and fragmentation of ecosystems, above a threshold, damages the ecosystem and biodiversity, connections between the ecosystem fragments can ameliorate the impact. The best connector of habitat patches is a physical corridor composed of the remnant habitat. A study that assessed the extent and distribution of habitat and connecting corridors was done for the eight-state southeast region of the US. The habitat (5,000 acre minimum) and connectivity assessment revealed that 43 percent of the total land and water area was composed of habitat patches (30 percent) or connectors (13 percent). Some of the habitat and connectors were in protected conservation areas (22 percent) and a substantial area of open water (12 percent) and wetlands (14 percent) had a lesser degree of protection. The remainder (52 percent) of the habitat and connector network is vulnerable to development. This assessment was based on data from the early 1990s and there has not been a new assessment to establish a trend.[4] If all of the vulnerable area is developed, the viability of the ecosystem will be destroyed. Retention of 25–30 percent of the original, undisturbed ecosystem area is a general minimum guiding conservation planning.

Wetland ecosystems

Wetlands, streams and rivers are important ecosystems for hydrological, ecological and economic reasons. Since rivers and streams are linear, they connect habitat types

UNIVERSITY
OF SHEFFIELD
LIBRARY

Figure 3.6
The US National
Wetland Inventory
provides accurate
assessment of the loss
or gain of many types
of wetlands. This image
shows the location of
at least eight types of
wetlands in the coastal
city of Everett,
Washington.

as well as provide habitat for aquatic and terrestrial species. They are part of the hydrological cycle and play a role in flood control and sediment distribution. Fresh and saltwater marshes and swamps have high rates of gross primary production and often serve as nursery areas for juvenile fish. The draining of wetlands to create land for agriculture and human settlement has a long history in the US. The edges of rivers and lakes are also very attractive as places for people to settle (Figure 3.6) and, until recently, the waterways were regarded as a convenient waste disposal network.

The extent of wetland ecosystems in the US is a fraction of the area covered by forests. There are 110 million acres (44.6 million hectares) of wetlands of all types in the nation. This amounts to half of the original wetland area. The historical loss of freshwater wetlands resulted in reduced hydrologic and ecosystem connectivity, and habitat loss and fragmentation. In some regions, the losses preclude reestablishment and watershed rehabilitation. Some of the recent wetland area loss is attributed to sea-level rise and climate change. The long-term loss of freshwater wetlands is continuing, but at a much slower rate than in previous decades. Between 2004 and 2009, wetlands of all types declined by an estimated 62,300 acres (25,200 ha). Ninety-five percent of existing wetlands are freshwater wetlands.[7]

In 2012 the US Fish and Wildlife Service sponsored an ecosystem service valuation study of wetlands in four wildlife refuges. These varied according to acreage and region of the country. Each wetland was analyzed according to services provided for storm protection, water quality, commercial fishing, habitat and carbon storage. Larger wetlands and those associated with higher human populations nearby provided the highest economic valuation. The total gross economic value per wetland acre per year ranged from $92 to $510. The total values of the four wetlands ranged from $13 million (Arrowwood Wetland) to over $4 billion (Okefenokee Wetland).[8]

Municipal- and county-scale green infrastructure networks can preserve the remaining wetlands and restore some of the wetlands that were lost or damaged in the past. Subsequent chapters present planning, design and implementation details for wetlands created to treat stormwater and wastewater. These can be augmented to provide significant habitat and ecosystem functions.

Soil structure

Understanding the scope and importance of processes and organisms supporting ecosystems is challenging but critical. Because fundamental or supporting ecosystem functions were well established before modern man evolved, they are often taken for granted. The development and maintenance of soils is a fundamental ecosystem function. Soils are critical for the cycling of carbon, nitrogen, sulfur and other substances. For example, the amount of carbon in soils is 1.8 times the amount held in plants, and nitrogen in soils is 18 times greater than in plants.[9]

Soils physically support and protect seeds before they sprout and hold nutrients, making them available to plants over time. Humus and clay particles (less than 2 μm in diameter) typically have a negative charge and hold positively charged minerals and nutrients (cations). Without this capacity, many of the nutrients and minerals needed by plants would be leached from the root zone. Conversely, without the buffering capacity of soils, nutrients in excessive amounts would be toxic to the plants.[9]

A great number and diversity of soil and other organisms are involved in the decomposition of dead organic matter and waste. They utilize the energy present in complex organic molecules by processing chemical compounds in the waste. The chemical bonds in these large molecules are broken by a series of organisms and the remaining substances are available for use by successive sets of organisms. At the

Figure 3.7
Some soils, such as this one in the arid climate of Utah, are very fragile. This one supports a twisted moss and can be considered an old growth soil.

end of this decomposition process, simple inorganic chemicals remain as nutrients for plants. Therefore, the fertility of soils results primarily from the activities of bacteria, fungi, algae, crustacea, mites, termites, springtails, millipedes and worms.

Soil formation is a critical and continuous process closely related to nutrient cycling, and is dependent on a rich biodiversity of microorganisms and plants, especially legumes and deeply rooted plants. Studies in Denmark found 50,000 earthworms and related species, an equal number of insects and mites and nearly 12 million roundworms inhabiting each square yard of pasture. Even less visible were the 30,000 protozoa, 50,000 algae, 400,000 fungi and billions of individual bacteria in each cubic inch of that pasture soil. Some bacteria even convert atmospheric nitrogen into forms usable by plants. This nitrogen is transferred from plants to animals and man. Some fungi form networks that connect the root systems of trees and provide them with nutrients. Ants and earthworms improve soil structure, aeration and drainage by mixing plant material and microbes. Annually, as much as 4.4 tons of worm casts are produced on each acre of land.[9] Compaction of soil, erosion and deposition of heavy metals or excess nutrients are all results of human activities and are threats to ecosystem health. Conversely, humans can take simple management steps to preserve and restore soil.

Chemical transformation and energy

Chemical elements, such as nitrogen, oxygen, sulfur and carbon, as well as substances such as water and carbon dioxide, cycle through ecosystems. There are often small, natural inputs of substances from outside the ecosystem, such as dust and nitrogen from lightning, that are important to the function and stability of the system. Unusual inputs or withdrawals resulting from natural or human activity often result in compromised or at least changed ecosystem functions. Measuring the flow of chemical substances into, through and out of ecosystems provides insight into ecosystem health.

The degree of internal cycling of energy within ecosystems is another indicator of their health. The interactions and transformations of energy and material flows are complex to describe and much more difficult to quantify, but computer technology and mathematical models based on ecosystem experiments are providing more accurate and useful results. The primary energy source for an ecosystem is its net primary productivity. This is the amount of carbon fixed through photosynthesis. The flow of energy and the carbon created by primary production support several fundamental ecosystem functions. The maintenance of the biodiversity of soil organisms, plants and habitat is an example of one of these fundamental or supporting functions. It is upon primary production and the associated supporting functions that ecosystems are built. Biodiversity is also critical to nutrient cycling, another basic ecosystem function. Supporting ecosystem functions, such as water cycling, operate at global and local scales.[10] Therefore, green infrastructure planning must connect local, regional and even national systems.

Acid rain caused, largely, by burning coal to generate electricity is an example of chemical inputs that stress species and ecosystems across the northeast US and areas of Europe. The rain across the northeast US region has an average acidity of pH 4. Some insects, amphibians and fish are sensitive to acidic water. For example, brook trout eggs will not hatch at pH 5 or lower. Increased acidity has caused the species to become locally extinct in parts of the northeast.[11]

Air quality and climate change

Oxygen and nitrogen are atmospheric elements that serve animals and people; carbon dioxide, nitrogen and filtered solar radiation serve plant associations. Atmospheric processes also extract gases, such as oxygen, nitrogen and others.[12] Clean air sustains natural ecosystems. Although pollutants up to certain thresholds don't have adverse impacts, highly polluted air, such as high levels of ozone and nitrogen oxide pollution, causes damage. Changes in the concentration of carbon dioxide (CO_2) in the atmosphere impacts the growth rate of plants and the energy balance of the system. Deposition of heavy metals and other pollutants from industrial activities or burning fossil fuels, such as coal, harm ecosystem functions and species.

High concentrations of ozone have negative ecosystem impacts. The mid-Atlantic and southeast regions of the US have the highest levels of ozone damage to forests. Of the sensitive species in these areas, as much as 12 percent display a high or severe degree of foliage damage due to ozone pollution. Ozone impacts vary by region, and two regions of the US show no ozone damage at all.[4] In the urban environment, ground-level ozone decreases production of tree biomass by 10 percent.[13] Ozone also decreases crop production. Significant reductions in soybean yield (9–19 percent) are expected by 2030 due to high ozone concentrations.[14]

The climate of the Earth has fluctuated dramatically, probably due to changes to its rotation and the energy output of the sun. Other historic causes of climate change may be from asteroid impacts, volcanic eruptions and uplifts caused by plate tectonics. However, the climate has been relatively stable for the last 10,000 years.[9] As life developed on the planet, mechanisms evolved to gradually warm the planet. In some cases these mechanisms moderate climate changes, but in others they are thought to accelerate it.[9,12] A regional cycle of daily plant transpiration along with evaporation and afternoon thunderstorms is an example of an ecosystem process that limits moisture loss and the rise of surface temperature. In the tropical rain forests of the Amazon, this process is responsible for 50 percent of the annual rainfall. Temperature is also moderated by the shading, insulation and wind barrier functions of forests to create regional greenhouse conditions.[9]

Anthropogenic emission of greenhouse gases has focused our attention on a climate ecosystem function that has been overwhelmed. The recent anthropogenic rise of 0.8°C will increase to 1.5°C unless significant reductions in greenhouse gas emissions are made immediately. We must act quickly to avoid a projected 3°C rise by 2050 if we are to avoid great disruption to human society and ecosystems worldwide.[12] Despite efforts advocating these changes during the past 20 years, no positive changes have been adopted in the US. In fact, all greenhouse gas emissions continue to rise[15] (with the exception of a small drop in CO_2 emissions in 2012 due to a shift from coal to natural gas for electrical energy production).

Human activities have increased the concentration of three greenhouse gases. The global concentration has increased for carbon dioxide (39 percent), methane (159 percent) and nitrous oxide (18 percent) during the period from 1750 to 2005. The US is responsible for about 18 percent of the carbon dioxide emitted into the atmosphere, although it contains less than 5 percent of the world population. Carbon dioxide represents 83 percent of the greenhouse gases emitted by human activities and is most responsible for climate change. In the US, carbon dioxide from the burning of fossil fuels is responsible for 94.6 percent of the carbon emitted. The transportation sector is responsible for one-third of this, and nearly two-thirds of the transportation emissions come from personal vehicle use. Electricity generators (primarily coal-fired power plants) are responsible for 41 percent of the carbon emissions from fossil fuel combustion.[15]

However, methane has a significant impact even though it amounts to only 14 percent of the greenhouse gases emitted, because it is 21 times more effective in trapping heat in the atmosphere.[15] Soot is another greenhouse element responsible for about 16 percent of global warming. These elements last in the atmosphere for a shorter amount of time than CO_2, so their control could yield climate change mitigation results more quickly than CO_2 reduction measures. Political and economic resistance to regulation of carbon emissions has resulted in the increase of CO_2 between 1990 and 2009. Since we urgently need to make progress, perhaps simultaneous reduction targets for carbon dioxide, methane and soot will yield both medium- and long-term results.

Implementing 14 measures for reducing methane and soot worldwide, including capturing gas that escapes from coal, oil and natural gas mining and processing facilities, stopping leaks in gas pipelines, capturing methane from landfills and waste-water treatment plants, frequent draining of rice paddies and better management of manure would reduce the anticipated global warming by 0.9°F (0.5°C) by 2050. Without the implementation of these measures the projected rise in the average global temperature is expected to be 2.2°F. With the proposed methane and soot reduction the average global temperature increase is estimated to be 1.3°F (0.7°C), which is below the 2°F threshold representing major economic and ecological disruptions. Secondary health and agricultural benefits of the proposed methane and soot reductions are very significant. The economic benefit of reducing methane and soot are many times greater than the cost of implementation.[16]

Water quality and quantity

The annual volume of water from precipitation on the land surface is equal to a 3-foot depth over the entire land area, and all of it supports natural ecosystems in one way or another.[9] Of course, the precipitation isn't distributed evenly, which is one of the primary factors distinguishing ecosystems from one another (Figure 3.8). Global warming is already changing the amount and form of precipitation that various regions and ecosystems receive. This will continue to cause the boundaries of ecosystems to shift. Research demonstrates that organisms are already shifting their territories toward the poles. This natural climate adaptation will increase the frequency

Figure 3.8
Wetland ecosystems are especially important for purification of water and provision of clean water habitat for birds, fish and other aquatic organisms.

of pest and disease outbreaks in stressed ecosystems.[5] If these changes in precipitation are rapid, ecosystems will suffer.

Healthy ecosystems depend on relatively clean water for optimum health. Naturally occurring nutrients due to soil-forming processes and decomposition of vegetation are removed from water and soil by a host of microorganisms and plants. These substances are transferred up the food chain to serve the metabolic functions of mammals, fish and birds. Evaporation of water from surfaces and transpiration of water from plants is another water purification mechanism and part of the water cycle. Acidic rain and the results of other atmospheric pollution compromise the water cycle and damage ecosystem health.

Contaminants and excess nutrients acquired by water flowing over the agricultural and urban landscape enter aquatic ecosystems. Wastewater treatment plants and conventional agriculture are the primary sources of such large amounts of carbon, nitrogen and phosphorus that lakes, rivers and coastal waters become eutrophic. The excess nutrients cause rapid growth of phytoplankton, algae and bacteria, which damage the natural ecosystem and cause changes in its structure and function. Excessive growth of phytoplankton can lead to oxygen levels in the water that are too low to support freshwater and marine fish and many other aquatic species. This situation has already led to coastal dead zones as large as 27,000 square miles (70,000 km^2) near South America, Japan, China, Australia, New Zealand and the west coast of North America. The number of these zones is doubling each decade.[5]

Phosphorus accumulation in ecosystems has increased 40–95 percent above levels during the preindustrial period. Most of the accumulation occurs in soils, but this nutrient eventually makes its way to aquatic systems. Phosphorus from artificial fertilizer and household detergents also cause eutrophication of freshwater ecosystems, especially in temperate climates. Unfortunately, the use of synthetic fertilizers is expected to increase at the rate of over one million tons per year until 2030.[5]

Biological diversity

Biological diversity (biodiversity), like habitat, is both the result of healthy ecosystems and a means of measuring ecosystem health. The assessment of biodiversity includes the variety of genes, species, populations and communities and ecosystems. The biodiversity focus tends to change at different scales. The regional focus is often on species, while national and international conservation efforts focus on ecosystems. Despite the focus, variety, quantity, quality of habitat and distribution are biodiversity assessment considerations.[5]

There is no nationwide assessment of biodiversity or its trends in the US, although there is considerable information on most mammal and bird species (Figure 3.9) and their population trends. However, the biodiversity of the entire group of native freshwater fish and its change over time is measured and can serve as one indicator of general biodiversity. At least 12 freshwater fish species are extinct and another three may be extinct. These extinctions or, more likely, local extinction of population groups are the cause of reduced fish biodiversity in various regions. Only 12 percent of the area of the contiguous US has the historical biodiversity of fish fully intact. Watersheds extending over 24 percent of the US have lost 10 percent of their fish biodiversity, with reductions in the southwest particularly severe.[4]

Within an ecosystem the number of species grows in response to increasing ecosystem complexity and the exploitation of habitat niches as organisms compete and evolve. The number of species in an area is one way that biodiversity is expressed (Figure 3.10). This is called species richness, variety or diversity. The number of individuals of a single species is called abundance and is another common measure of ecosystem health.

Figure 3.9
The endangered Kirtland Warbler has very specific habitat requirements that make it vulnerable to habitat loss and extinction. They breed in Michigan and require at least 160 acres of dense, young Jack pine (*Pinus banksiana*) forest.

However, overall, species richness and abundance is declining in developed and developing countries across the globe. Many species within the five categories of organisms (bacteria, single-celled organisms, fungi, plants and animals) are faced with extinction. These extinctions are caused by habitat loss due to the expansion of agriculture, timber harvest and urbanization.[5] At least for perching birds and songbirds in the US (Figure 3.9), the previous extinction rate estimates have been revised downward, based on new research. The recalculated extinction rate is 625–6,250 times normal.[3] As noted in Chapter 1, the number of threatened species in the world has more than doubled in the last 15 years.[17] Of course, extinctions reduce the biological diversity of an ecosystem and will eventually compromise its health and that of the organisms, including man, that depend on them. Extinctions at the unprecedented current rate indicate a dramatically unsustainable relationship between man and other creatures.

The ecosystem role that species play is an important consideration for ecosystem health. Species can be organized into functional categories. If all species within a functional category, such as pollinators, become extinct then there would be a significant negative impact on the ecosystem, even if the total number of species remained high. This understanding suggests that maintenance of complex ecosystems and the breadth of species populations is a wiser approach than targeting specific species for conservation.[9] Nevertheless, high-profile species (Figure 3.11), or better, a guild of species selected from all functional categories, is often highlighted as an indirect indicator of ecosystem health or the success of conservation efforts.

Figure 3.10
Two ways to measure ecosystem health are to assess the variety of species and the number of individuals within the species. Species can be organized into functional groups. Some species may perform the same ecosystem function, such as nectar production.

Figure 3.11
The northern spotted owl is a specialist species and highly dependent on old growth forest at least 150 years old in California, Oregon, Washington and British Columbia. It is an interior species requiring a large habitat area. Its offspring often fail to survive migration to fragments of old growth forest. This species was listed as threatened with extinction because of commercial timber harvests on public land in 1990 and ignited a clash between advocates of economic forest use and advocates of ecosystem protection. Its numbers continue to decline.[18]

Since a number of species within an ecosystem might perform similar functions, the extinction of one species may not impact the health of the ecosystem significantly, especially if the populations of the remaining species within the functional group expand. Because of this dynamic, it is very difficult to study and test the impact of biodiversity loss until most or all of the species in the functional group are gone.

The abundance of individuals across species relates to population dynamics at the landscape scale. Population that declines beyond a typical fluctuation indicates significant stress, just as declining species diversity does. Local extinction means that the entire population of a species has disappeared and indicates that the entire species may be threatened. The presence of rare or endemic species is another indicator of ecosystem health. The loss of species within these groups suggests that the capacity of the ecosystem is compromised even if the abundance and variety of species has not changed much yet.

Local populations of most species are not well defined, but the long-term population trends for birds in the US are known due to the periodic North American Breeding Bird Survey that began in 1966. Sets of species in 12 environment or habitat groups (trends for five of these groups are presented in Table 3.1) are defined according to *significant positive*, *positive* and *significant negative* population trends. Data from this study also provide the trend for individual species and for individual states/provinces and regions. The data is geographically organized so that changes

Table 3.1 Population trends for indicator bird guilds in the US and southern Canada as a percentage of species with positive or negative population trends, 1966–2010.[19] For more information see www.mbr-pwrc.usgs.gov/bbs/bbs.html.

Species Group	Significant Positive	Positive	Significant Negative	Number of Species
Grassland	4	21	54	28
Shrubland	13	31	40	87
Woodland	31	57	28	131
Urban	27	33	67	15
Water and Wetland	19	50	17	86
All Species Groups	21	45	32	424

in population trends can be displayed on maps. Species threatened with extinction or those of concern are identified along with the pressures that force them toward extinction. Similarly, factors leading to population growth are collected. The most recent ten-year trend can also be compared to the full trend.[19] Comprehensive and long-term data of the sort collected for birds in the US and Canada are one reason that birds are often selected as indicators of ecosystem health.

Since populations of species are groups of individuals separated from other groups, they may reflect differences in genetics. Data on populations of waterbirds that depend on wetlands and other freshwater habitat are the best-studied set of species. Therefore, waterbirds suggest trends that may be occurring in the populations of other species. Worldwide, 41 percent of known waterbird populations are decreasing, 36 percent are stable and 19 percent are increasing. In North America the populations of 88 species of waterbirds are stable, 62 are increasing and 68 are declining. Large mammals in Africa are another well-studied group. Over 60 percent of their populations are declining, while only 4 percent are increasing. Similarly large population losses of amphibians (almost 71 percent) are occurring in species worldwide.[5]

Maintaining biological diversity

One of several goals of the following chapters is to show how to maintain or enhance biodiversity at the landscape and municipal level through the use of green infrastructure. Maintaining biodiversity is a challenge, since many species are negatively impacted by human activity or require large territories. In fact, some species require huge territories virtually undisturbed by humans in order to sustain viable populations (Figure 3.11). For example, grizzly bears occupy overlapping home ranges, but their density in the Yellowstone ecosystem is about one bear per 34 square miles.[20] Other species are extremely sensitive to human presence and activity (Figure 3.12). For these species, a country residence in the forest can reduce the presence of these species for as much as 600 feet into the forest.[21]

Figure 3.12
The hermit thrush
(*Catharus guttatus*) is a
forest interior species
and highly sensitive to
human presence and
activity. Its presence is
reduced around country
residences in the forest
for as much as 600
feet.

In contrast, many species do adapt to the presence of people and the land-use changes they establish. Some species seem to adapt to fragmentation of their habitat. The scarlet tanager is an interior forest bird, but it seems to breed in forest fragments less than 25 acres (10 ha) in size when its preferred interior habitat is diminished.[10] Some species, such as crows, are even considered completely urbanized and flourish in cities even to the point of becoming pests, as is the case with rats and cockroaches. Biological diversity within urban areas can be higher than it is within the surrounding, more natural, ecosystems. This is explained by the many exotic or invasive species that are encouraged or supported by human activities. Exotic plants, whose original habitats are distributed across the globe, usually dominate the ornamental landscape of urban centers and residential gardens. The biodiversity of native species is always much lower within urban and suburban environments. However, the variety of native species and the number of individuals supported in these environments can be maximized through careful urban planning and design, as discussed in the following chapters.

Invasive species

Non-indigenous species that become established within natural ecosystems threaten the healthy function of the system. Invasive species in the US, such as kudzu, zebra mussels, grass carp, starlings and nutria, have damaged ecosystem health.[4] As for biodiversity assessment, there is no national mapping and monitoring of all invasive species and their impact, although for some areas and habitat types more information is available. The assessment of the aquatic ecosystems (soft-bottom estuaries) along the coast from northern California to Canada can serve as an indicator of the impact of invasive species. A study of this region measured the abundance of benthic (organisms living on the sediment or in sediment) invasive species. It revealed that the invasive species had a higher negative impact on the ecosystem than sedimentation or eutrophication, which are also anthropogenic in origin. About 15 percent of the monitored sites within this region contained a greater number of invasive than native organisms. Another 20 percent of the monitored sites were moderately invaded by non-native species.[4]

Ecosystem resilience

Ecosystems are subject to shocks from natural and man-made catastrophes. Some ecosystems are quite vulnerable to perturbation. Some, such as fire-adapted communities, even invite certain kinds of dramatic change. Other ecosystems have a greater capacity to adsorb shocks while maintaining ecosystem functions, but recover slowly.[5] This variability of vulnerability and resilience leads to a regional landscape of dynamic ecosystems. Thus regions are composed of disturbed, recovering and mature ecosystems that form a landscape mosaic. The biological diversity present in ecosystems before perturbations occur is related to their resilience. Each species extinction, whether local or global, represents a potential loss of ecosystem resilience. Extinction of a functional group of species can be a severe impact to ecosystem functions.

Resilience is the ability to return to the stable state after disturbance. If the disturbance is severe, it can cause the ecosystem to change states and represents long-term declines in species composition and ecosystem functions. Resilience can be expressed as a measure of the time it takes the ecosystem to return from the stressed state to the original condition, or expressed as the return of the network of species in the undisturbed system.

Climate influences ecosystem resilience, so climate change could increase or decrease recovery rates. At the local scale, resilience is reduced if infiltration, soil moisture and nutrient cycles diminish. Therefore, soils structurally resistant to change contribute to high resilience.[22] Sustainable use and management of forest ecosystems requires protection of soils and preservation of seed sources and the rapid migration of seed into damaged landscapes. Since commercial forestry and damage associated with climate change, such as fires and insect infestations, have large impacts on expanses of forest, attention to the resilience of this ecosystem is urgent. Poorly resilient ecosystems that are damaged may require active management and restoration by humans (Figure 3.13), such as thinning stands, fuel load reduction, erosion prevention and re-vegetation.

The resiliency of the ecosystems damaged by hurricanes has been studied. Publicly available remote-sensing data (moderate resolution imaging spectroradiometer, MODIS) was used to monitor the recovery of the landscape after Hurricane Rita. Rita came ashore on 24 September 2005 and caused considerable damage to southwestern Louisiana towns, crops and natural ecosystems. This study established a baseline of gross primary biomass production derived from data collected between

Figure 3.13
A helicopter on a recently burned forest in Arizona drops a 900-pound bale of straw to control erosion and flooding. One ton of straw per acre was placed over 25,000 acres seeded with barley and other plants to help restore damage from the largest forest fire in the history of Arizona.

2000 and 2005. Gross primary production was measured for several ecosystem types for the 12 months following Hurricane Rita and this was compared to the baseline. This study really traces the regeneration of the landscape, which is slightly different from resilience since only one ecosystem function is being measured. Nevertheless, the study demonstrated that ecosystem biomass recovery was surprisingly rapid for coastal wetlands and several other ecosystems. The exception was evergreen forests, which remained below the baseline for the entire year. The most resilient ecosystem was the shrub/scrub type. As during Hurricane Katrina, it was resistant to storm damage.[23]

The Louisiana study also demonstrated links between the resilience of the ecosystems and recovery of human systems. Businesses linked to ecosystem services, such as fisheries, agriculture and forestry, were least resilient when tied to the least resilient ecosystem types. Conversely, the resilient wetlands and croplands were linked to higher business resilience.[23]

Indicators

The study above used an indicator of ecosystem health, assuming that other aspects would match the performance of the indicator. Ecosystem resilience is even more complex to demonstrate and monitor than ecosystem health. To simplify the process, reduce cost and communicate more clearly with citizens and decision makers, the use of ecosystem indicators simplifies data collection, assessment and communication. Many people are familiar with the concept of indicator species. The presence, abundance and distribution of the indicator species are used as proxies for the whole system. For example, the condition and number of plants of a native buckwheat species has been used in California as an indicator of sustainable human recreational use of a natural area because it is sensitive to trampling.

Indicators are numerical values that define the state and trend of a system. Generally, several indicators are necessary to describe complex systems or relationships. The most critical and difficult task is establishing the set of indicators and testing that they reliably describe the system. For example, a set of indicators was proposed to define the health of the urban forest in and around Gainesville, Florida and its provision of ecosystem services. Of course, the forest was mapped and data were collected from sample plots. The data were entered into a widely used forest health model (UFORE) that estimated ecosystem health, including the impact of pollution levels. The model characterized the effects of various land uses. The result was an understanding that the indicators of tree cover, soil pH and soil organic matter were most useful for defining sustained provision of ecosystem services. Which ecosystem services are prioritized will vary by region. In Florida, storm abatement was a very important ecosystem benefit. Therefore, the ecosystem benefit is storm protection and the indicator is forest structure. The quantifiable expression of the indicator is tree density and percent coverage within designated sample plots. In a different region, abatement of particulate pollution might be a more highly prioritized ecosystem service benefit and a different indicator would be developed. These examples focus on ecosystem services, but other indicators would target ecosystem health. Once the indicators are validated they can be measured regularly at a low cost to communicate ecosystem health in relation to changes in use, management or community goals.[24] This approach to assuring continued ecosystem service is an alternative to the

Figure 3.14
Removal of invasive species and other management activities may be required to sustain healthy ecosystems within the green infrastructure.

economic assessment of value to humans, but is compatible and could be directly tied to processes that estimate economic value.

In municipalities the creation of a green infrastructure will involve preservation of existing habitat and corridors, but will also require newly designed or restored landscapes. Existing habitat in the city will require management to mitigate the impacts of pollution and human use, as well as controlling invasive species (Figure 3.14). New or restored landscapes can increase rare ecosystems, such as wetlands, and build the components that lead to healthy ecosystems, such as improvements to soil and vegetation structure. Resilient designed landscapes depend on a high diversity of native plants, soil restoration, varied topography, a perennial water source, microclimate situations and other measures appropriate to the climate, region and native species. However, green infrastructure in the urban setting will require monitoring and management. Guilds of indicator species should be identified and monitored to measure the success of restored landscapes and the health of existing habitat. Subsequent chapters address many of these planning and design issues, but first a discovery of the services and benefits to humans provided by ecosystems is covered in the next chapter.

References

1   Gomez-Baggethun, "Natural Capital and Ecosystem Services," in *Ecosystem Services, Issues in Environmental Science and Technology*, vol. 30, Cambridge: Royal Society of Chemistry, 2010.

2   Millennium Ecosystem Assessment, *Ecosystems and Human Well-Being: Biodiversity Synthesis*, Washington, DC: World Resources Institute, 2005.

3   F. He, "Species–Area Relationships Always Overestimate Extinction Rates from Habitat Loss," *Nature*, vol. 473, pp. 368–371, 2011.

4   US Environmental Protection Agency (EPA), "EPA's 2008 Report on the Environment," National Technical Information Service, Environmental Assessment EPA/600/R-07/045F, 2008.

5   R. M. Hassan, S. R. Carpenter, K. Chopra, D. Capistrano and Millennium Ecosystem Assessment, *Ecosystems and Human Well-Being*, Washington, DC: Island Press, 2005.

6   L. Fahrig, "Effects of Habitat Fragmentation on Biodiversity," *Annual Review of Ecology, Evolution, and Systematics*, vol. 34, no. 1, pp. 487–515, 2003.

7   T. Dahl, *Status and Trends of Wetlands in the Conterminous United States 2004 to 2009*, Washington, DC: US Fish and Wildlife Service, 2010.

8   D. Patton, J. Bergstrom, A. Covich and R. Moore, *National Wildlife Refuge Wetland Ecosystem Service Valuation Model, Phase 1 Report: An Assessment of Ecosystem Services Associated with National Wildlife Refuges*, Washington, DC: US Fish and Wildlife Service, 2012.

9   G. Daily, *Ecosystem Services: Benefits Supplied to Human Societies by Natural Ecosystems*, Washington, DC: Ecological Society of America, 1997.

10 A. Fitter, "An Assessment of Ecosystem Services and Biodiversity in Europe," in *Ecosystem Services, Issues in Environmental Science and Technology*, Cambridge: Royal Society of Chemistry, 2010.

11 US Fish and Wildlife Service, "Contaminants," 8 October 2010. [Online]. Available: www.fws.gov/r5crc/Habitat/Contaminants.html (accessed 15 March 2013).

12 J. Thornes, "Atmospheric Services," in *Ecosystem Services, Issues in Environmental Science and Technology*, vol. 30, Cambridge: Royal Society of Chemistry, 2010.

13 "Surface-Level Ozone Pollution Set To Reduce Tree Growth 10% By 2100," *Science News*, 10 December 2008. [Online]. Available: www.sciencedaily.com/releases/2012/10/121030161523.htm (accessed 1 March 2013).

14 "Ozone's Impact on Soybean Yield: Reducing Future Losses," *Science News*, 30 October 2012. [Online]. Available: www.sciencedaily.com/releases/2012/10/121030161523.htm (accessed 1 March 2013).

15 US EPA, "Inventory of U.S. Greenhouse Gas Emissions and Sinks: 1990–2009," EPA 430-R-11–005, 2011.

16 D. Shindell, "Simultaneously Mitigating Near-Term Climate Change and Improving Human Health and Food Security," *Science*, vol. 335, no. 6065, pp. 183–189, 2012.

17 International Union for Conservation of Nature and Natural Resources, "Summary Statistics," 2011. [Online]. Available: www.iucnredlist.org/about/summary-statistics#Tables_1_2 (accessed 8 March 2013).

18 US Fish and Wildlife Service, "Species Fact Sheet: Northern Spotted Owl, *Strix occidentalis caurina*," 5 November 2012. [Online]. Available: www.fws.gov/oregonfwo/Species/Data/NorthernSpottedOwl (accessed 8 March 2013).

19 J. R. Sauer, J. E. Hines, J. E. Fallon, K. L. Pardieck, D. J. Ziolkowski and W. A. Link, "The North American Breeding Bird Survey, Results and Analysis 1966–2010," 2011. [Online]. Available: www.mbr-pwrc.usgs.gov/bbs/bbs.html (accessed 8 March 2013).

20 F. Craighead, "Grizzly Bear Ranges and Movement as Determined by Radiotracking," in *Bears: Their Biology and Management*, vol. 3, Binghamton, NY, and Moscow: JSTOR, 1974.

21 M. J. Glennon and H. E. Kretser, "Size of the Ecological Effect Zone Associated with Exurban Development in the Adirondack Park, NY," *Landscape and Urban Planning*, vol. 112, pp. 10–17, 2013.

22 H. Yan, J. Zhan and T. Zhang, "Resilience of Forest Ecosystems and Its Influencing Factors," *Procedia Environmental Sciences*, vol. 10, pp. 2201–2206, 2011.

23 A. E. Frazier, C. S. Renschler and S. B. Miles, "Evaluating Post-Disaster Ecosystem Resilience Using MODIS GPP data," *International Journal of Applied Earth Observation and Geoinformation*, vol. 21, pp. 43–52, 2013.

24 C. Dobbs, F. J. Escobedo and W. C. Zipperer, "A Framework for Developing Urban Forest Ecosystem Services and Goods Indicators," *Landscape and Urban Planning*, vol. 99, no. 3–4, pp. 196–206, 2011.

CHAPTER FOUR

Ecosystem services

Introduction

In contrast to the previous chapter, the sections below concentrate on the potential ecosystem services and the actual benefits to man. When humans directly or indirectly use the environment and products from it, they are receiving ecosystem services. Examples of ecosystem products include clean water, food, lumber, minerals, fibers, etc. (Figure 4.1). Non-product services include water purification, waste treatment and intangible elements such as recreation and beauty. An ecosystem benefit is the human valuation of an ecosystem service.[1]

The Millennium Ecosystem Assessment divided ecosystem services that benefit humans into four classes: (1) supporting; (2) regulating; (3) provisioning; and (4) cultural. Supporting ecosystem services indirectly benefit humans but are fundamental to the other three categories of services that are more directly enjoyed by people.[2] "Ecosystem services" is a deliberately anthropocentric phrase that frames the argument for preservation of natural systems in the cost–benefit terminology of economics. It is hoped that this language and demonstration of economic value will foster an understanding of the true value of healthy ecosystems and lead to greater commitment and investment in their conservation. This chapter provides many examples of the economic valuation of ecosystem benefits.

Green infrastructure organizes several elements that provide human and ecosystem benefits. This chapter establishes the typology of ecosystem services and benefits, as well as threats to them, in the context of green infrastructure at the municipal and landscape scale. Components that are managed ecosystems for the explicit purpose of maximizing certain ecosystem products, such as wastewater treatment, are the subjects of later chapters. The eight functions and services identified in Figure 1.5 interact with each other as discussed below. They are organized according to the Millennium Ecosystem Assessment categories.

Human benefits from supporting ecosystem functions

The provision of seafood, timber, fodder and other commonly traded natural products are ecosystem services provided on a scale that is larger than generally associated with green infrastructure. However, networks of corridors, spaces and habitat areas

within the city and county have an impact on these more distantly derived products. Community agriculture and forestry, and certainly residential and public landscapes, depend on the maintenance of supporting ecosystem services,[3] such as soil formation and nutrient cycling. Habitat provision, water cycling and primary production are three more examples of supporting ecosystem services tied to human activities at a scale somewhat larger than cities but linked to them. Some of the topics in this chapter will be familiar since they relate to ecosystem health as discussed in the previous chapter, but this discussion approaches the topics from an anthropocentric perspective.

Habitat for humans

In contrast to habitat definitions for animals and plants, it is surprisingly difficult to define and understand what a human habitat is. We cannot use the same parameters of temperature, food sources or associated species as we can for other organisms. Of course, *Homo sapiens* evolved in a particular habitat, but the species long ago exercised its ability to modify its environment to allow expansion of the population into areas where excessive heat, cold, wind or the lack of supportive vegetation and animals would normally limit habitation. Through the use of natural materials, and

Figure 4.1
Products, like lumber, food and medicine, are the most obvious of the ecosystem benefits, but there are many other important services including air and water purification, waste decomposition, soil and nutrient cycling, climate and radiation regulation, habitat provision, noise pollution control, aesthetic and cultural.

later synthetic ones, man extended the range of environments that he could occupy far beyond his evolutionary home.

Modification of the environment is not an activity peculiar to man. Most organisms modify the environment to protect themselves and to better support their offspring. For example, over time redwood forests modify the soil chemistry, moisture and temperature, humidity and amount of sunlight reaching the ground in ways that support redwood trees and not others that might compete for space, light or nutrients.

For man, environmental control is conscious and sometimes long term, wide ranging and requiring continuous or occasional use of natural resources. This store of resources and our ability to use them to ameliorate hostile environments might be regarded as man's contemporary habitat more correctly than any association with native plant and animal groups or climatic conditions. Building materials, energy and technology to modify the environment are globally available in the modern economy. Therefore, the location or origin of the resources do not define human habitat geographically. Nevertheless, some cities and towns are more desirable places for people to live than others. Since all cities are artificial environments of human manufacture, we can study why some are more benign. The keys to understanding optimum human habitat are the dimensions of human health. Many ecosystem services contribute to human health and habitat, as discussed below.

Despite the enormous number of plant and animal species, man depends on relatively few of them for food. In fact, a small set has been selected and modified through hybridization (and more recently genetic modification) to better serve our needs. Dependence on this small group of plants and animals erroneously caused us to behave as if only they are all that are required for human wellbeing. When one or more of the basic set of plants or animals is diminished through flooding, drought or disease, the result is often hardship or starvation. Similarly, if a basic natural resource, such as oil, is temporarily unavailable, this can cause great suffering, especially in the extreme environments where man lives comfortably only through the constant expenditure of the resource.

Human habitat, then, is increasingly the occupation of land locally incapable of supporting the population without reliance on modified, anthropocentric plants and animals, imported energy, and sometimes imported water, and other materials from sources beyond the region. Man has committed himself to this model and, in terms of population growth over the centuries, it has served the species. However, the more reductionist the model becomes, as the store of resources declines due to their unrenewable character or demand from an ever-growing population, then the more vulnerable human societies become. Reducing our risk could come from population reductions, increases in resources or both. We have used technology and fossil fuel subsidies to increase resources and largely ignored the population side of the equation.

More productive hybrids or genetically altered strains of commodity plants and animals, more herbicides, pesticides, artificial fertilizer and specialized farm equipment and expanding the area dedicated to agriculture may enhance our ability to produce more food. However, it is apparent that this is an increasingly artificial system with an ultimate capacity. More clear is the limit of fossil fuel reserves and the dramatically increasing global demand for oil. Global commodity agriculture is increasingly dependent on fossil fuel but will, presumably, be prioritized as the oil supply decreases.

Since human settlements are increasingly urban and require the support of regional and even global resources for sustenance, huge areas for agriculture and forestland are needed. These land areas, energy production and infrastructure, both nearby and far away, should be included in the definition of human habitat. Although increasingly modified, these systems ultimately are based in nature. Hybridized plants, which would be unrecognizable to the humans that first cultivated the species, still require a soil substrate, nutrients, reasonably pure water and light. We substitute naturally occurring nutrients with artificial fertilizers, but these are also derived from natural resources. The sections below remind us that indispensible materials and processes are provided to humans by natural and managed ecosystems.

Soil and nutrient cycling

Regulating the flow and availability of nutrients, gases and water by soil is an amazing ecosystem service that is emphasized only rarely, but is evident in the control difficulties when attempting hydroponic culture of plants. Consideration of simply physically supporting vegetation hints at the magnitude of costs associated with soil destroyed by pollution. The cost for physical support products used in hydroponic agriculture is $22,000 per acre. Of course, soils have been damaged by human activities such as pollution, compaction and erosion. In fact, soil damage by human activities is widespread, impacting almost 20 percent of the vegetated land area of the planet.[4]

Nutrient cycling is an ecosystem service to humans, especially in regard to the huge amount of solid waste produced by humans. Waste arising from household garbage, sewage, industry, agriculture and forestry constitute about one-third of the 143 billion tons of dead organic matter produced each year. Organisms decompose this organic waste in addition to soaps, detergents, pesticides, oil, acids and paper. Some materials are detoxified, or the disease-causing bacteria, viruses and other pathogens are removed by microbiotic activity.[4] This is certainly an ecosystem service that we must preserve and one that we can make greater use of to reduce the cost of maintaining a healthy city. The decomposition products are often materials like nitrogen or mulch that can be reused for human benefit. For example, domestic sewage can be "mined" to recover the large quantities of phosphorus it contains for reuse in agriculture. Another emerging prospect is the development of bio-plastics from treated sewage byproducts.

There are many ways to foster soil preservation or soil formation and the natural cycling of nutrients in residential and public landscapes. Prevention of wind and water erosion and the damage to soils during construction of buildings and landscapes is an obvious opportunity. Reducing the use of artificial fertilizers and pesticides benefit aquatic environments as well as soil fauna and flora. Using mulch and compost to cover exposed soil reduces erosion and provides the carbon needed by soil organisms to create fertile, healthy soil and nutrients for plants. Threats to natural soil formation and nutrient cycling include deposition of heavy metals, acid rain, herbicides, pesticides, soil compaction, erosion and eutrophication of water bodies.

Water cycling

Water is cycled through phase changes involving local, regional and global systems. Water is concentrated, transported, purified and distributed to human settlements, primarily through seven processes. Water evaporates from surfaces and transpires (Figure 4.2) from plants to enter the atmosphere as clean water vapor. It condenses on, or precipitates to, surfaces as relatively pure water. Some of the surface water infiltrates into the soil and is available to plants, while another fraction percolates to recharge aquifers or moves underground to sustain the base flow of streams and rivers during the dry season.

We can increase the benefit of clean water for human use by encouraging infiltration, percolation, groundwater recharge and base flow through many landscape practices within green infrastructure. Large sedimentation and infiltration basins are usually operated by counties, but small and numerous applications at each residence or commercial building can significantly slow runoff of stormwater, reduce flooding, reduce stream channelization and increase soil infiltration. Planting vegetation as a primary component of green infrastructure has a positive impact on the movement of water into and through the soil. Similarly, plants have a positive impact on the movement of water through evapotranspiration. Plants slow the surface runoff rate and velocity. The example of forest clearing illustrates the impacts of plants on runoff. In a New Hampshire study, the average stream flow increased 40 percent and the peak runoff was five times more than before a forest area was cleared.[4]

Unfortunately, often the benefits of green infrastructure are needed to compensate for damage caused by human activity elsewhere. We can anticipate the need for an increase of green infrastructure to address changes to the water cycle caused by global warming. In the UK, climate change will cause water cycle impacts. These include higher rainfall intensity, which is expected to rise by 40 percent by 2080. The cost of dealing with the associated flooding will be four to eight times the current amount.[5] New and retrofitted landscapes designed to detain or retain the increased storm volumes can protect property and reduce the extent and frequency of flooding.

Figure 4.2
The tree plantations in this image provide multiple benefits. The trees transpire the water and, along with soil organisms, remove excess nutrients (nitrogen and phosphorus) from the treated wastewater and sludge that is sprayed on the plantation. The trees are suitable for milling into molding or as pulp for paper, and can be harvested on a short cycle.

Human benefits from regulating ecosystem services

Wind, temperature and oxidation processes in the atmosphere provide a regulating service through their capacities to clean the air and disperse pollution. Most trace gases emitted into the air are removed through oxidation in a process that would normally maintain the current composition of the atmosphere and climatic characteristics.[6]

Climate and radiation

Climate regulation is an ecosystem service. The atmosphere provides four supporting ecosystem functions, including its natural warming. The density of the atmosphere and the ozone layer protect us from radiation, plasma and meteors. It also redistributes the water resources. Finally, the density pressure of the atmosphere allows direct use for sound communication and transportation. Natural ecosystems respond to changes in climate and may in turn moderate them. For example, global warming increases biomass production and decomposition rates. This could decrease or increase the release of carbon dioxide. The importance of these buffering measures is uncertain in the context of the emerging climate instability. It is clear that climate and ecosystems are closely paired and that the stability of their interactions is important.[4]

Green infrastructure can support the efforts to adapt to climate change or mitigate its impacts through encouraging alternate transportation and the sequestration of carbon. Although reduction in fossil fuel emissions is the most effective measure leading to climate change mitigation, other measures support this effort. For example, 13 tons of carbon dioxide is removed from the atmosphere annually for each set of 100 large mature trees.[7] Since the average per capita carbon emission in the US is more than 17 tons per year, it's clear that planting trees in urban forests or reforestation of public lands with millions of trees every year is required to make a significant contribution to climate change mitigation. However, Figure 4.2 illustrates that there are opportunities to plant millions of trees to serve multiple purposes. Clearly, reduction of CO_2 emissions must be tied to reduced use of fossil fuels and to other mitigation efforts, including reforestation.

In Europe, where CO_2 emissions are much lower (9.6 tons per capita in Germany) than in the US, carbon sequestration is a somewhat more hopeful measure. Urban forestry associated with green infrastructure contributes to a more positive carbon balance through the preservation of dense stands of trees or large-scale replanting of deforested areas. High carbon storage in a district of Leipzig, Germany (Figure 4.3), which contains multi-story residential buildings adjacent to a forested riparian corridor, demonstrates that high population density and high carbon storage can occur in the same urban district. The average carbon storage for the city is 11 metric tons of carbon per hectare, while for the district shown in Figure 4.3, it is 30.5 metric tons of carbon per hectare.[8]

In the past, regulations to reduce harmful emissions have been successful. For example, the Montreal Protocol established the direct global regulation of ozone-depleting chemicals used principally in refrigeration. The Antarctic and Arctic holes

Figure 4.3
High carbon storage of
this urban forest in
Leipzig is associated
with high-density urban
living. The riparian
woodland also offers
many biological
diversity and cultural
services to the city.
Photo 51°19'35.41" N
12°21'43.30" E, 13
August 2012 (accessed
14 May 2013) by
Google Earth.

in the ozone layer have now stopped growing in size, but have not yet begun to shrink.[6]

Temperature

Consideration of the ecosystem services of the atmosphere shows that the natural capture of heat by the atmosphere resulted in a 33°C shift from −18°C to an average surface temperature of 15°C. This natural rise in the average temperature resulted in a stable climate for the last 10,000 years and supported the evolution of existing ecosystems.[6] The climate today is less stable due to the effects of anthropogenic emission of greenhouse gases. Climate change is compounded by the heat island effect in cities and results in higher summer temperature for extended periods. Unless mitigated with green infrastructure and other measures, this will decrease human comfort, work productivity, water resources and wildlife. Increased mortality and health problems requiring hospitalization will result. These were the impacts of a heat wave in Europe in 2003. It was responsible for 30,000 more deaths than in other summers. The 2003 conditions are expected to be the new normal for Europe by 2050.[9]

The heat island effect is the elevated temperature in cities and nearby areas caused by urban materials and poor air circulation. The absorption and radiation of heat by

metal, concrete and asphalt increase the average temperature in cities. Green infrastructure reduces the impact of the heat island through shading surfaces, lower absorption of radiation and transpiration of water.

The heat island increases the demand for energy to cool buildings. For example, in Athens, Greece the heat island effect triples the amount of electricity demand for cooling. In US cities, each 1°F increase in temperature causes 1.5–2 percent increase in the peak electrical demand.[10] The higher albedo (reflectance) and higher evaporation and transpiration of water through vegetation and soils from green roofs and street trees reduce urban temperatures.

Studies show that green roofs reduce the maximum ambient temperature above the roof. Direct measurements in one study, at 5 p.m., revealed a maximum temperature reduction of 7.6°F at 1′ above the roof surface. If widely implemented at the city scale, green roofs could reduce the average ambient temperatures by between 0.5–5.4°F. Green roofs on tall buildings have little effect on the heat island effect.[10] Replacing asphalt, concrete and metal roofing with water-holding material, such as permeable asphalt embedded with absorbent fibers, also significantly reduces temperatures above roofs.[11] The design and performance of green roofs is the topic of Chapter 9.

Figure 4.4
Human activities have overwhelmed the atmosphere's capacity to provide a stable climate or protect us from harmful ozone depletion.

Wind

Windbreaks and shelterbelts provide green infrastructure benefits for human comfort and the protection of crops (Figure 4.5). A dense windbreak can reduce wind velocity for a distance as much as 30 times the height of the windbreak. There are additional benefits to be gained: prevention of snowdrifts on highways and reduced heating costs of buildings with well-placed windbreaks.[12]

Figure 4.5
Green infrastructure, in the form of windbreaks, protects the crops in the windy Columbia River basin while the ridgeline turbines create energy from this ecosystem service.

The increasing investment in wind energy projects worldwide highlights the ecosystem benefit of this natural phenomenon to humans. Competing demands for highly productive locations for wind farms sometimes place recreation, agriculture and wildlife in conflict, in both terrestrial and marine settings. Wind also benefits us in cities, where it disperses air pollutants, and in agriculture, where it pollinates crops such as corn and wheat. Of course, wind is sometimes also an ecosystem disservice, associated with hurricane and tornado storm damage to human settlements and wildlife habitats. In this case, forests and wetlands can mitigate the destructive force of wind-driven storms.

Global wind patterns are created by temperature and moisture differences at various latitudes. Global temperature changes due to climate change and the melting of polar ice are likely to cause a change in wind patterns. These changes will impact marine systems due to nutrient upwelling, as well as impacting terrestrial and human ecosystems.

Humidity

Changes in humidity impact both humans and natural ecosystems. A human comfort zone can be described as an interaction of temperature and humidity. Mortality rates increase due to stress on cardiovascular and respiratory systems, during periods of extreme temperature and humidity. Very low humidity is more problematic than high humidity.[13]

Plants and animals are also affected by changes in humidity. Climate change predictions include precipitation, temperature and humidity differences. For example, in Northern Europe an increase in air temperature of 2.3–4.5°C and an increase in precipitation of 5–30 percent will probably occur by 2100. The increase in precipitation will be accompanied by an increase of cloud cover and frequency of days with rain or snow, resulting in higher humidity. Warmer temperatures will also increase the water-holding capacity of the air. A study of the impact of an increase in humidity of 7 percent on fast-growing trees (aspen and birch) revealed considerable changes in tree respiration rates, photosynthesis, water-use efficiency, biomass allocation, growth, sap flow and other measures. These findings suggest that increased humidity due to global warming will change the functions of forest ecosystems. Adaptation to a new climatic condition may require revision of the usual planting palette in the green infrastructure of cities. Climate models have predicted the temperature and precipitation impacts on various regions. This will allow us to make long-term adaptation plans, which may include planting species to replace those that will die due to an altered climate.

Disease and pest regulation

Pests and disease occur in cycles that are dampened in healthy ecosystems but sometimes exacerbated in stressed ones. The example of the mountain pine beetle (*Dendroctonus ponderosae*) in the US and Canada illustrates an interaction of insects and their host population that seems to be out of equilibrium. The beetle is native and formally the number of trees it attacked and killed was limited. However, the current outbreak, which began in the middle of the 1990s, has affected an area ten times larger than any other infestation on record. The beetle infestations have killed huge tracts of forest (Figure 4.6). For example, 34.6 million acres (14 million hectares) have been affected in British Columbia. Cold temperatures in winter and cool temperatures in summer previously limited the range of the mountain pine beetle. Winter extremes of –40°C limit the population. Lodgepole pines (*Pinus contorta*) are the principal host trees, but other species of pine are also susceptible to attack. Once they are attacked, the trees defend themselves by increasing pitch flow, but trees that are stressed from drought or other causes are particularly susceptible and overwhelmed by swarms of the insects. The changing climate seems to be involved in this ecosystem change. The natural range of the beetle is expanding due to warmer temperatures, and the pines are more susceptible to attack because they are exposed to more severe drought conditions.[14] The natural ecosystem functions that limited the impact of the beetle have been compromised by human-caused changes to the climate.

Substantial ecosystem benefit can still be obtained from the beetle-killed forest tracts without compromising the regeneration of the forest. Since the insects attack mature stands, a great amount of merchantable timber can be harvested. While these salvage operations reduce the number of emerging seedlings, their numbers are sufficient for stand regeneration. The harvest of the dead trees generates biomass in the form of tree tops and branches, just as it does during the harvest of healthy stands. If left in place, the woody material could foster ground fires that would kill the saplings.[15] However, the harvest slash can be the source of additional human benefits, since the woody biomass can be collected and used to make isobutanol or

Figure 4.6
This photo shows the harvesting of trees killed by mountain pine beetle along roads in the Beaverhead-Deerlodge National Forest of Montana.

made into chips or pellets to fuel furnaces or wood stoves. Retention of some vertical snags and large trunks or branches on the ground preserves habitat niches within the recovering forest after the salvage operation is complete.

While the outbreak of the mountain pine beetle is, in some ways, an ecosystem disservice to humans, insects more often play a positive role. Natural enemies regulate 95 percent of the 100,000 arthropod (invertebrate animals with an exoskeleton) species that can be pests in the world's agriculture and forestland. The ecosystem benefits of biological pest control can be readily calculated. Each year the value of the biological control of pests in global agriculture is $400 billon.[16] In contrast, there are also significant ecosystem disservices in relationship to agriculture. Either before or after harvest, insects and other organisms destroy 25–50 percent of the world's crops. Similarly, human attempts to manage the ecosystem for food production are constrained when weeds compete alongside planted crops for water, sunlight and nutrients.[4]

Water regulation and purification

In the past when we have pursued economic gain, without the long-term goal of sustained productivity, we have damaged the ecosystem to our detriment. Deforestation is one of the most extensive examples of this shortsighted approach to human wellbeing. Flooding, soil erosion, siltation of reservoirs, streams and canals, and sometimes even the loss of the capacity of the forest to regenerate, disrupt the regulation of the water cycle and deprive us of clean water and other resources of economic value.[4]

Only about 1 percent of the water on the planet is available for human use. The remainder is seawater, ice, clouds and vapor in the air. About 70 percent of the available freshwater is used in agriculture. The water used directly by people is very valuable and the value can be easily calculated. In Britain, the cost of a cubic meter of fresh water is about $1.55 (£1). The cost of bottled water is much higher at about $1,086 (£700) per cubic meter. Even at the lower rate, the value of global precipitation is $776 billion (£500 billion). The cost of freshwater is expected to rise in response to global warming to a cost of $1 trillion per year by 2020.[6]

The experience of New York City water agency illustrates the economic and ecosystem benefits of green infrastructure to city residents. Today the city provides about one billion gallons of potable water to residents and visitors each day from its Catskill watershed (Figure 4.7). During the 1990s the potable water supply source for New York City was becoming increasingly polluted due to agriculture, urbanization and the discharge of effluent from wastewater treatment plants within the watershed. Faced with the choice of constructing a filtration plant to treat the increasingly polluted water, the city embarked on a watershed protection alternative instead. The city allocated $300 million for land acquisition and purchase of conservation easements in 1997. An additional $241 million was dedicated to this purpose in 2007 to fund activities through 2017. Since 1997, the city has added 121,000 acres (49,000 ha) to the 45,000 acres (18,000 ha) it already owned around the drinking water reservoirs. The state owns an additional 200,000 acres (81,000 ha) of protected watershed in the city catchment areas.[17] An official from the US Environmental Protection Agency estimated that the watershed investments by the city avoided the cost of building a $6–8 billion filtration plant, and hundreds of millions of dollars of operating cost, to clean polluted water flowing from an unprotected watershed.[18]

Figure 4.7
The Catskill–Delaware system (upper left) and the Croton watershed (lower right) are the watersheds that supply New York City with its drinking water. Together the two watersheds cover over 2,000 square miles. Photo base 41°26'47.73" N 73°36'10.42" W (accessed 14 March 2013), Google Earth.

Assessment of septic tanks and drain fields and the construction of 70 stormwater management facilities contributed to sustained water quality excellence within the watershed. Secondary ecosystem benefits are biodiversity protection and the provision of 75,000 acres (30,350 ha) of public land available for diverse recreational pursuits.[17] Investments in the watershed environment were the best way to ensure a long-term source of pure water for New York City and acquire additional ecosystem benefits.

Humans consume the greatest amount of water indirectly (70 percent is agriculture). Irrigated agriculture occupies about 18 percent of the agricultural land area and accounts for 40 percent of its economic value. The supply of water for agriculture, and its purity, is an ecosystem service of enormous value. However, it is very susceptible to reduction due to global warming.[16] Therefore, aquifer recharge, as well as measures to purify and reuse water, is a strategy to sustain this ecosystem service benefit.

Protection from storm hazards

Green infrastructure can provide substantial protection from flooding hazard. The case of New Orleans before and after 1930 is an instructive example. When New Orleans was founded, extensive forested swamps and wetlands of various types protected it from the devastating storm surges of hurricanes and tropical storms. A storm surge is a bulge of water that is several feet higher than mean sea level. This wall of water is driven inland by high winds. However, storm surges attenuate as they pass over wetlands. The reduction of the height of the storm surge is variable due to differences in storm characteristics, route and wetland characteristics, but a conservative estimate is that five miles of wetlands reduce the height of the storm surge by one foot.[19] The shortest distance from New Orleans to the Gulf of Mexico is about 30 miles. Therefore, a healthy wetland buffer would produce a six-foot reduction in a storm surge. Levees contain the Mississippi River since it annually flows at 14 feet (4.3 m) above sea level through New Orleans, which is at or below sea level (Figure 4.8). In this situation, reducing storm surges by six feet or more is a critical component of the city's flood protection system. The storm surge delivered by Hurricane Katrina was estimated at 10–20 feet.

Unfortunately, the Louisiana wetlands that previously buffered the city had been either eliminated or were unhealthy when Hurricane Katrina struck in 2005. It is really the loss of wetlands due to human alteration and management of the Mississippi River and its delta that caused the city to be overwhelmed.

While it is true that all of the engineered flood protection measures, including the levees, flood walls and drainage pumps failed during Hurricane Katrina, the tragic loss of property and 1,500 lives can be assigned to the loss of 1,800 square miles (39 square miles per year) of wetlands due to man's activity since the 1930s.[20] The wetland loss was caused by oil and gas exploration and extraction, levee construction resulting in loss of annual sediment supplied to the wetlands, land subsidence and more recently sea-level rise due to global warming. Construction of drainage canals for decades converted swamps and wetlands for agriculture and urbanization. Then levees to protect the dewatered land from flooding deprived other wetlands of the

Figure 4.8
The Mississippi River and the City of New Orleans.

annual sediment that built and sustained them. Today, the sediment is captured behind dams on the Mississippi or settles to the bottom of the thickening riverbed or is discharged beyond the continental shelf in the Gulf of Mexico. Historically, the distribution of river sediment more than compensated for the natural subsidence of the river delta. Without it, salt marshes became seawater coves connected to the gulf, while more inland freshwater ponds and lakes expanded and new ponds submerged previous wetlands. Furthermore, storms pushed saltwater farther inland, damaging the remaining freshwater wetlands. Wide and deep navigation channels connecting the gulf to the city funneled undiminished storm surges into New Orleans.

There are also natural causes of wetland loss. Hurricanes Katrina and Rita in 2005 destroyed nearly 140,000 acres (56,656 ha) of wetlands, although these are quite resilient. Marshes are also damaged by invasive species. The nutria (native to south America) has caused substantial damage by feeding on marsh vegetation.[21] These impacts also need to be mitigated to maintain the landscape infrastructure.

Calculations of the economic value of wetlands as a flood protection measure for New Orleans are reliable because we know that annual maintenance of flood control structures is $461,000 per year[22] and that the federal government estimated the damage caused by the 2005 Hurricanes Katrina and Rita and pledged $100 billion to rebuild the gulf coast region around New Orleans.[20]

There are other human benefits to be gained from the restoration of the Louisiana wetlands (Figure 4.9) as well. The biologically dead zone in the Gulf of Mexico, caused primarily by nitrogen-rich runoff from agriculture that is discharged by the channelized Mississippi River, is nearly 8,000 square miles (20,720 km²) in size.[22] Reducing the nitrogen levels by discharging water into the delta wetlands and other upstream measures would reduce the nitrogen concentration and restore the once prolific fishery in this oxygen-depleted zone.

The freshwater marshes are much less productive in the contemporary delta than marshes elsewhere that have river inputs (Figure 4.9). The Mississippi delta net primary production will be only half of its potential by 2050. This loss of productivity is a significant economic and food security issue for humans. The productivity of a healthy wetland ecosystem is illustrated by the saltwater marsh near Galveston, Texas. The 1,080-acre (437 ha) saltwater marsh produces 16 million brown shrimp, 15.5 million white shrimp and 11.3 million blue crab each year.[22] The Mississippi delta represents the largest fishery and most important bird migration flyway in the

Figure 4.9
Coastal wetlands have large economic benefits derived from storm protection and food production and other ecosystem benefits. Louisiana is estimated to have lost 1.2 million acres (485,623 ha) of coastal wetlands during the 100 years between 1900 and 2000.[21]

US due to its 9,650 square mile (24,993 km²) size and its productivity potential. Just three coastal ecosystem services – (1) abundant fish and wildlife, (2) high capacity to treat polluted water and (3) high storm protection value – illustrate the wealth contained in the Louisiana wetlands.

The flood control and other ecosystem service values of Louisiana wetlands are calculated to be $5,200 per acre per year. Therefore, restoring or recreating the 1,800 square miles (4,662 km²) of wetland lost in the area since 1930 would yield $6 billion of value to humans each year.[20] A similar case can be made for the restoration of the barrier islands near the Louisiana coast. There is also an amenity economic benefit to wetland restoration. Four case studies in the Mississippi river delta demonstrated amenity values of $2.95 per acre. This means that every one-acre increase in wetland areas close to residences (within the census block) increases the housing value by $2.95. This value per acre declines as distance between the home and the wetland increases.[21]

Today, subsidence in the Mississippi delta is about 0.5" per year[22] and sea-level rise due to global warming adds another 0.5" per year to the problem. Within the next 50–100 years, the relative sea-level rise anticipated at the Louisiana coast is 0.5–1 m.[23] Clearly, corrective measures need to be taken, especially given the vulnerability of the man-made flood control structures and devices. Fortunately, efforts are underway to re-establish lost wetlands and enhance damaged ones. The US Army Corps of Engineers is implementing a plan to restore and protect 58,861 acres (23,820 ha) of wetlands east of New Orleans. The cost will be $2.9 billion for construction, not including engineering and design costs, and real estate acquisition.

Pollination

Pollination is one of those ecosystem services that is critical to human wellbeing but often taken for granted. It is important because about 75 percent of the plant species that humans consume require insect pollinators, although some commodity crops

Figure 4.10
This pollen-covered bee is a reminder of the enormous economic benefit of pollinators to commercial agriculture and ecosystem functions.

(wheat, rice and maize) do not require insect pollination.[16] The economic value to the production of the 30 percent of crops that require pollination is almost 10 percent of the value of world agricultural output.[16,4] Another assessment of the economic value of pollination is illustrated by beekeeping businesses. In Switzerland, raising bees generates $213 million of economic benefit each year. One hive of bees ensured $1,050 worth of fruit and berries, in addition to the $215 value of its honey, beeswax and pollen it produces in a single year.[24]

Thoughtful conservation of natural habitat and the planting of green infrastructure in urban areas can support bees and the other 100,000 species of pollinators. Threats to pollinators are habitat loss and environmental pollutants. A parasitic mite (*Varroa destructor*) has reduced the unmanaged honey bee colonies in Europe and the US.[16] The damage caused by the mite is thought to be associated with poor hive health due to the impact of pesticides. Another threat to honeybees in the US is the aggressive African honeybee, which was accidentally released in Brazil in 1956. Through competition and hybridization the African strain threatens the species of honeybee in North America, which was introduced from Europe.[4]

The natural ecosystem viability is also dependent on pollinators, since over 90 percent of plant species require animal species, such as bats, bees, beetles, birds, butterflies and flies, for pollination and successful reproduction. Species of natural pollinators from at least 60 genera are threatened, endangered or extinct.[4] Planning for the availability of a wide range of habitat types for the food, breeding and other requirements of pollinators will yield significant benefits to humans.

Water treatment

The potential to use green infrastructure for the treatment of polluted water is tremendous since human settlements generate enormous amounts of stormwater and wastewater. Shifting the approach to treatment of these polluted waters to distributed, biological methods, within green infrastructure, has the potential to generate

Figure 4.11
Land application of
treated wastewater to
reduce phosphorus is
an economic alternative
and provides additional
green infrastructure
benefits.

substantial savings and many secondary ecosystem benefits. For example, a conventional sewage treatment plant in Oregon faced the prospect of upgrading the facility in order to comply with higher standards that limited the amount of phosphorus, nitrogen and temperature of the outflow. Instead, the organization implemented a landscape solution (Figure 4.11).

In a great example of forward thinking, the wastewater authority had purchased 340 acres (137 ha) of former agricultural land, including degraded wetlands and upland oak/grassland vegetation on valley slopes years earlier for eventual use as a biological treatment component (Figure 4.11). Water, which already meets secondary water quality standards, is pumped from the wastewater treatment plant and is contained in a newly constructed 2-acre (0.8 ha) wetland for a day. Then the water is distributed over 258 acres (104 ha), including 60 acres (24 ha) of restored native wetlands and 23 acres (9 ha) of created wetlands.[25,26]

The project cost about $10 million, compared to an estimated $100 million for upgrading the conventional plant. The savings were probably even greater since a comparable plant upgrade project in another municipality resulted in a final cost of approximately $150 million. The public debt repayment period for the project is three to five years.[26] The amazing economic benefit of this green infrastructure project is matched by the habitat and biodiversity aspects. Land, which would have been developed for suburban housing according to the existing pattern of habitat fragmentation and decreasing connectivity, preserves rare habitats and connects to regional habitats along the adjacent river corridor. The potential to add recreation facilities as the city expands in the future is high.

The multifunctionality of landscapes created to treat polluted stormwater runoff offer opportunities similar to those in the wastewater treatment project discussed above. Trees, plants and soil organisms have the capacity to clean stormwater and influence its flow. Mature trees of selected species can absorb as much as the first 0.5" of rainfall. When multiplied by many trees the effect is substantial. In the US Pacific Northwest 100 trees capture about 54,900 gallons of rainwater, thereby reducing municipal infrastructure costs.[7]

Waste decomposition

Solid waste management consumes a significant portion of the budget of every city and town. Separation of waste into streams with different treatment requirements and economic values supports the opportunities to recover and reuse the resources. Construction and demolition and other sources of wood waste provide opportunities to create biofuels or bioplastics. Even the managed biological processes of high-rate composting provide materials that improve fertility, soil structure and biodiversity when applied to farmland or degraded sites.

Human benefits from provisioning ecosystem services

Food

Community agriculture is an emerging and valuable part of green infrastructure in cities. To avoid conflicts with adjacent residential use and to respond to an alternative market, farmers within and adjacent to the city limits often adopt organic horticultural methods. Avoiding the use of chemical herbicides, pesticides and artificial fertilizers establishes a sustainable practice that supports ecosystem health on the farm and in the neighborhood. Community agriculture including community gardens and small-scale farms supplement the global food network and increase local food security (Figure 4.12). Having residents with farming skills increases the social capacity of the city while the local sale and purchase of products supports the local economy to a greater degree than sales in the global economy. Most communities have the capacity to greatly expand the proportion of high-value products such as fresh vegetables that are produced and consumed locally. This may require the adjustment of zoning laws, and the creation of new networks of food producers, processors and distribution systems. Chapter 10 addresses community agriculture in more detail.

Beyond the city the production impacts of agriculture determine whether the provision of food is an ecosystem service or threat. New concepts of ecological agriculture promote sustainable soil structure and fertility, water quality and biodiversity of pollinators, birds and animals. Production and harvest of crops, fruit, fungi, nuts, livestock, fish and shellfish is an ecosystem service even when there are artificial inputs of energy and chemicals, but long-term damage to the environment compromises the ecosystem service eventually. Instead, all agriculture needs to achieve multiple functions. Biological diversity, recreation, education and aesthetics are compatible with profitable agriculture. The use of hedgerows and shelterbelts and a mosaic of habitat patches, within a matrix of fields, supports biodiversity and recreation.

Figure 4.12
This one-acre organic farm produces 45 varieties of vegetables and salad greens for sale in the local farmers market.

Constructed wetlands that remove excess nitrogen from agricultural tailwater are another example of an ecosystem health measure that can be implemented without reducing growing area while supporting wildlife. Subsurface wetlands using wood chips as the bed media are very effective for the removal of nitrates from water that runs off fields.[27]

Because machinery, artificial fertilizer, pesticides and irrigation artificially support so much of agriculture, we tend to ignore the fundamental ecosystem functions that continue to make food production possible. The free ecosystems services provided for the 1.4 billion acres (566,559,900 ha) of global cropland include filtered solar radiation, precipitation, nitrogen, natural global warming and pollination. Basic provision of water, carbon dioxide and oxygen make photosynthesis and respiration possible. As noted earlier, soil and nutrient cycles are important even in the production of agricultural commodities.[16] It is hard to imagine that humans are capable of disrupting such fundamental natural process, but the decline of some of the systems that provide these services are well documented.

Addressing agriculture is important because it affects a large portion of the primary production, which is the basis of food and energy flows through ecosystems. In fact, humans harvest about 30 percent of the net primary production of the planet. Livestock grazes about one-third of this and the production of livestock is expected to double by 2050. Marine fisheries are another major protein source, as they provide nearly half of the human population with a significant portion of its protein. Marine fisheries are entirely dependent on natural ecosystem services. About one-quarter of the total supply of fish now comes from inland fisheries and aquaculture. Like other domestic livestock operations, aquaculture requires artificial inputs of food, pesticides and antibiotics to support high-volume, commercial production. As in other agriculture, the treatment of wastes from these operations is required as part of a larger effort to maintain ecosystem health. This is as critical to the future capacity to meet growing demand for food as improved strains of seeds, efficient irrigation or other production enhancements.[16]

Preservation of plant biodiversity is necessary for future ecosystem benefits to humans. Existing biodiversity is a source of genetic material that could be of great importance in the future for breeding of crop varieties to improve resistance to drought, disease and insect damage.[16]

Land-use changes have ecosystem benefit implications for humans. Conversion of forest and other habitat into pasture or other agriculture provides food businesses, but they can also involve large negative impacts, especially in the tropics. An example is the loss of tropical forest due to conversion to grassland for cattle grazing. The biodiversity impact is significant and the loss of carbon sequestration is a deficit that can't be accommodated in the current climate change situation. Similarly, the conversion of prime agricultural land to suburban development is a foolish reduction in our capacity to produce necessary food.

Conflicts over water resources are common in the semiarid and arid portions of the US. Hydroelectric power generation, water demand for agriculture and preserving minimum flows necessary to support ecosystem functions produce complex challenges. More efficient power generators, less water consumptive irrigation technologies, new crop varieties, runoff controls and reclamation and reuse of water are ways to meet some of these challenges.

Increasing land area for agriculture, plant hybrids and dependence on artificial inputs has led to amazing increases in agricultural productivity since 1950. Worldwide, 25 percent of the land area is in cultivation, but the demand for food will increase by as much as 50 percent by 2030. In fact, the demand for food products has increased faster than the population. Over the course of history, about 6,000 species of plants have been cultivated for food, but today only 30 crops comprise 95 percent of the world's food calories. This dependency on only a few species is really even greater since wheat, rice and corn account for 50 percent of the calorie intake. Similarly, only 14 species of livestock provide 90 percent of global production.[16] In the future we will need to continue the use of artificial fertilizer and monoculture of crops to produce the necessary food. However, it is important to understand that this is primarily an artificially supported system that has significant environmental impacts. It can be managed better to serve multiple functions and to mitigate the impact of unsustainable practices.

Energy

Fossil fuels are, of course, ecosystem benefits even if the geologic time scale is involved. While fossil fuels are our primary source, other energy sources are also increasingly important. Even biomass is globally important since it provides about 15 percent of the world's energy supply and as much as 40 percent of the energy resources in developing countries.[4] Surprisingly, biomass is the fastest-growing sector of renewable energy sources in the US. New technologies are likely to increase its importance.

The development of the process for creating ethanol and, more recently, isobutanol from plant and wood material represents another significant link between the ecosystem and energy. Isobutanol is a very high-quality energy liquid that can be used as jet fuel. It represents a carbon-neutral energy supply for military and commercial aircraft that will be available in the near future. The feedstock for the production of isobutanol is woody biomass that is currently piled and burned after commercial forest harvest operations. The biomass can also be generated from fuel reduction operations to reduce wildfires, from thinning forest stands to improve forest health, and from harvesting of millions of acres of trees killed by beetles.[28]

The direct use of wood as a cooking and heating fuel has been discouraged because of its inefficiency and the particulate air pollution it creates. In the US there are 12 million residential fireplaces and wood stoves. As many as nine million of these are outdated designs that are very inefficient and emit high levels of particulates, polycyclic aromatic hydrocarbons (PAH) and other pollutants. For example, old wood stoves produce 30 grams or more of particulate pollutants per hour (about the same rate as diesel trucks). This is a significant air pollution contribution in cities. In fact, wood burning is the primary source of urban particulate pollution in winter. Contemporary pellet stoves produce the least particulate pollution and are about 80 percent efficient. The best-performing pellet stoves produce about 1 g of particulate pollution per hour. Modern wood stove designs, with and without a catalytic converter, often approach the performance of pellet stoves. Electrostatic precipitators seem to offer the most promise for secondary pollution control, but the technology is expensive and systems are still being developed for the residential market.[29]

Advances in the design of pellet stoves make the prospect of using renewal biomass fuel as the primary heat source acceptable. Using biomass directly, rather than using it to create liquid fuel or electricity, is cost efficient. If the biomass is derived from a sustainable growth and harvest system, then the energy is carbon neutral, which reduces climate change impacts. Using efficient pellet stoves reduces the per capita CO_2 emissions by 10–20 percent for Americans. This finding is supported by an Austrian study demonstrating that wood pellet stoves reduce annual household CO_2 emission by as much as 11 tons compared to other fossil fuels. The improved performance of stoves, furnaces and boilers burning woody biomass suggests that community forestry programs might increase the local supply of energy resources and mitigate climate change trends, especially in non-metropolitan counties. Using woody biomass left after commercial timber harvest to make pellets for stoves provides an additional benefit, since this slash is generally burned, creating large amounts of particulate pollution and emitting CO_2. Oil and gas furnaces produce less particulate pollution compared to the best-performing pellet stoves, but oil and natural gas both produce CO_2 and exacerbate the climate change problem.

Live vegetation, rather than harvested biomass, also contributes to reduced energy consumption and reductions in CO_2 emissions. The positive impact of trees and green roofs on the heat island effect and the temperature of cities have associated energy benefits. Landscape measures reduce energy demands for heating and cooling buildings. In the residential setting in the US northwest, a single large tree placed on the west or south side of the building reduces home air-conditioning cost by an average of $7 each year ($16 per year in the south).[7]

Creation of carbon-neutral fuels from biomass derived from the culture of algae is an experimental technology. It is an attractive area of research because seawater and wastewater can be used to produce the crop instead of freshwater. Currently, high capital costs limit the commercial applicability of the biofuels, but within a decade or two the technology and lower cost are expected to allow competition with traditional fossil fuels. An atmospheric provisioning service comes from the direct use of wind and waves for power generation. In 2007 the value of global energy created by wind-powered generators was $37 billion. In the same year, $50.2 billion was invested in the technology. With the addition of two million new wind turbines, wind power could provide about 20 percent of world energy requirement by 2050.[6]

Fibers

The ecosystem provides resources that are the basis of several industries, including pulp for paper, cotton for textiles and lumber for building construction. The residential and commercial building industry is a significant portion of the national economy fueled for two centuries by the harvest of forests in a rapid and unsustainable march across the US. The largest annual harvest of timber in the US for all products was in 1989 (18.8 billion cubic feet). Since this peak, harvested amounts have gradually declined over the last two decades. Only the southern regions of the nation increased harvest volumes during the last decade. By 2002, slightly more than 15 billion cubic feet were being harvested annually. Only 1.5 billion cubic feet of this came from publicly owned land in 2002, compared to about four billion cubic feet in 1989. The timber harvest figures, above, represent all wood products, including fuelwood and pulpwood.[30].

Forest health, measured as forest cover, has recovered one-third of the loss from previous rapid deforestation of the US. Today, forests occupy 31.2 percent (641 million acres) of the US and dominate the landscape of the northeast, New England, mid-Atlantic, southeast and northwest regions of the country.[31] More recent concepts of sustainable harvest levels and the management of forests for multiple benefits, including recreation, water supply and wildlife, have reduced forest harvest amounts on public land dramatically compared to the widespread clear-cutting practices of the 1980s. Sustainable harvest on public land combined with private commercial forest operations can easily supply the demand for lumber in the future. This is evident since excess lumber is still being exported. Log and lumber exports from the west coast of the US amounted to almost five million cubic feet during the first quarter of 2012.[32]

Biochemical

Nature is the source of material for new products and the inspiration for others. The extraction of oxygen, nitrogen, argon and other gases from the atmosphere is a thriving global industry. Most drugs are based on natural sources such as plants,

Figure 4.13
Crystal nanostructures on the wings of the emerald-patched cattleheart butterfly (enlarged 20 times).

fungi and bacteria. Pharmaceuticals are the obvious examples of important bio-chemical ecosystem services, but there is also a long history of study and invention based on natural elements. For example, scientists at the Argonne National Laboratory are attempting to manufacture crystals that are environmentally benign for use in paints, fiber optics and solar cells. The inspiration for this work is the emerald-patched cattleheart butterfly. Figure 4.13 shows the crystal nanostructures on the butterfly's wings that selectively reflect green colors.

Genetic material from wild plants is being used to increase productivity of crops by conferring resistance to disease, drought, pests and other limitations. Biodiversity is the storehouse of this material and will probably have even greater importance as we try to adapt agricultural production to the new circumstances that global climate change will establish. Already, the use of genetic modifications to adjust crop resistance to perturbation is adding about 1 percent to crop productivity and one billion dollars of value to agricultural production annually. We will certainly need the thousands of varieties of mold and rice that were researched to derive commercial quantities of penicillin and a rice variety resistant to the grassy stunt virus, as new diseases and agriculture challenges arise.[4] These brief examples suggest that preservation of biodiversity serves us and that efforts to save species from extinction are worthwhile investments in our future wellbeing.

Air purification

Vegetation within a green infrastructure improves air quality either directly or indirectly to benefit humans. Nitrogen dioxide and sulfur dioxide are absorbed through leaf surfaces, while particulate matter is intercepted by the leaves and then deposited when leaves are washed by rain or fall to the ground. Pollution is particularly problematic where high densities of tall buildings create urban canyons where pollutants can concentrate. Recent research indicates that increasing the planting of these canyon spaces with green roofs, green walls and trees would increase the rapid and sustained deposition of nitrogen oxides and particulates. The ecosystem benefit is a reduction of these pollutants by as much as 40 percent for nitrogen oxides and 60 percent for particulates.[33]

Reduced temperature due to transpiration and shading reduce ozone levels. Similarly, air quality is indirectly improved when vegetation shades buildings in the summer and prevents heat loss in the winter and, therefore, lowers pollution generated by energy production (especially energy from coal-fired power plants). An assessment of the ecosystem service benefit of sets of 100 trees in the urban ecosystem reveals that pollutants (123 lb in the Pacific northwest, 137 lb in the south) are removed from the human environment.[7]

Human benefits from cultural ecosystem services

Aesthetic and spiritual

People respond to landscape beauty and scale. We love the textures, colors, variety and harmony found in the landscape and even images of the landscape. We want to experience the majesty of the Grand Canyon and the mystery of the microscopic landscape. We want to engage all of our faculties to touch, smell and listen to pristine nature. We want to engage our minds and muscles in the experience of a special landscape or a common and familiar bit of nature.

The image of the Santiam River in Figure 4.14 suggests the sound and dynamic pattern of the rushing water. We can almost bathe in the cool, green color of the forest and draw in the fragrant, humid air. The landscape is unified by the dominance of the enclosing forest, but we can find a variety of evergreen and deciduous plants. There is the energizing suggestion of danger in swift whitewater and deep pools. A mystery to be solved is presented in the turn of the river beyond our view. We are drawn to explore the gravel bank with its tenacious young tree, to lift the stones to find the mayfly larva in their traveling homes of cemented sand. Surely there are polished pebbles from miles upstream that are captured here. There is also a stone ruin of a man-made structure that hints at the story of a people who lived near this place long ago. The experiential use of the image and, better, a heightened experience in the physical landscape, is healthy and satisfying. We want the green infrastructure network to lead us from where we live to places like the Santiam River in the Niagara County Park.

Figure 4.14
The riparian scene along the Santiam River.

Human components of the urban landscape can have effects as powerful as those we experience in natural settings, such as along the Santiam River. There are astounding achievements in architecture and engineering that are beautiful and amazing. They are testaments to our ability to create and to build. Some of these artifacts of human history are contemporary, while others carry the heritage of our civilization. A great building is a frozen bit of social, political, economic or religious history. Seeing and using them should make us want to understand that cultural history better. Historic districts provide an even more complete and varied history of human habitation and endeavor. We want the green infrastructure to lead us to great buildings and through the cultural landscape.

Art and religion abound with reference to natural ecosystems as a source of wonderment, inspiration, peace and rejuvenation. Activities drawing on this source of fulfillment include ecotourism, hiking and camping, bird watching, photography, boating, fishing and hunting (Figure 4.15). More domestic examples of this ecosystem service are pets, feeding birds and gardening. The cultural category of ecosystem services applies to we humans who experience the natural world with our senses and interpret or appreciate it with our minds. Visual perception dominates our suite of sensory experiences and nature rewards us with daily stimulation.

Health and recreation

The landscape provides an opportunity for the physical activity that, as the chapter on human health illustrated, is inadequate in the lives of most people living in industrialized counties. When the landscape encourages physical activity it imparts a valuable human benefit. The economic value of physical activity is high. In England, the annual cost of a sedentary lifestyle is over $12 billion (£8 billion) annually. Inactivity due to obesity adds a burden of another $3.8 billion (£2.5 billion) per year. If adult residents of the UK would increase their physical activity by a modest 10 percent, it would save the nation more than $761 million (£500 million) per year.[9]

This economic understanding doesn't capture the full value of open space and recreation in cities, but these are clearly not frivolous amenities to be avoided in the pursuit of acreage for commercial or residential development. Instead they are critical to our physical and psychological health. A second British study found that, in areas where levels of greenery are high, people were three times more active and 40 percent less obese. The positive contribution of the landscape to physical health was confirmed by a study in Scotland. The evidence revealed a strong relationship between access to open space and improvements in mental health and lessening symptoms of chronic disease.[9]

Figure 4.15
Nature photography (of a heron in this case) is a joyful example of a cultural ecosystem service.

Parks are public resources that citizens use instead of purchasing these opportunities in the private sector. A study of Denver showed that the value of using public recreation facilities (Figure 4.16) by citizens is $452 million per year. The health benefits of public parks calculated for Denver confirms the economic importance that the British study found. The physical activity opportunities in parks can be expressed as the value of avoided medical costs. For Denver this amounts to $65 million per year.[34] The question of how much land a city should provide as recreation and open space is the topic of Chapter 7.

Education

Although urban areas express human values primarily, there is an overlap between the presence of other species and people that is especially important in cities. People are most likely to have experiences with nature if it is present near where they live and work. Here is where daily pleasure, restoration and even education about the natural environment and native species can occur. The city of Austin, Texas capitalizes on the twilight flight of 1.5 million free-tailed bats (*Tadarida brasiliensis*), and the 100,000 visitors that they attract annually, to provide education as well as foster tourism and civic pride (Figure 4.17). A local environmental group provides literature and interpretive programs about the ecology of bats and the service that they provide to humans. Riverboat tours and an annual festival organized around seeing and celebrating bats has extended to a bat mascot for a sport team and even a statue of a bat as a expression of sense-of-place and civic pride.[35]

Figure 4.16
Citizens use recreation centers, playgrounds (like this one at Stapleton), trails and sports fields provided and maintained by the city and avoid the cost of purchasing these opportunities in the marketplace.

Figure 4.17
Crowds gather to view
the Congress Avenue
Bridge flight of bats in
Austin, Texas.

That the bats have a constituency that understands their needs bodes well for the animals. Environmental education of the type we see in Austin can be extended. Citizens can engage in science projects gathering data on the presence of species and their numbers. The annual breeding bird count is a long-term example of citizen science in the US. There are many other environmental monitoring opportunities, such as the regular review of American rivers by the citizen group River Watchers. More direct activities include ecosystem restoration of streams, wetlands and forests. Examples of these activities are abundant in Chicago and the Chesapeake Bay watershed (Figure 4.18). In and near Chicago, thousands of volunteers engage in the Chicago Wilderness Habitat Project (www.habitatproject.org). The skills and interests of the volunteers are matched to programs that monitor populations of birds, dragonflies, butterflies, frogs and native plants. Volunteers working with professional scientists and resource managers collect seeds, restore habitats and eradicate invasive plants.

Tourism

Global tourism was valued at $856 billion in 2007. Not all of this is related to the natural environment, but a large portion of both winter and summer tourism for skiing or adventures in a warmer climate are economic benefits of a green infrastructure.[6] Even tourism at a municipal scale is economically important. Tourists often dedicate part of their travel to visiting high-quality parks and recreation facilities. This is illustrated by Central Park in New York City. It attracts 40 million visitors each year and is a top tourist destination.

The Trust for Public Land was commissioned by the city and county of Denver to estimate the economic value of the 6,200 acres (2,509 ha) of parkland and recreation assets within their jurisdictions. Economic benefit accrues from property tax, direct

Figure 4.18
Volunteers work to
restore habitat within
the Chesapeake Bay
Watershed.

use, tourism, clean air, clean water, human health and the social environment. The increased property tax, generated by an increase in value of residences because of their proximity to parks, amounts to more than $4 million annually. Sales tax revenue from non-residents visiting to use city facilities is over $3 million per year. The value of property owned by city residents increased by $30.7 million due to park effects. Similarly, residents receive $18 million in net income from tourist spending. The costs of stormwater treatment ($804,000) and air quality improvement ($129,000) were saved by the city due to the effects of park vegetation and soil infiltration. "Friends of" groups are organizations of citizens that improve parks and neighborhoods at a very low cost to the city. These groups provide services that are socially and economically valuable. For example, reductions in antisocial behavior and degraded public facilities reduce city costs by an estimated $2.7 million. The park system of Denver thus has an economic benefit of approximately $569 million.[34]

Economic value of ecosystem services

Economic development and vitality are cultural factors that can be supported or diminished by the use of land. The traditional view is that only industrial or commercial developments add economic value to a city. This chapter illustrates that the ecosystem directly provides much of the economic value to society and indirectly supports many economic activities. Existing healthy ecosystems provide humans with a great range of products of economic value. Restoring degraded landscapes can also be justified by the economic value of the ecosystem services that they provide. The example of the new National Forest in the UK confirms this observation. The National Forest is a 200 square mile (518 km²) region of central England. It is being transformed from a degraded landscape into a multifunctional green infrastructure with commercial forestry, tourism and other benefits. The total project cost $54.5 million (€41,974,755). Maintenance and management costs about $7 million (€5,391,253) per year. This investment has created or secured many new jobs in forestry (333 jobs), tourism and service sectors in a region that was economically depressed. Millions of visitors now come to the area every day, establishing a $432 million (€321 million) tourism benefit, based on an analysis of the period from 1991 to 2010. The value of recreation during this period is estimated to be $845 million (€628 million) and lumber products are valued at $15 million (€11 million). Carbon sequestration $281 million (€209 million), biodiversity $75 million (€56 million) and landscape restoration and enhancement $154 million (€114 million); these represent a total value of $510 million (€379 million). In total, the economic value of the ecosystems services provided by the restored ecosystem is estimated to be $1.35 billion (€1.005 billion), with a benefits to cost ratio of 4.8 to 1. For the period 1990 to 2010 the benefit–cost ratio is 2.6 to 1.[24] For a discussion of recreation and biodiversity in the National Forest, see Chapter 7.

An early study of the relationship of open space and residential property has been confirmed many times. The city of Boulder, Colorado purchased thousands of acres of open space (Figure 4.19) using funds from a 0.4 percent city sales tax adopted by the voters. Sales of residential property within 3,200 feet of the newly acquired

Figure 4.19
Investments in open space have an economic benefit far greater than their initial cost.

greenbelt were analyzed. The study revealed that the average value of properties adjacent to the greenbelt were 32 percent higher than those 3,200 feet away. The value of residential property decreased $4.20 (1975) with every foot from the green-belt. In addition to the free public resource that open space offers all residents, private landowners are willing to pay a premium for proximity to the resource, just as they are willing to pay more for a home with more square footage.[36]

The increase in property value increases property tax revenue. Since the value of all the homes within the study area rose, property taxes reflect this increase. In fact, if taxes were collected in relationship to this increased value it would result in enough revenue to repay the cost of acquiring the greenbelt land within just three years. Assessment of property value for taxing purposes sometimes doesn't properly reflect causes for value increases, but it could certainly be organized to reflect the effect of proximity to publicly provided resources.[36] The Boulder assessment of property values associated with proximity to the greenbelt is confirmed by similar studies in Europe. A 2004 study in the Netherlands found that a view of a park raised house prices by 8 percent, and having a park nearby raised house prices by 6 percent.[24]

At the scale of the residence, green infrastructure also provides economic benefits that vary by region according to environmental conditions, energy costs and property values. For example, a single large tree in the urban Pacific northwest is worth $2,820 ($4,240 in the south) in property value, energy and environmental benefits over its lifetime. This value represents a benefit to cost ratio ranging from 3:1 to 4:1. Over an average lifespan of 40 years, 100 trees in the northwest provide an ecosystem benefit worth $190,320 ($316,120 in the South).[7]

It is paradoxical that we energetically calculate the economic cost of environmental and weather disasters, while ignoring the value of ecosystem services. For example, the cost of the Hurricane Katrina disaster is estimated at $90 billion. Weather-related damage costs in the US average $23 billion per year. However, the less visible cost of climate change is much higher. The estimated cost of damage caused by global warming is anticipated to be $250 billion per year by 2050. The total economic impact of global warming is estimated at $3 trillion to $12 trillion. Clearly, the economic value of the services that maintain a stable climate is many times greater than the losses caused by unusual weather events, but sustaining these services is often ignored by decision makers at all levels of government. Overall, ecosystem services are estimated to be about twice the value of the gross world product (GWP; $18 trillion), while the total economic value of atmospheric services is between 100 and 1000 times the GWP.[6]

Sustaining ecosystem services

The ecosystem in general, and specifically the green infrastructure of the city and countryside, provides a host of benefits to people. Sustaining those benefits means attending to the health of the ecosystems that provide them. This chapter outlined services that are important but sometimes indirect and undervalued by society. In particular, supporting ecosystem functions are less visible and often taken for granted. In fact, the climate change controversy illustrates that we have difficulty even believing that the damage we cause to these less tangible aspects of ecosystem health can be caused by man and affect him so directly and dramatically. Ecosystems that provide economically traded products have a built-in indicator of system health. Gradual reductions in the numbers of oysters harvested, for example, signal an ecosystem health problem. But green infrastructure used for recreation isn't traded, so its value is sometimes discounted. This is why physical and psychological benefits and avoided-cost economic studies serve to remind us of the essential nature of green infrastructure for recreation.

The more obvious ecosystem benefits, such as sustained harvests of timber, crops or seafood, are more clearly linked to human wellbeing but are subject to pressure from human population growth, economic and political interests. Enumerating the species that provide products to man would create an overwhelming list. In turn, each of these species is embedded in an ecosystem that must be sustained for continued productivity. This exercise reminds us that we are sustained by the natural world.[4]

Our quality of life is, similarly, enhanced by the social and cultural opportunities presented to us in the urban setting. Celebrations of historical and contemporary civilization and technological innovation enrich us. Yet we need physical activity, recreation and natural areas that present the wonders of nature to enhance the quality of our lives. Actually, the enjoyment of nature for health and aesthetic purposes, or the cultural understanding and education opportunities of historic monuments, and even economic products probably now depend on human access to managed ecosystems. Sustained natural biodiversity may also require some degree of human management. These resources (recreational, aesthetic, historic, biological and economic) need to be distributed throughout our communities and metropolitan regions. Subsequent chapters will explore how to plan, design, engineer and locate green infrastructure components to sustain economic, social and environmental benefits.

References

1   E. Gomez-Baggethun, "Natural Capital and Ecosystem Services," in *Ecosystem Services, Issues in Environmental Science and Technology*, vol. 30, Cambridge: Royal Society of Chemistry, 2010.

2   R. M. Hassan, S. R. Carpenter, K. Chopra, D. Capistrano and Millennium Ecosystem Assessment, *Ecosystems and Human Well-Being*, Washington, DC: Island Press, 2005.

3   K. Tzoulas and P. James, "Peoples' Use of, and Concerns about, Green Space Networks: A Case Study of Birchwood, Warrington New Town, UK," *Urban Forestry & Urban Greening*, vol. 9, no. 2, pp. 121–128, 2010.

4   G. Daily, *Ecosystem Services: Benefits Supplied to Human Societies by Natural Ecosystems*, Washington, DC: Ecological Society of America, 1997.

5   United Nations Environment Programme, "21 Issues for the 21st Century Results of the UNEP Foresight Process on Emerging Environmental Issues," 2012.

6   J. Thornes, "Atmospheric Services," in *Ecosystem Services, Issues in Environmental Science and Technology*, vol. 30, Cambridge: Royal Society of Chemistry, 2010.

7   E. McPherson, J. R. Simpson, P. J. Peper and Q. Xiao, *Trees Pay Us Back in the Pacific Northwest Region*, Albany, CA: US Department of Agriculture, 2011.

8   M. W. Strohbach and D. Haase, "Above-Ground Carbon Storage by Urban Trees in Leipzig, Germany: Analysis of Patterns in a European City," *Landscape and Urban Planning*, vol. 104, no. 1, pp. 95–104, 2012.

9   L. Grant, "Multi-Functional Urban Green Infrastructure," The Chartered Institution of Water and Environmental Management, Briefing Report, 2010.

10 M. Santamouris, "Cooling the Cities: A Review of Reflective and Green Roof Mitigation Technologies to Fight Heat Island and Improve Comfort in Urban Environments," *Solar Energy*, in press.

11 T. Nakayama and T. Fujita, "Cooling Effect of Water-Holding Pavements Made of New Materials on Water and Heat Budgets in Urban Areas," *Landscape and Urban Planning*, vol. 96, no. 2, pp. 57–67, 2010.

12 J. M. Caborn, *Shelterbelts and Windbreaks*, London: Faber and Faber, 1965.

13 A. I. Barreca, "Climate Change, Humidity, and Mortality in the United States," *Journal of Environmental Economics and Management*, vol. 63, no. 1, pp. 19–34, 2012.

14 N. C. Coops, M. A. Wulder and R. H. Waring, "Modeling Lodgepole and Jack Pine Vulnerability to Mountain Pine Beetle Expansion into the Western Canadian Boreal Forest," *Forest Ecology and Management*, vol. 274, pp. 161–171, 2012.

15 J. M. Griffin, M. Simard and M. G. Turner, "Salvage Harvest Effects on Advance Tree Regeneration, Soil Nitrogen, and Fuels Following Mountain Pine Beetle Outbreak in Lodgepole Pine," *Forest Ecology and Management*, vol. 291, pp. 228–239, 2013.

16 K. Norris, "Ecosystem Services and Food Production," in *Ecosystem Services, Issues in Environmental Science and Technology*, vol. 30, Cambridge: Royal Society of Chemistry, 2010.

17 New York City Department of Environmental Protection, "New York City 2011 Drinking Water Supply and Quality Report," 2012.

18 A. DePalma, "New York's Water Supply May Need Filtering," *New York Times*, 20 July 2006.

19 T. V. Wamsley, M. A. Cialone, J. M. Smith, J. H. Atkinson and J. D. Rosati, "The Potential of Wetlands in Reducing Storm Surge," *Ocean Engineering*, vol. 37, no. 1, pp. 59–68, 2010.

20 R. Costanza, W. J. Mitsch and J. W. Day, "Creating a Sustainable and Desirable New Orleans," *Ecological Engineering*, vol. 26, no. 4, pp. 317–320, 2006.

21 S. G. Kim, S.-H. Cho and R. K. Roberts, "Identifying Priority Areas for Wetlands Restoration along the Louisiana Coast under the Coastal Wetlands Planning, Protection, and Restoration Act of 1990," *Canadian Journal of Agricultural Economics/Revue canadienne d'agroeconomie*, vol. 59, no. 2, pp. 295–320, 2011.

22 T. W. La Point, "Understanding One's Place in the Watershed: How Earth Science Can Inform Perceptions about the Future of the New Orleans Region," *Technology in Society*, vol. 29, no. 2, pp. 197–203, 2007.

23 J. M. Smith, M. A. Cialone, T. V. Wamsley, and T. O. McAlpin, "Potential Impact of Sea Level Rise on Coastal Surges in Southeast Louisiana," *Ocean Engineering*, vol. 37, no. 1, pp. 37–47, 2010.

24 European Commission, "The Multifunctionality of Green Infrastructure," 2012.

25 Roseburg Urban Sanitary Authority, "RUSA Farm: Natural Treatment Systems Project," 2011.

26 J. Baird, "Roseburg Urban Sanitary Authority, Land Farm," personal interview, 2011.

27 L. A. Schipper, W. D. Robertson, A. J. Gold, D. B. Jaynes and S. C. Cameron, "Denitrifying Bioreactors: An Approach for Reducing Nitrate Loads to Receiving Waters," *Ecological Engineering*, vol. 36, no. 11, pp. 1532–1543, 2010.

28 D. Johnson, "Woody Biomass Supply Chain and Infrastructure for the Biofuels Industries," presented at the 2011 Industry Studies Conference, Pittsburg, PA, 2011.

29 Institute for Process and Particle Engineering, "Survey on the Present Status of Particle Precipitation Devices for Residential Biomass Combustion," Graz University of Technology, Austria, IEA Bioenergy Task 32, 2011.

30 D. Adams, R. Haynes and A. Daigneault, "Estimated Timber Harvest by U.S. Region and Ownership, 1950–2002," US Department of Agriculture, General Technical Report PNW-GTR-659, 2006.

31 US Environmental Protection Agency (EPA), "EPA's 2008 Report on the Environment," National Technical Information Service, Environmental Assessment EPA/600/R-07/045F, 2008.

32 USDA Forest Service Pacific Northwest Research Station, "West Coast Lumber Exports Increase Slightly in the First Quarter of 2012," 21 May 2012. [Online]. Available: www.fs.fed.us/pnw/news/2012/05/lumber-exports.shtml (accessed 21 May 2012).

33 T. A. M. Pugh, A. R. MacKenzie, J. D. Whyatt and C. N. Hewitt, "Effectiveness of Green Infrastructure for Improvement of Air Quality in Urban Street Canyons," *Environmental Science & Technology*, vol. 46, no. 14, pp. 7692–7699, 2012.

34 The Trust for Public Land, "The Economic Benefits of Denver's Park and Recreation System," 2010.

35 D. C. Dearborn and S. Kark, "Motivations for Conserving Urban Biodiversity," *Conservation Biology*, vol. 24, no. 2, pp. 432–440, 2010.

36 M. Correll, J. Lillydahl and L. Singell, "The Effects of Greenbelts on Residential Property Values: Some Findings on the Political Economy of Open Space," *Land Economics*, vol. 54, no. 2, pp. 207–217, 1978.

CHAPTER FIVE

Planning and design processes

Introduction

To be functional, politically viable and economically feasible, green infrastructure needs to offer many benefits. To acquire diverse benefits the landscape infrastructure must be championed by citizens and by a range of interest groups that typically focus on single issues. This coalition of constituencies is vitally important to apply the political pressure to complete planning, secure the commitment of the elected officials and dedicate funds to implement a long-term plan. Planning and design professionals in the past have generally failed to program for the full range of benefits possible from green infrastructure due to single-use approaches to funding or piecemeal planning and design processes.

The creation of teams composed of citizens, business representatives, elected officials, municipal department heads and disciplinary experts is key to meeting the full planning potential. The discipline experts from finance, planning, ecology and landscape architecture should be participants charged with resolving the technical issues involved with planning, locating and funding. Since there is a host of green infrastructure demands to be simultaneously planned for, the process is similar to comprehensive planning at the municipal and county scale. The outcome of comprehensive planning documents is usually a set of articulated values, visions, goals and sometimes strategies to meet stated objectives. However, since green infrastructure is a structural and continuous network, it must be geographically located and implemented with the support of growth limit boundaries, conservation easements, transfer of development rights programs, subdivision ordinances, stormwater management requirements, rights-of-way agreements, land purchases or other planning measures. While development of a vision and goals are important first steps, creation of master plans supported by zoning, subdivision and development ordinances move the vision toward realization. The entire process is a long-term endeavor. To be economically, socially and environmentally viable, green infrastructure must be planned years, sometimes decades, in advance of development pressures.

Participatory planning: Stapleton case study

Participatory planning is a civic model that improves upon the common pattern in the US, where citizens react to private development proposals instead of articulating policy and physical planning goals in advance of private market objectives. The Stapleton redevelopment project in Denver, Colorado (introduced in Chapter 1) is a model of comprehensive planning processes in advance of planning proposals. The public had a particularly prominent role in establishing the vision, guidelines and conceptual plan for Stapleton, since the property was publically owned. In Stapleton a 35-person citizen group managed a two-year community planning process called Stapleton Tomorrow, beginning in 1989. In June 1991 they completed a concept plan for the redevelopment of Stapleton, which was incorporated into Denver's Comprehensive Plan.[1]

In order to create a detailed physical and financial development plan for Stapleton, several new entities were created to build on the Stapleton Tomorrow plan. The City of Denver joined with the Stapleton Redevelopment Foundation in 1993 to begin the development process. In the same year, Mayor Wellington Webb appointed a Citizens Advisory Board. It was established to work with the Stapleton Redevelopment Foundation. The Citizens Advisory Board was a partner in the preparation and publication of the *Green Book (The Stapleton Redevelopment Plan)*. Mayor Webb created a second organization in 1995. This was a private, non-profit group called the Stapleton Development Corporation. The Citizens Advisory Board was advisory to the Stapleton Development Corporation and placed a member on its board.[2]

More than 100 public events were incorporated into the public planning process for Stapleton. In 1995 the two groups published the *Green Book* with the assistance of a number of technical consultants, including engineers, planners, architects and landscape architects. The *Green Book* continues to provide the parameters for the development of Stapleton.[2]

Figure 5.1
The *Green Book* established the open space requirements for the redevelopment of the Stapleton property. The disciplinary consultants established the multiple use of the open space for recreation, habitat and stormwater management.

The *Green Book* allocated over 1,600 acres to parks, trails, recreation facilities and natural areas, including the restoration of Westerly Creek and a 365-acre Prairie Park in the northern portion of the site (Figure 5.1). Commercial and industrial use was allocated 1,200 acres of developable land. The residential density was specified to meet 12 units per acre in order to support public transportation systems. Neighborhood centers were planned with higher residential density to provide the population needed for neighborhood commercial and transit centers.[1]

The Stapleton Development Corporation is responsible for receiving parcels from the Denver International Airport (the public owner) after demolition and remediation of any toxic substances. The development-ready parcels are sold to the developer, Forest City, after covenants are added to the deeds. The covenants are measures that assure that the land is developed according to the *Green Book* master plan. Other reviews by the Stapleton Development Corporation during detailed planning and construction also align the outcome with the master plan.

Not all of the goals of the *Green Book* have been realized. For example, the development is less diverse in terms of economic strata of residents than the *Green Book* envisioned, and the 1,660-acre open space was reduced slightly. The community is also overwhelmingly auto-oriented rather than transit-oriented. However, a transit-oriented neighborhood has been planned around a future light rail station that will connect Stapleton to Denver city center and the international airport by 2015. The rail station will include an adjacent 16-bay bus transfer facility. The 0.5-mile radius area around the station will be the focus of high-density mixed-use development that Stapleton has failed to provide, except in a tentative way around the 29th Avenue Founders Park. There will be 45 acres of parkland within the half-mile radius of the transit station, providing an unusual mixture of high-density residential and commercial use and open space access.

The green infrastructure network at Stapleton was a structural element of the master plan. It was conceived as having multiple purposes ranging from separating and focusing the highest density development (Figure 5.2), to the restoration of habitat and connecting it to regional preserves and corridors. This orientation was the result of proactive planning by citizens, the city and economic development, environmental and social interest groups.

Activist planning

The activist character of the Stapleton planning process is as admirable and effective as it is unusual. What fostered this process at Stapleton and what impedes the application of this model elsewhere? There are at least two factors. First the Stapleton property was publicly owned and contained areas where toxic substances, such as solvents and hydrocarbons, required removal or remediation. Both of these attributes prevented the usual pattern of purchase and development of relatively small parcels of land by private developers without the benefit of a physical design (master planning). The second factor was the need to replace habitat completely destroyed by the previous land use. The presence of a nearby creek and an adjacent wildlife refuge encouraged planning for native biodiversity, habitat and connectivity within the city limits. Elsewhere, piecemeal development of smaller, privately owned parcels

and the absence of a regional vision (and physical master plan) result in reactionary planning processes, unintended cumulative impacts and poor-quality built environments.

The ability of the city of Denver to prepare parcels for development, attach development requirements and transfer the property to a developer guaranteed that the green infrastructure was implemented according to the binding development plan. Other cities should develop physical master plans for green infrastructure for the entire municipal area. County planning of green infrastructure will have somewhat different priorities but should be conducted in concert with the municipal effort for the necessary integration of planning scales. The cities should prioritize and then purchase the key parcels and transfer these to the private sector with development covenants where commercial and residential development can frame the open space at densities higher than typical of suburban development. This strategy limits the land area consumed by the built environment, supports public transportation and rewards residents, developers and business owners willing to occupy higher-density areas.

History shows us that citizen participation and commitment is necessary for the implementation of citywide open-space networks. The examples of Stapleton and Boulder, Colorado illustrate that consistent and long-term planning, funding and implementation results in high-quality urban environments (Figure 5.3). These places perform well economically, environmentally and socially. In a later chapter the case study of Stockholm, Sweden reinforces the process and development lessons learned in the Colorado examples.

Figure 5.2
The green infrastructure in the town center of Stapleton is framed by high-density mixed-use buildings.

Figure 5.3
Green infrastructure linking urban and natural spaces provides social and environmental benefits in Boulder, Colorado.

Planning tools in support of green infrastructure

While it seems clear that land acquisition is the most effective way to implement green infrastructure and establish an urban structure for a growing city (or shrinking city, for that matter), other planning tools should also be utilized. Acquiring conservation easements and the purchase or transfer of development rights are somewhat effective tools for the preservation of ranch and farmland. They can be effective for the conservation of biodiversity if ecological principles are required during the continued economic use of the properties. These techniques are less expensive than land acquisition.

Transfer of development rights programs

A city and county can cooperate to establish a market for the sale of development rights and their transfer to other properties. The purpose is two-fold. First, the density of residential or commercial development is intended to increase within the city limits. Second, within the county, farming, ranching, forestry, water supply, recreation and habitat are intended for protection from speculative suburban and exurban residential development. A transfer of development rights program establishes a sending area (in the county) and a receiving area (in the city). Then the city establishes an artificially low density requirement for the receiving area, with density increases permitted when development rights are transferred from the sending area. The program is market-based and has property value and property tax implications that serve both developers of city property and owners of large parcels of county land.[3]

Comprehensive planning, zoning and ordinances

Zoning is generally ineffective as a sustainability planning tool in the long term since it really protects existing uses rather than establishing future ones. Zoning is highly susceptible to political and economic manipulation and has a planning horizon that is generally too short to serve the creation of a system-wide green infrastructure. However, zoning that is the result of physical planning establishes real expectations of future land use. This planning tool is sometimes called a future land use plan. It is more effective than zoning that establishes temporary zones in anticipation of unspecified future development. For example, urban farming should be zoned as a use-by-right instead of a temporary or conditional use occupying land intended for suburban expansion. In this way, community agriculture can be located where it supports the local economy, contributes to the green infrastructure system and where it can be provided with the appropriate infrastructure. This method helps avoid conflicts with other land-uses and establishes the land value for taxation according to its agricultural use, not according to its speculative value as future suburban hous-ing. Purchase or transfer of development rights would support this community agriculture zoning and make permanent local food production a component of the civic economy and social capital.

Comprehensive plans are positive first steps but lack the authority to implement the green infrastructure values and goals expressed there. Subdivision and develop-ment ordinances that are established to implement green infrastructure goals articu-lated in a comprehensive plan or future land-use plan are more effective tools for creating long-term results. Without these, comprehensive plans and general zoning plans are often simply exercises of wishful thinking.

Resource protection and conservation subdivision ordinances

Natural resource protection ordinances are really development restrictions that could be reflected in the development or subdivision ordinances. Nevertheless, they can support a green infrastructure plan if the protected riparian areas, steep slopes, wetlands or other landscapes contribute to a continuous network of spaces and corridors. Conservation subdivision ordinances are useful if the conserved open space is required to be consistent with a green infrastructure plan established by the city or county. Clustering residential and commercial structures and preserving open space or habitat can decrease the impact of exurban residences on native species. However, if the subdivision open space is too small or isolated from ecological corridors and habitat fragments, it may offer little more biodiversity value than low-density suburban development.

Incentives and technical assistance

Tax incentives and technical assistance for private landowners are often valuable tools to encourage an expansion of the efforts that land acquisition and purchase of easements or developments rights put in place. University Extension Agents have served owners of agricultural land with technical assistance for many decades in the US, and this program could be expanded to provide technical support in other aspects of sustainability. Similarly, payment to landowners for the preservation of habitat, landscape restoration or ecological agricultural practices that support biodiversity are new tools that may become more common and effective in the US.[4]

Planning for biodiversity

Planning for biodiversity is certainly not a separate process from green infrastructure or municipal comprehensive planning, but the effort dedicated to it and the planning processes involved are of particular interest. Surveys of 84 municipal, county and tribal planning directors in Washington, Iowa and North Carolina demonstrate that almost all planning activity is related to development of the built environment, such as processing permits, and economic and housing development. The majority of the directors within the three regions noted that their staff dedicated less than 5 percent of their time to conservation or biodiversity issues. Only 14–28 percent of the jurisdictions surveyed in the three regions had an inventory of native plants or animals in their comprehensive plans and only 9–33 percent of the plans set specific goals to conserve native species. Within the three regions, 25 percent, 81 percent and 87 percent of the jurisdictions had comprehensive plans encouraging open space focused on habitat protection. In general, ordinances supported the comprehensive plan goals to a lesser degree, suggesting that the goals were not always coupled to enforceable measures. In contrast to focused biodiversity efforts, 52–86 percent of the jurisdictions created parks and open space with multiple functions that included biodiversity support. Similarly, 48 to 73 percent of the jurisdictions called for greenways that included recreation and biodiversity aspects. This study suggests that multifunctional green infrastructure is a higher priority than species or habitat conservation among planners at the municipal and county scale, but that the conservation measures taken are general rather than species specific.[5] Therefore, it is unclear whether meaningful biodiversity conservation is accomplished.

The nearly complete focus on development issues is not surprising since it is projected that the developed areas of cities and towns is expected to increase 79 percent in the US during the next 20 years.[5] Of course, the impacts of that development should also merit concern and mitigation activity. The development emphasis suggests that building green infrastructure that has transportation, recreation and urban form elements (support for commercial and residential structures) are important bases on which to add corridors and habitat areas for biodiversity.

Some regions of the US, and many more in European and Asian countries, have been densely settled for generations. In this setting, establishing green infrastructure that includes biodiversity support is especially difficult. A planning model for the analysis and promotion of biodiversity in regions where urbanization and human activity has permanently altered the original ecosystems is offered by Chiba City, Japan. This city near Tokyo engaged in a planning process that began by determining the species and their distribution in relation to four current land-use zones, in order to establish a sustainable development plan that includes conservation of species and restoration of habitat. The city has a population of nearly one million and a land

Figure 5.4
Formal waterfront park constructed on reclaimed land in Chiba, Japan.

area of 105.05 square miles (272.08 km²) that was transformed by filling Tokyo Bay to create industrial land, which eliminated almost all of the salt marshes and tidal wetlands habitat (Figures 5.4 and 5.5).

Inland the landscape is dominated by rice agriculture in fairly small plots. A comprehensive survey identified the flora (1,553 species) and fauna (2,838 species) of which 80 plant species and 62 animal species were classified as endangered. An additional 69 plant and 35 animal species were classified as threatened. A number of plant species (22) and animal species (17) were already locally extinct. The surprising diversity of species in this human-dominated landscape is due largely to the traditional rice agriculture in poorly drained paddies within narrow valleys surrounded by forest remnants of evergreen and broad-leaved trees, such as chinkapin (*Castanopsis cuspidata*), laurel (*Machilus thunbergii*) and live oaks (*Quercus myrsinaefolia*, *Q. acuta*, *Q. glauca*) (Figure 5.6).[6]

The distribution of 165 endangered and threatened plant and animal species was mapped and then the numbers of these species occurring within 1-km² cells were noted and compared to the city's four land-use classifications (urbanization promotion; parkland; agriculture and urbanization control; and agricultural promotion) and the percentage of green cover. The analysis revealed many cells with

Figure 5.5
Chiba has transformed
its coast for industrial
and residential use.
Photo 35°34′26.50″ N
140°08′55.09″ E, 25
October 2012 (accessed
14 March 2013), by
Google Earth.

Figure 5.6
The inland valleys
support small-scale
agriculture and
ecological corridors
connecting small
fragments of forest
habitat. Photo
35°28′34.28″ N
140°09′36.08″ E,
28 March 2012
(accessed 14 March
2013) by Google Earth.

more than ten endangered species; the top-ranking cell had 36 species present. The land-use zone with the greatest number of endangered species was the agriculture and urbanization control zone, which is land awaiting more intensive development. Cells with more that 50 percent green cover (and more than 25 percent of this as forest) contained the greatest number of endangered species. City parkland contained few threatened species, indicating opportunities for improvement.[6]

The biodiversity analysis clearly supports a green infrastructure solution for sustaining ecosystem services and biodiversity. Core areas (at least 250 acres in size) of the narrow valleys need protected status and require ecological corridor connections. The urban parks need to be re-vegetated to restore some habitat value and foster education and human–wildlife interactions within the neighborhoods. The restoration of coastal mud flats and marshes is possible in some areas and is necessary to mitigate past damage. Finally, traditional rice farming practices that support biodiversity need to be subsidized and the worst practices of more modern agriculture (dredging, channelization, seasonal draining and removal of stream and canal vegetation) need to be prohibited, mitigated or adapted to better support biodiversity.[6]

Statewide GIS planning

In contrast to the Chiba example, it is the federal and state governments that are most involved in the protection of species and habitat in the US. Cities and counties depend on state and federal ecologists and conservation biologists for data and technical information.[5] To support this process a statewide biodiversity map for Arizona was prepared using a geographic information system (GIS) and a process similar to that used in Chiba. Endangered and threatened avian species (101), mammals (61), reptiles (49), fish (35), crustaceans and mollusks (30) and amphibians (17) were identified and their potential habitat modeled according to actual occurrence based on field surveys and habitat requirements, according to the judgment of species experts. As in Chiba, cells (30 × 30 m) covering the state were coded for the presence of each target species to create a biological diversity map. Threats to each species were also considered and mapped. Therefore, each cell contained the degree of biological diversity and species threats. The interactions of these characteristics were ranked on a 16-point scale (Table 5.1). In the ranking system, 1 represents high biodiversity and low threat, while 11 represents high biodiversity and high stress. A score of 16 represents low biodiversity and high threat. The 16 categories can be grouped into four sets (see the quadrants in Table 5.1) to simplify the map for statewide or regional planning. Geographic areas characterized as low in diversity and high in threats are optimal zones for development. Species scores

Table 5.1 Habitat ranking system.[7]

	Low Threat	Moderate-Low	Moderate-High	High Threat
High Biodiversity	1	3	9	11
Moderate-High	2	4	10	12
Moderate-Low	5	6	13	15
Low Biodiversity	7	8	14	16

were weighted to emphasize the importance of the most endangered species, such as those under the protection of the US Endangered Species Act.[7]

Having a statewide GIS with much higher resolution than the Chiba map allows cities and counties, without conservation biologists on staff, to include biodiversity data and location when reviewing development proposals for planned unit developments, transportation infrastructure or especially a green infrastructure network of trails, parks, open space, recreation facilities, farm and forest protection, ecological corridors and habitat patches.

Using GIS for habitat conservation planning

The Arizona example emphasizes species indicators and identifies areas most suitable for preservation and other areas most suitable for development. It doesn't link species and habitat in a detailed way; presumably this activity was reserved for planning at the municipal scale. Planning for the conservation of habitat requires high-quality GIS data at the planning scale and field verification that the proposed habitat contains breeding pairs of the target species. In addition, a model must be developed, tested and applied to predict valuable habitat that might be preserved. The simplest model uses habitat area only, but more sophisticated models incorporate structural and functional corridors, the shape of habitat patches and seasonal factors. A demographic model considers factors influencing species population dynamics, especially territory and dispersal.

The use of a single species as a proxy for others of conservation interest is an efficient planning approach, but requires careful study to determine the correlation of other species' needs with those of the surrogate. This approach was taken in the creation of a biodiversity conservation map in Poland. The white-backed woodpecker (Figure 5.7) was selected as the umbrella species since it is sensitive to human activity and requires a large territory (0.5–1.5 km^2 per breeding pair) of broad-leaf forest with many standing dead trees. Its habitat needs correlate well with those of Eurasian lynx, gray wolf, European bison and brown bear. The plan alternative based on a

Figure 5.7
The white-backed woodpecker (*Dendrocopos leucotos*) is the indicator species for many others of conservation interest.

population model and forest areas of conservation value resulted in a better match between predicted and actual presence of breeding pairs than a simple habitat area model. In this planning effort the proposed conservation plan was verified by a second source. The alternative GIS outputs of predicted high-quality habitat were compared to actual occurrence of breeding pairs documented in a species atlas.[8]

When large and highly mobile mammals are chosen as indicator species the technical aspect of determining their home territory location is more difficult. Often, many individuals of the target species are captured and fitted with tracking collars. This was done in northwest Montana as part of a recovery plan for the Canada lynx. The movements of the animals were recorded over the course of a year using radio and global positioning technology. This established migration routes, winter versus summer ranges and potential conflicts with road corridors or other barriers and hazards. Separated populations were then determined. Preferred habitat and minimum size was determined and mapped from the data, along with the necessary ecological corridor locations and widths. The road crossing and mortality data influenced the selection of corridor routes and consideration of other management measures, such as fencing and wildlife overpasses.[9] For the lynx and other highly mobile species, it is clear that habitat preserves and less protected multiple-use land and private property will all play a role in sustaining the species.[10]

Large-scale planning studies map habitat based primarily on vegetation cover. This is cost effective and offers enough detail for state and regional planning. The initial planning information is collected by the US government using satellite sensors and is available at no cost. Figure 5.8 shows a small portion of a diverse landscape captured by Landsat 7 using the Normalized Difference Vegetation Index (NDVI). This image type renders vegetation differences in enough detail to map the most valuable habitat areas. The habitat maps derived from satellite imagery are combined with models that consider additional data, including scientific field studies to predict the presence, number and sometimes the variety of species. At the national and regional scale this process and the 30 × 30 m resolution guides biodiversity planning efforts effectively. Figure 5.9 illustrates another NDVI Landsat image of Everett, Washington along with its hinterland. Urbanization, agriculture, wetlands, forest and other vegetation and land uses are easily distinguished. The image is certainly valuable for understanding the existing pattern of urban and suburban settlement and the habitat fragments and ecological corridors. A conceptual green infrastructure could be effectively developed using an enlargement of this image as a base.

However, for planning at smaller scales, finer resolution is necessary to capture the detail needed for conservation of endangered and threatened species, as well as the potential parks and recreation facilities connected by corridors. In this case light detection and ranging (LIDAR) imagery and aerial photographs would provide additional detail (Figure 5.10). LIDAR images can be derived from satellite sensors or from aircraft. The technical processes required for working with LIDAR data are more complex than those used to create the Landsat images since a bare earth terrain is created to depict the topography and then the height of vegetation is added using other data sensors. However, the output is useful for several different purposes. LIDAR data is particularly valuable when mapping

Figure 5.8
This NDVI image from NASA illustrates the wide range of vegetation types that can be distinguished using multiple sensors that collect different infrared and other wavelengths.

Figure 5.9
This Landsat image is an NDVI output with good definition of urban, agricultural and natural elements.

Figure 5.10
This image is derived from a 1 m pixel resolution NASA LIDAR combined with other map data. This map distinguishes 19 different land and vegetation classes for a barrier island off the coast of Virginia. Note the docks in the lower left corner.

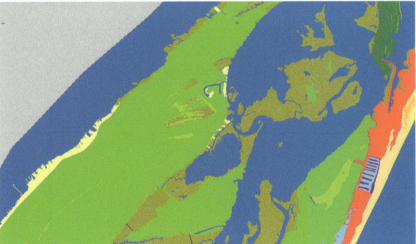

biomass density and aquatic vegetation, especially where an estimate of water depth is necessary. The resolution of LIDAR images from aircraft is 1 m^2, which is very effective for detailed habitat mapping.

Although conservation research at the municipal scale often uses a single species as the indicator of habitat for other species, this approach may not be valid for the most detailed planning scale. When habitat is highly fragmented and when conservation of very different taxa is the planning goal, then different methods may provide more accurate results. An Israeli study demonstrated that micro changes within areas of continuous habitat type were more important than the habitat classification for predicting the presence of some species. For example, the roughness of the topography, presence of leaf litter and stones were important predictors of some organisms, especially ones that were locally rare.[11]

Detailed design and planning information for habitat, corridors, open space, stormwater, wastewater, community agriculture and green roofs is presented in the following chapters.

References

1   City and County of Denver, Stapleton Redevelopment Foundation and Citizens Advisory Board, "The Stapleton Development Plan," 1995.

2   B. Palmberg, "Planning for Large Scale Urban Infill: The Case of the Stapleton Redevelopment," Masters Project, University of North Carolina, Chapel Hill, 2006.

3   J. Howe, E. McMahon and L. Propst, *Balancing Nature and Commerce in Gateway Communities*. Washington, DC: Island Press, 1997.

4   European Commission, "The Multifunctionality of Green Infrastructure," 2012. [Online]. Available: http://ec.europa.eu/environment/nature/ecosystems/docs/Green_Infrastructure.pdf. (accessed 15 March 2013).

5   J. R. Miller, M. Groom, G. R. Hess, T. Steelman, D. L. Stokes, J. Thompson, T. Bowman, L. Fricke, B. King and R. Marquardt, "Biodiversity Conservation in Local Planning," *Conservation Biology*, vol. 23, no. 1, pp. 53–63, 2009.

6   T. Nakamura and K. Short, "Land-Use Planning and Distribution of Threatened Wildlife in a City of Japan," *Landscape and Urban Planning*, vol. 53, no. 1–4, pp. 1–15, 2001.

7   J. G. Underwood, J. Francis and L. R. Gerber, "Incorporating Biodiversity Conservation and Recreational Wildlife Values into Smart Growth Land Use Planning," *Landscape and Urban Planning*, vol. 100, no. 1–2, pp. 136–143, 2011.

8   T. Edman, P. Angelstam, G. Mikusi-Ñski, J. M. Roberge and A. Sikora, "Spatial Planning for Biodiversity Conservation: Assessment of Forest Landscapes of Conservation Value Using Umbrella Species Requirements in Poland," *Landscape and Urban Planning*, vol. 102, no. 1, pp. 16–23, 2011.

9   J. R. Squires, N. J. DeCesare, L. E. Olson, J. A. Kolbe, M. Hebblewhite and S. A. Parks, "Combining Resource Selection and Movement Behavior to Predict Corridors for Canada Lynx at their Southern Range Periphery," *Biological Conservation*, vol. 157, pp. 187–195, 2013.

10 J. Hilty, *Corridor Ecology: The Science and Practice of Linking Landscapes for Biodiversity Conservation*. Washington, DC: Island Press, 2006.

11 Y. Mandelik, T. Dayan, V. Chikatunov and V. Kravchenko, "The Relative Performance of Taxonomic vs. Environmental Indicators for Local Biodiversity Assessment: A Comparative Study," *Ecological Indicators*, vol. 15, no. 1, pp. 171–180, 2012.

CHAPTER SIX

Habitat and ecological corridors

Introduction

A municipal green infrastructure is composed of diverse elements that must be planned simultaneously. However, the requirements of habitat and ecological corridors are somewhat more demanding than many of the man-made aspects of the system. This is because the system needs to be a continuous, and ideally complex, network of the highest value ecosystems. Other elements, such as recreation trails, stormwater management areas and playfields, can be attached to the habitat and corridor alignment, or form additional strands or spaces in the network. Therefore, habitat and corridors are presented first and separately from open space as a matter of convenience, but not to minimize the need for comprehensive planning.

Habitat

The introductory chapter and the chapter on ecosystem health presented the startling rate of species extinction[1] and its primary cause, habitat loss. Urbanization is joined by the expansion of agricultural production and timber harvest to form a triumvirate of habitat loss agents. To mitigate their impacts, an ecosystem approach is adopted to prevent species extinctions (Figure 6.1).

Some land areas provide the conditions for the evolution of robust ecosystems, some of which are quite rare. These precious ecosystems are gems of our natural heritage and merit concerted conservation effort (Figure 6.2). Other ecosystems are more common, often extending across hundreds of thousands of acres. Both the rare and the extensive ecosystems must be preserved as continuous entities large enough to ensure the viability of species populations, including the prospect of perturbations and catastrophes. To be viable, the regional preserves must be connected to others like them to provide for migration, distribution of offspring and exchange of genes. Therefore, these ecological connectors must be accommodated through, or at the edges of, cities.

The previous chapter introduced regional planning processes; more detail about ecosystem planning and wildlife conservation at the regional scale is beyond the scope of this book, but the connectors between the regional preserves are not. These ecological corridors can mitigate the fragmentation and loss of habitat.[2] Regional corridors are even more important with the prospect of ecosystem adjustments to a

changing climate. It will cause many species to shift their territories northward (in the northern hemisphere). In fact, this is already occurring based on studies showing a 40-mile northward migration by some species. This adaptation to climate change by wildlife is only possible if favorable routes to new habitat exist. In Europe, where roads, settlements and agriculture have fragmented habitat more than anywhere else in the world, an ecological network of habitat patches and linking corridors is critical.

At the regional scale identification and conservation of large mammals, birds of prey and habitat specialists are the focus of ecologists as a strategy to preserve the increasingly large number of threatened species.[3] When this fails, the focus expands to address the critical needs of endangered species, such as the Canada lynx discussed in the previous chapter.

At the municipal scale, the habitat requirements of all native species can't be met, but access between regional habitats can be provided. A municipal network of spaces and corridors can reduce the loss of many native species. This, of course, buffers them from extinction pressures. Urban biodiversity also has a critical human component. Near home is where most urban residents have frequent opportunities to encounter native and other species (Figure 6.3). The interaction and educational opportunities this provides may translate into an appreciation for the value of nature and a willingness to support its preservation outside the city, where the resident visits less frequently.

Of course, there are species and habitat areas that benefit from the shared attention of landscape and urban biodiversity planners. Some ecosystems are not

Figure 6.1
In this image of the Italian landscape, the corridors and habitat are woven through the agricultural enterprise. The woodland provides wildlife habitat while serving the human residents with erosion protection, forest products and pure water.

Figure 6.2
This round-leaved sundew (*Drosera rotundifolia*) is an example of the exquisite beauty and fascinating biology that is part of our natural heritage. The plant grows in a bog ecosystem, which is rare and vulnerable to damage.

Figure 6.3
This pure water and habitat is the result of wetlands restored to a site previously used as a military base and landfill. Today it treats urban stormwater runoff and supports wildlife and provides beauty in a public landscape in a densely settled urban area.

extensive and can be accommodated within or near cities. For example, freshwater habitat in England is among several key ecosystem types that are at risk[4] and can be fostered in urban areas (Figure 6.3). When, as in Europe, almost half of the wildlife species are declining in population and important ecosystems are unhealthy, then the role of habitat and corridors within the cities becomes more critical. As urgent as the needs of some habitat types and species are, ecologists believe that with planning and design, biodiversity loss can be arrested and reversed by as early as 2020.

The context of urban habitat

Worldwide, but especially in the US, where the average density is 4.2 dwelling units per acre, it is population growth coupled with housing choice that results in rapid conversion of land to urban use (Figure 6.4). If land in the US continues to be consumed for development at the same rate as between 1982 and 2007, then an additional loss of 64 million acres (26 million hectares) of farm, forest and habitat will occur during the next 40 years.[5]

Given the already compromised habitat and the populations of native species that it supports, further loss of land to suburban development is especially damaging. Reducing human population growth rates is necessary everywhere, but especially in many developing countries, where population growth has been unsustainable for decades. Similarly, the conversion of existing urban land to higher-density use is the responsible course, despite the opposition that this strategy will surely generate among business sectors seeking to develop pristine land to acquire a maximum profit. Development of greenfield sites (agriculture, forest or habitat areas) may be required to accommodate population growth, but it should be permitted only after infill, redevelopment and brownfield options are exhausted. Furthermore, identification of marginal forestland, poor agricultural soils and areas of low biodiversity as suitable places for urban development would minimize the adverse impact of urban development.

Figure 6.4
This image illustrates the loss of forest habitat and connectivity due to fragmentation by roads, reduction of habitat due to exurban housing development and complete loss of ecosystem values due to low-density suburban development. Photo 48°01′55.46″ N, 122°04′46.88″ W by Google Earth (accessed 15 May 2013).

The economic value of land for urban development exceeds the value of the land for agriculture, forestry and habitat. The lack of land-use controls to protect these uses beyond the boundaries of incorporated cities and towns, and the American aversion to such controls, has led to the constant erosion of all but urban land use. Human, and especially economic, interests usually dominate planning efforts since the process is anthropocentric.[6] The promotion of higher-density residential and commercial districts through the development of new mixed-use and housing products has had little impact over the last 20 years. In fact, the planning discussions and economic pressures are often focused on suburban versus exurban options rather than on urban densities. For example, a recent study in Indiana revealed that most residents and planners opposed developers and realtors regarding exurban residential developments. Residents and planners favored lower dwelling unit densities and requirements for open-space dedications. Real-estate agents and developers advocated suburban densities (four units per acre) and no requirements for common open space.[7]

Exurban housing impact of biodiversity

The sense that exurban densities preserve biodiversity is not consistent with the results of ecological studies. Measurements of biodiversity dip precipitously downward at densities of more that one residence per 40 acres (16 hectares). The presence of a road network, people and dogs combined with removal of native vegetation cause reductions in wildlife numbers and species around exurban dwellings. The low biodiversity associated with exurban development is confirmed by a study demonstrating that native bird species are detected around exurban residences at the same diminished rates as in suburban subdivisions. Similarly, urbanized birds are more present around exurban homes than in the natural landscape nearby.[8]

Therefore, for the purpose of preserving biodiversity, county land use plans and ordinances should prohibit residential subdivisions at densities of 1 unit per 40 acres (16 hectares) and greater. An alternative is to require clustering of homes into higher-

Figure 6.5
The landscape of this town, Keswick, England, is knit together by hedgerows connecting habitat fragments to regional habitat. In contrast to most towns in the US, even this small town has quite high residential densities.

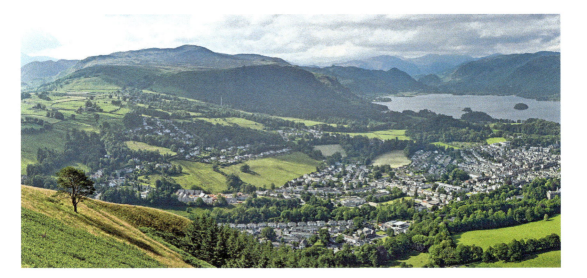

density hamlets with protected habitats and corridors separating them, as is common in Europe (Figure 6.5).

Types and uses of ecological corridors

Since urban development fragments habitat and creates a hostile environment between the remnant patches, movement of individuals and populations of species becomes difficult, even impossible and fatal. Movement through corridors between habitat patches is necessary for organisms to acquire food, disperse offspring, assure genetic diversity and adapt to natural perturbations.

The use of corridors is a very common pattern in undisturbed natural areas, where organisms use them to move within their home range or between habitats as they search for food. Evident even in birds, this instinctive activity is thought to reduce competition between groups. The need for an ecological corridor is greater if the urban matrix is hostile. If the area an organism needs to cross is in great contrast to its habitat, then the corridor is more valuable. In order to reduce predation, or other danger, organisms tend to cross more quickly when crossing a hostile matrix than when moving through a corridor. Similarly, the time spent moving through corridors of low quality is shorter than the movement time through high-quality corridors. An ecotone can be established to make ecological corridors more multifunctional. An ecotone is a transitional area (Figure 6.6) that can serve as either a filter or a barrier to separate human uses from habitat.[9]

The studies cited below illustrate the value of corridors for wildlife. A study of wolves in the US identified habitat fragmented by a golf course. Wolves traveled around the development at a higher elevation, on steep slopes where prey was scarce, rather than through the golf course, where prey was abundant. A corridor averaging 330 meters wide was established through the golf course. In the first two years after construction, wolf tracking showed that 81 percent and 51 percent of the movement between habitat areas was through the golf course, compared to only 1 percent

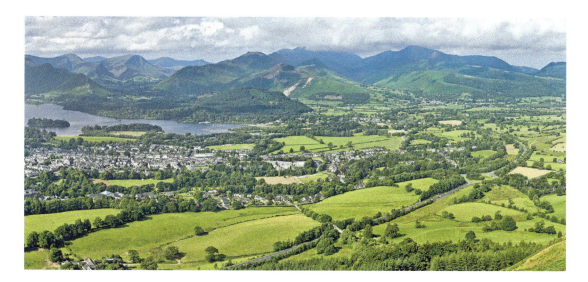

Figure 6.6
A newly restored
stream corridor in
Stapleton. There is an
ecotone between the
riparian and prairie
habitat and a visual
barrier between people
and habitat that could
be extended.

before the corridor was created. The area within the corridor did not serve as habitat for wolves, but as a link between two high-quality habitat areas.[10] Similarly, coyotes in an urbanizing area of southern California follow corridors along ridgelines, fences, road rights-of-way, railroad beds and storm drains.[11]

A Dutch study of butterfly species with good and moderate dispersal characteristics found that they would colonize a neighborhood area from a natural source area. Well-connected patches and road parkways were preferred routes. The implications of the study are that urban development impacts can be mitigated by preservation of core habitat at the edge of the neighborhood and routes through it. The presence of butterflies and other species with moderate or better dispersal characteristics, such as amphibians, reptiles, most flying insects, most small mammals and some bird species, can be further enhanced by creating habitat corridors and patches within the neighborhoods and varying the characteristics of the green spaces within the neighborhood. The study demonstrated that, for butterflies specifically, flowering shrubs and trees within the suburban and urban environment could be more valuable than the core habitat at certain life stages.[12]

Deforestation in England in the eighteenth and nineteenth centuries left red squirrels (*Sciurus vulgaris*) isolated in islands of trees. Furthermore, competition from the larger American gray squirrel reduced their numbers until they were endangered. Reforestation allowed red squirrels to migrate from one patch of forest to the next. The results of genetic tests show that red squirrels did travel between habitat islands up to about 1.5 km apart.[13] This study demonstrates that ecological corridors and closely spaced patch remnants do lead to the dispersal of species and to the increase in biodiversity.

Although many animals make use of corridors when they are available, many species, including most plants and others that are not very mobile, will not benefit from corridors between habitat areas.[14] In this case protection of critical habitat is necessary.

Based on the studies cited above and other research, a typology of ecological corridors can be established. Corridors can be differentiated by function and habitat type. Commuting, migration and dispersal corridors differ by function. The wolf study identified a commuting corridor used for daily movement between foraging areas. Dispersal corridors are of two types. One allows offspring to migrate between two habitat preserves. A second type connects large habitat preserves but is too long to allow dispersal of organisms in one step. Instead, organisms colonize habitat fragments where they breed. Their offspring disperse further along the corridor to the next habitat fragment and so on until the distance between the preserves is bridged. The red squirrel study described this corridor type. Migration corridors are the final functional type. Bird and fish migration between breeding and wintering sites are well-known examples.[14] The habitat type (riparian, forest, grassland, etc.) further distinguishes the corridor type.

Planning background

The concept of linking regional habitat preserves with corridors and providing a network of corridors through small- and large-scale agriculture was formulated and applied by Russian geographer Boris Rodoman. This system was designed to restore ecosystem functions destroyed by collectivization of farms in the former Soviet Bloc countries.[15] This concept can be extended to neighborhoods and cities for the preservation of biodiversity, since urban development can be as destructive to biodiversity as agriculture.

Urban planners and landscape architects need ecological information to plan for the location, spacing and dimensions of corridors. Techniques for mitigating corridor breaks due to road crossings are explained in a later section, but several hypothetical and constructed examples are available. Complicating corridor planning is the need for paths, stormwater treatment and other ecosystem services within some corridors. Planning the network of corridors and remnant patches, well in advance of urban development, yields better connectivity, optimum corridor lengths, less habitat fragmentation, better links to regional preserves and better control of patch size and shape.[16] In contrast to this preferred model, the example of the Cameron Run watershed near Washington, DC is similar to the majority of the urban watersheds in the US (Figure 6.7). A study of the watershed showed that a lack of comprehensive planning was evident within, and between, counties and cities. This led to the progressive, and perhaps irreversible, loss of biodiversity due to insufficient corridors and remnant habitat areas.[17] The watershed management plan for Cameron Run is comprised of many projects that attempt to mitigate the damage to the water quality and habitat caused by poorly planned large-lot residential development.

To avoid the poor result illustrated by Cameron Run, comprehensive planning that directs development and protects the ecosystem services is necessary. The entire watershed should be planned as a system with water quality and habitat safeguards established early. This would have avoided the cumulative impacts that polluted the waterways and destroyed virtually all of the habitat and corridors in Cameron Run. Planning for biodiversity preservation requires a longer time frame (decades) than

Figure 6.7
The 42 square mile Cameron Run watershed is outlined in red. Washington, DC is at the upper right. Photo 38°51'09.44" N, 77°09'32.92" W by Google Earth (accessed 16 June 2013).

the typical planning cycle (1–5 years).[18] Nevertheless, when planning for biodiversity improvements that need to occur quickly, within a highly fragmented urban area, ecological principles and spatial guidelines are needed to make informed decisions. In each planning and design phase an ecologist is a valued consultant but ecological assessments are expensive and time-consuming operations that are generally not supported in preliminary planning phases. For preliminary planning some guidance can come from previous ecological studies of the disturbance of species by human activity and species habituation to humans.[19] However, preservation of urban biodiversity requires long-term assessment by ecologists of the effectiveness of planning requirements, such as stream setback distances, habitat patch sizes, etc. This dialogue between ecologists, planners and landscape architects is necessary to adapt principles to local situations.

Regional corridors

Regional corridors and habitat areas should connect to the municipal green infrastructure system to encourage the maximum diversity and numbers of native species in the city area. A regional corridor plan for species preservation may lack some of the elements of the municipal green infrastructure in order to achieve biodiversity goals. Similarly, elements of the municipal system will primarily express human values. Elements such as stormwater management areas are appropriate for regional and municipal scales.

The corridor plan shown in Figure 6.8 connects three large blocks of preserved ecosystem (outlined in red). One of these is a small fragment (5,000 acres) isolated from other habitat areas. Wildlife movement between these areas is compromised

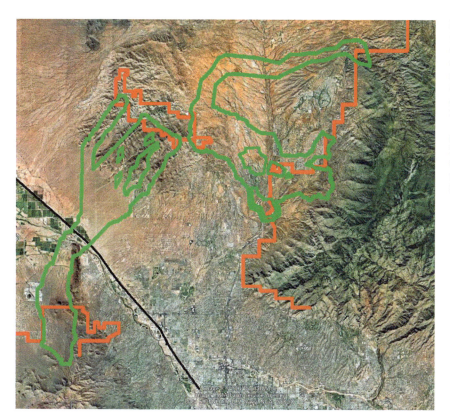

Figure 6.8
Proposed wildlife corridors outlined in green connect habitat preserves (outlined in red) near Tucson Arizona. Photo base 32°23'01.25" N, 110°51'30.78" W, 8 October 2012 (accessed 25 April 2013) by Google Earth, Adapted from Beier *et al.*, 2006.[20]

by suburban development from five rapidly growing towns and the city of Tucson. The urban area (shown as gray) has eliminated the possibility of corridor linkages throughout most of the region, but a few viable routes (outlined in green) remain.[20]

The corridor planners began by selecting 12 reptile and amphibian, 1 bird and 8 mammal species native to the region and sensitive to habitat loss and fragmentation. This group serves as the surrogate for all other species in the ecosystems. Using data on habitat needs and movement characteristics, the most viable corridor for each species was mapped using GIS. The species corridors were aggregated to create the network proposal.[20]

A minimum of 0.62 miles (1 km) was established as the minimum corridor width. This was necessary to accommodate the needs of all of the target species and to respond to several future threats. As urban development surrounds the corridor it will bring negative impacts with it. Two are the removal of native vegetation and the introduction of invasive species. Predation by pets and disturbance from artificial lighting and noise are other impacts that require a transition space. A buffer from these impacts is necessary to avoid an excessive reduction in the effective corridor width.[20]

The potential for man-made or natural perturbations of the corridor, especially fire, require a corridor width in excess of the minimum needed by the species. If a network of alternate routes were possible, as it is in two places in the proposed design, then the corridor width can be reduced somewhat. Climate change is another anticipated future impact that will change the vegetation and cause organisms to shift their territories in ways that we can't predict yet. A wider corridor is necessary due to this uncertainty. The wide corridor also anticipates the demand for trails for people to use as the human population in the region grows.[20]

The eastern portion of the network contains several barriers or impediments. These were evaluated in the field to determine mitigation measures. Since roads, an interstate highway, power lines, ditches and vegetation loss compromise even the best corridor alternative, there is an urgent need to secure the 14 mile (23 km) length of the corridor and implement the mitigation measures before the corridor opportunity is permanently lost.

This corridor proposal is one of 16 planning projects carried out in Arizona since 2006. That year 100 participants, including non-profit groups and several state and federal agencies, identified corridors that are needed to preserve biodiversity across the state. The necessary corridors were prioritized and planning for these was initiated. State, federal and private conservation land already dedicated to wildlife preservation and improvements to them represent a substantial public investment in ecosystem preservation. The proposed corridors protect this investment.[20] The absence of an ecological corridor along the river that runs through Tucson (visible in the lower portion of the image and along the interstate highway, shown as a black line) illustrates a lost opportunity for urban biodiversity and other ecosystem benefits.

Response to disturbance

Whether in the urban area or the regional landscape, human activity impacts almost all species. Disturbance is often expressed as the flushing distance (the horizontal dimension between an approaching person and a bird or animal that causes it to flee), or the alert distance (the dimension that causes the species to become wary and stop foraging).

The species studied for flushing distance are predominately birds, partly because they are somewhat easier to study than other animals. Some of the flushing distances are so long, such as 820 feet for the bald eagle (Figure 6.9), that a corridor around (as proposed for Tucson) rather than through a town or city is indicated. This conclusion leads to consideration of a spatial hierarchy of corridors in order to accommodate both sensitive and human-adapted species. Two studies demonstrated that as the size of the bird increased, so did the flushing distance and the distance the bird flew in response to disturbance.[25,22]

Some species exhibit a great deal of habituation toward human activity, which explains the flushing distances of 1,312 feet (400 m) and 29 feet (9 m) reported for elk. Many researchers have identified that the amount of vegetative cover or visibility has a significant impact on flushing distances. For example, an endangered grouse in Europe flushed at 75 feet (23 m) when visibility was 25–50 percent, compared to 29.5 feet (9 m) when it was 76–100 percent.[21] This finding has important implications for the design of ecological corridors, as well as for the design of urban parks.

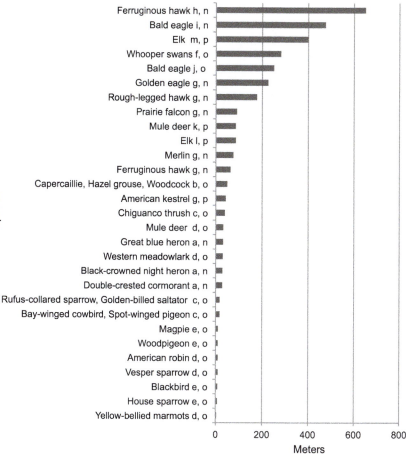

Figure 6.9
Average flushing distances. a, Rodgers and Smith, 1995[33]; b, Thiel, 2007[21]; c, Fernández-Juricic et al. 2007[34]; d, Ward et al., 1980[35];Miller, S; Knight, R; Miller, C. 2001[32]; e, Fernández-Juricic et al., 2001[22]; f, Rees et al., 2005[23]; g, Holmes et al. 1993[36]; h, Keeley and Bechard, 2011[24]; i, Fraser et al., 1985[37]; j, Stalmaster et al., 1980[38]; k, Freddy et al., 1986,[39] Ward et al., 1980[35]; l, Schultz and Bailey, 1978[40]; m, Cassirer et al., 1992[41]; n, people walking directly toward nest; o, person walking directly toward animal or bird; p, person walking toward animal or bird in winter.

Corridor dimensions

The data presented in Figure 6.9 is useful but limited by the small number of species represented and the paucity of data on habituation to human activity. However, one can conclude that 30–90 feet (10–30 m) wide corridors are sufficient for species moderately or highly adapted to human activity. The variability of the animal species, climate, vegetation and topography of different cities may require adjustments to these minimum dimensions. Corridors as narrow as 66 feet (20 m) can serve as home range habitat for some rodent and snake species. Fencerow corridors only a few meters wide reduce the probability of extinction within woodland habitat patches

Figure 6.10
Each species listed in Figure 6.9 and shown here has a different flushing distance characteristic. The rough-legged hawk flushes at a great distance from approaching people, while the capercaillie and especially the marmot tolerate people quite close to them once they are habituated.

for white-footed mice. Two California native birds use corridors only one meter wide and three native chaparral bird species use habitat strips only 30 feet wide.[11] This understanding emphasizes that all connectivity is beneficial, but increasing width increases the number of native species.

Ecologists, geographers and designers in the Czech Republic developed and applied a system of planning standards calibrated to the local (see Figure 6.12) and regional (see Figure 6.13) context. Based on scientific study and the realities of a fragmented and urbanizing landscape, their system is intended to restore damaged ecosystems and connect remnant habitat patches with ecological corridors to improve viability of species populations within a cultural context.[26] A study of birds in urban parks in Spain confirms the Czech neighborhood corridor standard. In the Spanish study, the average flushing distance of four species studied was 23–36 feet (7–11 m) (Figure 6.9),[22] equivalent to a suggested corridor width of 46–72 feet (14–22 m). This method of determining a minimum urban corridor results in a width that is only slightly more than the 30–60 feet (10–20 m) minimum recommended by the Czech standards. In addition, the bird flushing distances suggest a 72 feet (22 m) minimum spacing between pathways in urban parks to allow multiple use by birds, humans and a number of other animals.

A Tucson, Arizona study of bird biodiversity within a range of natural and human-dominated residential settings resulted in three planning recommendations. The study investigated 334 plots along 33 transects with housing densities ranging from zero to eight dwelling units per acre. The first recommendation of the study was to retain native vegetation as the housing density increases. This is the opposite of the typical pattern, where increasing housing density is accompanied by more exotic and ornamental plantings. Six of the native bird species studied could not survive in areas dominated by exotic plants. Second, riparian and other native vegetation corridors must be intact and undisturbed, especially within high-density housing areas. The study results showed that these remnant landscapes sustained the species richness of native birds and depressed non-native species. Third, retention of 2.5 acre (1 hectare) patches that are distributed not more that 1,650 feet (500 m) apart would

Figure 6.11
Corridors for biodiversity can include other uses. This stormwater management area is incorporated into a restored riparian corridor in Stapleton.

sustain bird species sensitive to human development where the patches were not connected by ecological corridors.[8] This distance confirms the maximum separation of habitat patches proposed by the Czech recommendations (see Figure 6.12)[26] Parks and other areas landscaped with non-native plants did not support these sensitive species.[8]

A study of breeding pairs of birds in corridors with recreation trails was conducted in North Carolina. The study identified 48 species and documented their presence in corridors of varying width. Most of the species were present in corridors at least 164 feet (50 m) wide, but three species were found only in corridors greater than 164 feet, while two more were present only in corridors greater than 328 feet (100 m) and one species was present only in corridors greater than 984 feet (300 m) wide.[27] In the Czech standards a 164 feet wide corridor is at the top of the scale for the rural setting. However, it should be noted that the North Carolina study focused on breeding birds. The corridors at the widths reported served not only as movement corridors between patches, but as habitat itself. Nevertheless, the findings suggest that for planners a hierarchy of corridor widths is indicated to achieve urban biodiversity and preservation of species sensitive to human activity.

Applying corridor and patch standards

Neighborhood scale

The set of Czech standards recognize that the width and length of an ecological corridor are related. Therefore, the maximum distance between even connected patches is limited. At the neighborhood scale the recommended maximum length of 3,270–6,335 feet (1,000–2,000 m) is paired with a minimum width of 33–66 feet (10–20 m) (Figure 6.12). At the rural scale (Figure 6.13) the recommended maximum length of 1,300–6,335 feet (400–1,000 m) is paired with a minimum width of 66–164 feet (20–50 m).[26]

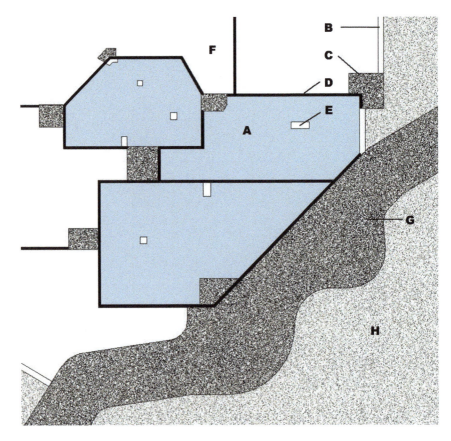

Figure 6.12
Urban remnant habitat patches and corridors organized to promote biodiversity. Austin, 2011. A, commercial and residential development; B, 164 feet (50 m) community perimeter and ecological corridor (city limit); C, neighborhood habitat remnant 1.2–12.4 acres (0.5–5 ha) minimum; D, 66 feet (20 m) wide ecological corridor with 3,270–6,335 feet (1,000–2,000 m) maximum length; E, commercial or residential plazas; F, future urban neighborhoods; G, 1,640 feet (500 m) wide river corridor or wildlife migration route (connection to regional preserve); H, commercial agriculture or forestry. Graphic by author for standards reported by Kubei, 1996.[26]

The schematic neighborhood plan, drawn to scale, shown in Figure 6.12, is a graphic representation of a biodiversity plan based on the Czech standards. The 66 feet wide ecological corridors (item D) form the edges of neighborhoods or internal greenways within them. Additional width and buffering would be added to the ecological corridor dimensions shown where recreational pathways are desirable. The neighborhoods are conceptualized as having mixed uses and mixed housing densities.

The element marked "E" on the plan represents parks, community agriculture or plazas with low ecological values. The element marked "C" on the plan represents patches of remnant habitat that link the neighborhoods. A recent Australian study suggests that if the urban matrix is low-density residential, then the vegetation in private gardens and street trees provide for biodiversity levels equivalent to that of patches four acres (1.6 ha) and smaller in size. Patches 12.3–24.7 acres (5–10 ha) bridged the gap between suburban biodiversity levels and those in continuous forest.[28] Another study found diversity of native bird species grew as habitat size increased above five acres (2 ha).[16] Space would be added to the habitat fragments (item C) to accommodate stormwater management areas (see Figure 6.11), sports fields, mown turf picnicking areas, etc.

Item B on the plan represents the ecological corridor (164 feet wide) along the city limit, but a wider corridor should be planned for the area of impact (sphere of influence) boundary (Figure 6.12).

Rural scale

The schematic plan in Figure 6.13 also uses the hierarchical system of Czech standards to estimate ecosystem benefits and development impacts that include rural

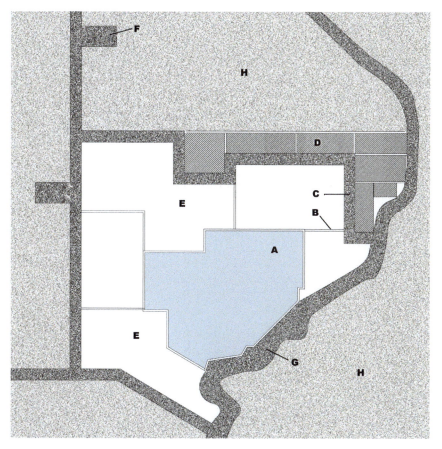

Figure 6.13
Schematic biodiversity plan with connections to regional habitat, Austin 2011. A, urban development within city limit; B, 164 feet (50 m) wide local corridors of remnant vegetation; C, 1,000 feet (304 m) outer ring corridor (urban growth limit); D, community agriculture; E, future urban development in area of impact; F, 124 acres (50 ha) patches of remnant habitat spaced 6,335 feet (2,000 m) apart maximum; G, 1,640 feet (500 m) wide riparian corridor; H, commodity agriculture. Graphic by author for standards reported by Kubei, 1996.[26]

components. More optimum patch and corridor sizes are suggested at the urban edge, where providing the space for the species more sensitive to human activity is spatially and economically feasible (Figure 6.13). Connections to the regional habitat and a corridor network are key components, since many species do not adapt to living in proximity to humans. For example, only somewhat more than 25 percent of North American bird species are defined as urbanized or urbanizing.[29] The plan includes three corridor types. The regional connection, such as a riparian corridor, is 1,640 feet (500 m) wide, the outer ring corridor is 1,000 feet (304 m) wide and the interior corridors around the city limit and separating the neighborhoods is 164 feet (50 m) wide. The perimeter habitat patches (item F) are 124 acres (50 hectares) and are connected by substantial corridors.

Roads

Roads fragment habitat and present barriers to movement of wildlife, in addition to generating a very high mortality rate for animals attempting to cross. A four-year study of a two-lane road in Arizona's Organ Pipe Cactus National Monument revealed that at least 36 snakes were killed by vehicles per mile per year.[20]

Overpasses or underpasses may be required to increase the effectiveness of ecological corridors. They are becoming common features of urban and rural landscapes in Europe (Figure 6.14) and North America. Even in urban centers, parks that have been fragmented by roads can be knit together with raised wildlife crossings. The Mile End Park in East London features a bridge that spans five traffic lanes. This 75 feet wide corridor links parkland and collects rainfall that is reused to irrigate the plantings on the bridge. Both humans and animals use the bridge to access pieces of the 90 acre (36 ha) park.[4]

Ecological corridors and compact growth

A planning concern is that ecological corridors are inconsistent with the need for higher urban density to make residential areas more sustainable. The exercise

Figure 6.14
Wildlife crossings that bridge highways remove barriers and hazards from ecological corridors.

presented here demonstrates that densities much higher than the American average and higher than required to sustain public light rail or bus transportation can be achieved while adopting ecological corridors based on the standards discussed above. An ecological network of corridors and remnant habitat patches within cities is possible if residential densities are moderate. For the plan in Figure 6.13, the total area of impact (exclusive of the perimeter corridor) is about 9,500 acres (3,845 ha). If a gross density target of seven dwelling units per acre is accepted to achieve a gross density of 19 people per acre (47.5 per hectare), then the total number of units equals 66,500. If 30 percent of the city area is reserved for habitat and multi-use corridors, and if roads and other infrastructure consume another 15 percent, then 5,225 acres (2,114 ha) are available for urban development. Maintaining the target of 66,500 units for the reduced development area would cause the average density to rise to 12.7 units per acre. This density is three times more compact than typical suburban developments. The density of 12.7 units per acre is easily achieved with a mixture of single-family residential housing on small lots, duplexes, row housing (Figure 6.15) and multistory condominiums and apartments (see Figure 6.16 for a block-scale density example). Of course, a range of housing options within the city would be offered at various densities. Residential buildings with 30–50 units per acre in the neighborhood and city centers would allow lower densities elsewhere. A view of permanent open space and immediate access encourages people to live at higher residential densities.[30]

A population density of at least 19 persons per acre is required to make light rail transportation economically viable in residential districts. In mixed-use areas a combination of residents and jobs equaling 19 per acre is sufficient for feasible light rail systems.[31] Therefore, high-density neighborhood and city centers with many jobs and residents could subsidize somewhat lower residential densities elsewhere if this were desirable.

Figure 6.15
This attractive neighborhood is composed of public housing. The density is several times higher than single-family detached housing achieves. This density allows for public open space for recreation and biodiversity as well as public transportation.

Figure 6.16
Ecological corridor separating housing blocks. This image illustrates a 66 feet wide corridor in a moderate-density residential neighborhood.

The perspective view in Figure 6.16 shows a proposed ecological corridor between and at the rear of row house units, such as those shown in Figure 6.15. The corridor is in the local category (33–66 feet/10–20 m wide) and in this illustration a 66 feet wide vegetated corridor is illustrated. The homeowner's access to the rear of the units is separated from the wildlife area with a continuous hedge (preferably of a native species). The perspective view in Figure 6.16 illustrates that compact growth and urban biodiversity can be achieved with careful planning. Two-story single-family homes attached at the garage can achieve 900–2,200 square feet (84–204 m²) with a small private outdoor space. Separated by a 66 feet wide ecological corridor at the rear of the property, this configuration achieves 8.7 net dwelling units per acre and a population density of 23.5. Row housing densities would be about 20 units per acre. The resulting block width is 360 feet.

Dense urban mixed-use development is desirable, since it consumes less land, but it is not the preferred residential situation for the great majority of Americans. Nevertheless, these high-density cores should be provided and improved to attract more residents as part of a set of sustainable strategies. Other housing choices and densities must also be provided, but these lower densities should be calibrated to foster public transit systems and urban biodiversity. Wider ecological corridors and larger habitat preserves should be combined with the most damaging residential densities (four units per acre to one unit per 40 acres).

Urban corridor design details

Planting design, material specification and stormwater measures must support the location and width standards to achieve the highest biodiversity benefit. The planting design should include a visual and physical barrier made of native shrubs at the corridor edge. The corridor is best as a remnant of native habitat. Therefore, location of the corridor and the native plants and a preservation plan to protect them during construction will be necessary. If the site is a redevelopment project then re-vegetation of the corridors with primarily native plants would be necessary to create the required vegetative cover and habitat structure. A mixture of deciduous and evergreen trees in a range of heights will maximize species diversity. An understory of deciduous and evergreen shrubs will also expand the number of habitat niches. Trees should be composed in groves, and thickets of shrubs will be beneficial. Openings with herbaceous plants will add to the heterogeneity of the habitat. Native trees should be specified in adjacent private yards to extend or buffer the habitat. Invasive exotic plants should be removed from the corridor. Lighting should be limited to ground-level path lights. The corridor should be used to hold and clean stormwater runoff from roofs and impervious surfaces and create water basins. Permanent pools of water are desirable.

Materials and plants for ecological corridors

Attention to planting design in urban parks can reduce flushing distances. The presence of shrubs and deciduous and evergreen trees (with some very tall) improves the capacity of the landscape to serve both birds and people.[22] One study found that the presence of shrubs (habitat diversity) and extensive tree canopy even in properties adjacent to a greenway resulted in higher biodiversity within it.[27]

On brownfields (Figures 6.6 and 6.11) or former agricultural land the corridor should be planted to approximate the pattern of dominant and subordinate species of nearby ecosystems. The planting design should be reconsidered for each functional group of species to assure that fruit, nectar, seed and shelter resources are available in each season.

Leaf litter and humus salvaged from other construction sites should be used to inoculate the new planting areas with the native bacteria, fungi and seed. Breaks in the forested corridor should include shrub and grass associations to encourage a full range of species, such as pollinators and butterflies. Vertical snags and felled logs with holes and hollow sections will encourage bird nests and ground-dwelling animals and birds. Natural depressions should be exploited and enhanced to create bio-retention basins for water-quality treatment of road and parking lot runoff in particular. Mercury vapor lighting should be avoided and all lighting should be only bright enough to provide safety, with motion activation preferable to continuous lighting.

References

1 F. He, "Species–Area Relationships always Overestimate Extinction Rates from Habitat Loss," *Nature*, vol. 473, pp. 368–371, 2011.
2 R. M. Hassan, S. R. Carpenter, K. Chopra, D. Capistrano and Millennium Ecosystem Assessment, *Ecosystems and Human Well-Being*, Washington, DC: Island Press, 2005.
3 International Union for Conservation of Nature and Natural Resources, "Summary Statistics," 2011. [Online]. Available: www.iucnredlist.org/about/summary-statistics# Tables_1_2.
4 L. Grant, "Multi-Functional Urban Green Infrastructure," The Chartered Institution of Water and Environmental Management, Briefing Report, 2010.

5   US Department of Agriculture, "Summary Report: 2007 National Resources Inventory," 2009.

6   K. Nilsson, "Ecological Scientific Knowledge in Urban and Land-Use Planning," in *Ecology of Cities and Towns: A Comparative Approach*, Cambridge: Cambridge University Press, 2009.

7   B. Johnson, "The Mis/Alignments of Exurban Land Use Controls with the Preferences of Varied Development Interest Groups," *Spaces and Flows Journal*, vol. 1, no. 2, pp. 27–46, 2011.

8   S. Germaine, "Relationships Among Breeding Birds, Habitat, and Residential Development in Greater Tucson, Arizona," *Ecological Applications*, vol. 8, no. 3, pp. 680–691, 1998.

9   A. Farina, *Principles and Methods in Landscape Ecology: Toward a Science of Landscape*, Dordrecht: Springer, 2006.

10 B. Shepherd, "Response of Wolves to Corridor Restoration and Human Use Management," *Ecology and Society*, vol. 11, no. 2, n.p., 2006.

11 J. Lyle, "Ecological Corridors in Urban Southern California," in *Wildlife Conservation in Metropolitan Environments*, Columbia, MD: National Institute for Urban Wildlife, 1991.

12 R. Snep, "How Peri-urban Areas Can Strengthen Animal Populations Within Cities: A Modeling Approach," *Biological Conservation*, vol. 127, no. 3, pp. 345–355, 2006.

13 M. Hale, "Impact of Landscape Management on the Genetic Structure of Red Squirrel Populations," *Science*, vol. 293, no. 5538, pp. 2246–2248, 2001.

14 I. Bouwma, "Ecological Corridors on a European Scale," in *Ecological Networks and Greenways*, Cambridge: Cambridge University Press, 2004.

15 G. Bennett and K. Mulongoy, *Review of Experience with Ecological Networks, Corridors and Buffer Zones*, Montreal: Secretariat of the Convention on Biological Diversity, 2006.

16 C. McGuckin, "A Landscape Ecological Model for Wildlife Enhancement of Stormwater Management Practices in Urban Greenways," *Landscape and Urban Planning*, vol. 33, p. 227, 1995.

17 M. M. Bryant, "Urban Landscape Conservation and the Role of Ecological Greenways at Local and Metropolitan Scales," *Landscape and Urban Planning*, vol. 76, no. 1, pp. 23–44, 2006.

18 K. Lofvenhaft, "Tools to Assess Human Impact on Biotope Resilience," in *Ecology of Cities and Towns: A Comparative Approach*, Cambridge: Cambridge University Press, 2009.

19 C. Duerksen, *Managing Development for People and Wildlife: A Handbook for Habitat Protection by Local Government*, Denver, CO: Colorado Division of Wildlife, 1998.

20 P. Beier, E. Garding and D. Majka, "Arizona Missing Linkages: Tucson – Tortolita – Santa Catalina Mountains Linkage Design," Arizona Game and Fish Department, Northern Arizona University, 2006.

21 D. Thiel, "Effects of Recreation and Hunting on Flushing Distance of Capercaillie," *Journal of Wildlife Management*, vol. 71, no. 6, pp. 1784–1792, 2007.

22 E. Fernández-Juricic, M. Jimenez and E. Lucas, "Bird Tolerance to Human Disturbance in Urban Parks of Madrid (Spain): Management Implications," in *Avian Ecology and Conservation in an Urbanizing World*, New York: Academic Publishers, 2001.

23 E. C. Rees, J. H. Bruce and G. T. White, "Factors Affecting the Behavioural Responses of Whooper Swans (*Cygnus c. cygnus*) to Various Human Activities," *Biological Conservation*, vol. 121, no. 3, pp. 369–382, 2005.

24 W. Keeley and M. Bechard, "Flushing Distances of Ferruginous Hawks Nesting in Rural and Exurban New Mexico," *The Journal of Wildlife Management*, vol. 75, no. 5, pp. 1034–1039, 2011.

25 E. Fernández-Juricic, R. Vaca and N. Schroeder, "Spatial and Temporal Responses of Forest Birds to Human Approaches in a Protected Area and Implications for Two Management Strategies," *Biological Conservation*, vol. 117, no. 4, pp. 407–416, 2004.

26 J. Kubei, "Biocentres and Corridors in a Cultural Landscape: A Critical Assessment of the Territorial System of Ecological Stability," *Landscape and Urban Planning*, vol. 35, p. 231–240, 1996.

27 J. Mason, C. Moorman, G. Hess and K. Sinclair, "Designing Urban Greenways to Provide Habitat for Breeding Birds," *Landscape and Urban Planning*, vol. 80, no. 1–2, pp. 153–164, 2003.

28 C. Catterall, "Responses of Faunal Assemblages to Urbanisation," in *Ecology of Cities and Towns: A Comparative Approach*, Cambridge: Cambridge University Press, 2009.

29 R. Johnston, "Synanthropic Birds of North America," in *Avian Ecology and Conservation in an Urbanizing World*, Boston, MA: Kluwer Academic Publishers, 2001.

30 C. Anderson, "Reset and Recovery: Shifting Markets and Opportunities for Rocky Mountain Communities," Sonoran Institute, 2013.

31 E. Guerra, "Cost of a Ride: The Effects of Densities on Fixed-Guideway Transit Ridership and Capital Costs," University of California Transportation Center, 2010.

32 S. Miller, R. Knight, "Wildlife Responses to Pedestrians and Dogs," *Wildlife Society Bulletin*, vol. 29, no. 1, 2001.

33 J. A. Rodgers, Jr. and H. T. Smith, "Set-back Distances to Protect Nesting Bird Colonies from Human Disturbance," *Conservation Biology*, vol. 9, pp. 89–99, 1995.

34 E. Fernandez-Juricic, R. Vaca and N. Schroeder, "Spatial and Temporal Responses of Forest Birds to Human Approaches in a Protected Area and Implications for Two Management Strategies," *Biological Conservation*, vol. 117, pp. 407–416, 2004.

35 A. L. Ward, N. E. Fornwalt, S. E. Henry and R. A. Hodorff, "Effects of Highway Operation Practices and Facilities on Elk, Mule Deer, and Pronghorn Antelope," *Federal Highway Office Research and Development Report FHWA-RD-79-143*, 1980.

36 T. L. Holmes, R. L. Knight, L. Stegall and G. R. Craig, "Responses of Wintering Grassland Raptors to Human Disturbance," *Wildlife Society Bulletin*, vol. 21, pp. 461–468, 1980.

37 J. D. Fraser, L. D. Frenzel and J. E. Mathison, "The Impact of Human Activities on Breeding Bald Eagles in North-central Minnesota," *Journal of Wildlife Management*, vol. 49, pp. 585–592, 1985.

38 M. V. Stalmaster and J. R. Newman, "Behavioral Responses of Wintering Bald Eagles to Human Activity," *Journal of Wildlife*, vol. 42, no. 3, pp. 506–513, 1978.

39 D. J. Freddy, W. M. Bronaugh and M. C. Fowler, "Responses of Mule Deer to Disturbance by Persons Afoot and in Snowmobiles," *Wildlife Society Bulletin*, vol. 14, pp. 63–68, 1986.

40 T. D. Schultz and J. A. Bailey, "Responses of National Park Elk to Human Activity," *Journal of Wildlife Management*, vol. 42, pp. 91–100, 1978.

41 E. F. Cassirer, D. J. Freddy and E. D. Ables, "Elk Responses to Disturbance by Cross-Country Skiers in Yellowstone National Park," *Wildlife Society Bulletin*, vol. 20, pp. 375–381, 1992.

CHAPTER SEVEN

Green infrastructure network

Introduction

The previous chapters established the need for green infrastructure to support both ecosystem health and human physical and psychological health. Rather than green infrastructure focused on preservation of native species and ecosystems, this chapter focuses on the planning and implementation of open-space networks primarily expressing human values. Often the open-space elements and networks are not planned. They are created piecemeal as parcels are developed rather than in a systematic way that optimizes space according to size, location, character and connectivity. In many cases green infrastructure elements with a dominant human focus can and should be attached to the edges of ecological corridors and habitat fragments. However, sometimes there is cause to separate the ecosystem and human values into dedicated spaces. Urban plazas and boulevards are two examples of open-space components where human values define the design and materials (Figure 7.1).

The charter of the Congress of New Urbanism neglects the issue of urban biodiversity (Figure 7.2) and one of its founders claims that green infrastructure will lead to the ruralization of cities and towns.[2] This chapter demonstrates that multifunctional corridors at the urban scale are compatible with compact growth while offering a number of important ecosystem benefits to urban residents.

The development of green infrastructure in America

The first planned and implemented multifunctional corridor in the US was the Emerald Necklace in Boston. Designed by Frederick Law Olmsted in the 1880s, the Emerald Necklace is a 1,100-acre (445-hectare), seven-mile-long sequence of waterways and six parks, including Franklin Park and the Arnold Arboretum. In contrast to isolated, urban parks, such as Central Park in New York and Prospect Park in Brooklyn, the Boston sequence focuses on connectivity of natural open space, recreation and flood control within the urban context.[3,4] Charles Eliot expanded the system in the 1890s to form a regional open space system. Several other cities followed, with plans for public open spaces linked by linear parks.

As American cities grew into metropolitan areas, access to natural open space was eroded. Urban expansion also fragmented natural landscapes into increasingly smaller and isolated remnants. The loss of open space and concern for the health

Figure 7.1
Human values dominate
this neighborhood
center at Stapleton.

of Americans led to the President's Commission on Americans Outdoors by the Lyndon Johnson administration in 1987.[5] The commission report advocated a national network of corridors connecting residential districts to rural and natural landscapes. Its multi-purpose focus was popularized by *Greenways for America* in 1990.[6] The pursuit of opportunities offered by the abandonment of railroad rights-of-way resulted in more than 10,000 miles of greenway[3] focusing primarily on pedestrian and bicycle access, but sometimes serving as wildlife corridors between habitat areas. In contrast, European nations and cities have focused on the biodiversity aspect of ecological corridors, particularly after the 1992 United Nations Convention on Biological Diversity.[7]

Multifunctional urban green infrastructure includes trails, stormwater management, community gardens, recreation fields, utility easements, dog parks, wildlife habitat and potentially other features. This chapter investigates the spatial, material and functional characteristics of open space designed by landscape architects and others.

Traditional planning and development in most cities and towns has considered neither urban nor naturalistic open space as a system to structure human settlement patterns. Instead, vehicular transportation routes and, more recently, transit-oriented development with light rail establish the scale and pattern of urban growth. In the first case, linear strip commercial and auto-dependent (pedestrian-hostile) environments are the result. In the case of transit-oriented development, a more sustainable pattern of high-density commercial and residential nodes is established, but open

Figure 7.2
Mixed-use development often focuses on high residential density as a sustainability measure but often neglects the multifunctional green infrastructure that contributes to a high quality of life. Juanita Bay Village in Kirkland, Washington.

space is often not used to structure the pattern of development. Figure 7.3 illustrates an exception to the common development pattern by using an urban open space to focus social and civic life while multistory, mixed-use buildings frame the space.

If green infrastructure, including spaces like urban plazas and boulevards (Figure 7.4), were planned with a multifunctional and network motivation, we would find that commercial, institutional and residential buildings would occur at higher densities and frame urban and naturalistic open spaces. This is a formula for environments that are more sustainable, and that provide a higher quality of life than the traditional paradigm, where cities sacrifice social and environmental qualities. The physical footprint of buildings and paved surfaces can be reduced, while the magnitude of the ecosystem services provided to citizens can increase with the adoption of green infrastructure as a structural planning method.

The physical activity, health and wellbeing of citizens in the urban setting can be fostered through planning and physical design. Open-space standards have long been the primary measure of the sufficiency of parks and paths and a metric comparing the desirability of living in one city or another. However, user satisfaction and levels of use of provided open space resources are more complicated ways of considering open space.

There are 12 factors that influence use of urban open space. These are: (1) park access and quality; (2) recreation facility location and variety; (3) the mix of land uses and desirable destinations; (4) residential density; (5) street connectivity; (6) ease of pedestrian transportation; (7) walking and biking facilities; (8) traffic speed and

Figure 7.3
Planned and serendipitous meetings at the neighborhood center are part of the civic experience.

Figure 7.4
Row houses frame a beautiful boulevard space in Stapleton.

volume; (9) pedestrian safety elements; (10) the degree of neighborhood civility or order; (11) threat of crime; (12) presence of vegetation.[1] This chapter will illustrate positive applications of these factors to form high-quality open-space systems, using Stapleton as a primary example. At the metropolitan scale open space systems provide regional connectivity for humans and wildlife.

Green belts and community definition

As mentioned in the first chapter, the garden city concept and its implementation in the early 1900s is an expression of green infrastructure to influence the character of urban settlement. Greenbelts of productive agriculture, nature parks and landscape malls, boulevards and promenades (Figure 7.5) were implemented in England for the towns of Letchworth and Welwyn. Both towns integrated a systematic open-space system with a transit focus on the railroad station. The greenbelts separated the town from adjacent communities, preserving a separate identity and sense of place while assuring local access to agricultural products. These communities are terrifically successful examples of comprehensive urban and open space planning. Applying the lessons from these places to the planning for new neighborhoods would result in urban and residential districts with a balance of moderate density and outstanding landscape amenities (Figure 7.6). If rebuilt today, we would incorporate higher development density, construct buildings with better energy performance, substitute light rail for the heavy rail line and perhaps adjust the programming of the open-space system, but at nearly 100 years old these towns continue to offer a higher quality of life than the vast majority of American towns and neighborhoods.

Beginning in the 1930s, the UK began designating greenbelts to curb suburban expansion and they now account for 13 percent of the land area in the country. They have added to the density of urban areas, but sometimes this increase was not planned or implemented in a sustainable way. Nevertheless, greenbelts in England are multifunctional and have the potential for an expanded set of uses and values that have not yet been realized.[2]

A more recent and ambitious green infrastructure project is the 200 square mile (518 km²) UK National Forest in central England. This project focuses on an entire region that includes urban development. The original forest had been clear-cut and replaced by coal and clay mines, quarries and agriculture. When the government established the forest boundary in 1990, only 6 percent of the forested land remained. Because of the natural resource and agricultural heritage and the presence of about 200,000 people living in towns within the new forest boundary, the project goal is to establish a multifunctional landscape that supports economic development, social benefits and environmental restoration of brownfields, forests and other habitat types. Urban dwellers, farmers and other land owners partner with public agencies to plant trees and other native vegetation. Land acquisition, grants and planning and technical services support the restoration of large and small parcels even within the urbanized areas.[3]

In addition, future commercial forestry and enhanced biodiversity are project goals articulated in action plans that guide the creation or restoration of 16 habitat types, including heath, wetlands and meadows. Biodiversity improvements are

Figure 7.5
The mall in Welwyn, England established the primary axis of the town linking the college, commercial center, park and agricultural greenbelt. The commercial center cross axis is punctuated by the fountain in the distance.

Figure 7.6
A promenade extends from the Letchworth railroad station through the town center and into the recreation space. The city hall is on the right.

Figure 7.7
Existing forest habitat is preserved and managed, while degraded forest is restored and new tree plantations expand patches until they meet nearby patches. This image shows new tree plantations and restored forest parcels connecting existing forest. Two results are increased interior habitat and future commercial forestry. Photo 52°42′31.03″ N 1°13′53.67″ W, 2 July 2006 (accessed 25 April 2013) by Google Earth.

Figure 7.8
Existing forest habitat fragments are being connected functionally by nearby patches or directly by ecological corridors and hedgerows. Species movement between patches, dispersal routes and recreation benefits are three results. Photo 52°46′56.68″ N 1°28′52.63″ W, 31 December 2009 (accessed 25 April 2013) by Google Earth.

measured by the number of acres of habitat planted and managed and by tracking the population and distribution of nine protected species: otter, bat, adder, bluebell, black poplar, rudder darter dragonfly, water vole, redstart and barn owl.[4] The restoration strategy is to enlarge isolated habitat fragments and connect them with others nearby (Figure 7.7). This will create a landscape mosaic where agriculture will remain the dominant land use, but with a much higher permeability for both people and wildlife. Ecological corridors, hedgerows and pedestrian and bicycle greenways will establish a continuous network (Figure 7.8). A secondary benefit is the sequestration of approximately 66,000 tons of carbon.[3]

Substantial progress has been made on National Forest enhancement since 1990. Over 15,000 acres (6,229 ha) of new woodland have been created through the planting of eight million trees. There are 55 miles (86 km) of new bicycle paths and 45 new sport and recreation facilities supporting residents and visitors. There are an additional 20 new tourism attractions that take advantage of the new green infrastructure and draw 8,686,500 visitors per year. The forest project is widely supported (84 percent approval) by the local citizenry.[3] The substantial economic benefits of this project were discussed in Chapter 4.

Physical infrastructure for promotion of health

Parks

Naturalistic open space provides the urban dweller with a broad range of services, including scenic, psychological, social, educational and scientific, as well as the opportunity to experience nature. Private development rarely provides public open spaces unless compelled by government. This is because the services listed above are health and quality of life interests that are often beyond the economic calculation of development products and profits. This is to say that developers are not held accountable for the costs of dangerous or unhealthy neighborhoods. Nevertheless, the impacts of these disservices are borne by individuals and the community. Since the free market fails to provide public open space, the public sector acts in the citizens' interest. When we consider that healthy ecosystems are also in the citizens' interest, then the preservation of biodiversity, flood protection and other services, such as open space, are justifiable planning and government concerns.[5] Nevertheless, open space generally follows an urban to rural gradient in respect to size and degree of human modification. This reflects land cost and the absence of systematic planning.

Although poorly distributed, open space is provided by public agencies including municipalities, counties, park districts and state parks. These agencies maintain over 20 million acres of land in the US. The majority of this is managed as state parks, but over six million acres is provided by municipal agencies. Two million acres of the municipal land is managed as informal open space (51.8 percent), habitat (34.3 percent) or preservation (4.9 percent).[6] It is clear that there is a substantial commitment to both formal recreation space and more naturalistic open space. Of course, the amount of formal parkland should not be reduced, but the acreage and thus the proportion of natural parkland within municipalities will need to grow in the future if urban biodiversity is valued.

Although open space is usually unplanned or an opportunistic provision, there are notable examples of deliberate open space systems that contain urban, as well as ecologically valuable, open space. These examples provide us with some of the most important demonstrations of the range and value of ecosystem services provided to urban residents.

Open space standards

Often open space in a city accumulates due to unplanned opportunities rather than deliberate physical planning that factors minimum size, location, residential density, connectivity or type of space. More often there is a piecemeal approach with a focus on meeting standards. Although very simple, the disadvantages of this approach are that it doesn't respond to the characteristics of the community or the unique qualities of the undeveloped landscape. Standards fail to account for opportunities for place making, multiple use or creating economic and other benefits for citizens. Many of these faults are due to an incremental rather than strategic approach.

Open-space standards reflect park acreage compared to city population. This simple formula has evolved to include access or service areas, in addition to acreage. This begins to address the unequal provision of open space by cities. In the UK, the first accessibility standard for open space was introduced in the late 1500s and specified that residents should be within three miles of open space. Several more recent standards have been promoted, including the ANGSt recommendations adopted by English Nature, a UK government agency. English Nature is promoting the adoption of these standards (Table 7.1) by all cities and towns. The standards specify at least five acres (2 ha) of green space within 1,000 feet (300 m) of each residence and a 50-acre (20-ha) space within 1.25 miles.[2]

In the US there are no national government requirements or guidelines for parks, open space, natural areas or trails, but the National Recreation and Park Association published guidelines in the early 1980s that set a standard of 6.25–10.5 acres per

Table 7.1 American and British open space recommendations.[8,2]

National Recreation and Park Association Standards – United States		
Park Type	Service Radius (miles)	Size (acres)
Mini-Park	less than ¼	0.06–1
Neighborhood Park	¼–½	5–10
Community Park	½–3	30–50
Large Urban Park	One per city	50 minimum, 75+ acres preferred
Nature Preserve	No recommendation	no recommendation
Sports Complex	One per city	25 minimum, 40–80 preferred

ANGSt Standards – United Kingdom		
Park Type	Service Radius	Size (acres)
Neighborhood	1,000' (300 meters)	5 (2 ha)
Community	1¼ miles (2 km)	50 (20 ha)
Large Urban Park	3 miles (5 km)	250 (100 ha)
Regional	6 miles (10km)	1,236 (500 ha)
Nature Preserve		2.5 (1 ha) for each 1,000 population increment

1,000 population for urban areas and 15–20 acres for regional parks.[7] The basis of this recommendation was subjective but widely adopted. These guidelines were revised in 1995 (Table 7.1). They suggest park types, sizes and service radii recommendations that many communities have adopted. The recommendations are clearly urban in orientation and there is no consideration of a networked system of parks. Park trails are classified by the association as single purpose, multipurpose or nature trails, but miles per 1,000 people or network density or other supply recommendations are not provided. Similarly, connector trails that are multipurpose but with a transportation focus are an identified trail type but, again, supply recommendations are not provided.[8] Neither the British nor the American standards recognize the opportunity to structure urban growth or the green infrastructure network potentials.

Cities meet the recommended standards to varying degrees. Seattle, for example, provides 4.8 acres per 1,000 population of developed parkland and 5.6 acres of natural parkland per 1,000 residents. Philadelphia provides almost seven acres of parkland per 1,000 people.[9] Often, smaller cities provide more park space per resident than large cities. For example, Boulder, Colorado, with a population of 103,600, provides 19 acres of urban parkland per 1,000 residents and 15 miles of greenway trails. Just beyond the city limit, the city provides 146 miles of trails and owns an additional 45,000 acres of natural open space and habitat.[10]

The Trust for Public Lands, a national non-profit organization in the US, developed a method to assess the 40 largest American cities according to the provision of parks. The organization combined several measures, which can serve as a guide for cities and towns that are planning park systems within their jurisdictions. As in the British method, both park acreage and access to it are important considerations. The study measured total acres of parkland within the city, but also determined the acreage as a percentage of the total city area. For the 40 cities, the range was 2.1 percent (Fresno) to 22.8 percent (San Diego) of the city area, with a median of 9.1 percent. The median park size ranged from 0.6 acres to 19.9, with a median size of 4.9 acres.[11] Even the best-performing city achieves less than the 30 percent open-space recommendation of this book for healthy human and ecosystem attainment. None of the largest US cities approach the 40 percent land area dedicated to parks achieved by Stockholm (see the case study in Chapter 12). This data suggest that American cities fail to provide the recommended park acreage and that the percentage of land area dedicated to open space is well below the amount necessary to provide for both recreation and habitat needs.

The Trust for Public Land also assessed the subject cities according to the public access to the parklands. They also distributed access according to economic stratification of the population. Access was defined as a ten-minute walk (0.5 miles) from the residence to the park entrance. The route needed to be free of obstacles, such as interstate highways, rivers, etc. The percentage of the urban population with this access ranged from 26 percent (Charlotte) to 98 percent (San Francisco), with a median of 57 percent.[11] This data shows that more that 40 percent of Americans do not have the recommended access to parkland.

The last measure considered by the Trust for Public Land is the level of service and investment in parks provided by the cities. The service component used playgrounds as a proxy since they reliably predict the provision of other park facilities.

Playgrounds per 10,000 residents ranged between 1 and 5, with a median of 1.89. Public investment ranged from $31 (El Paso) to $303 (Washington, DC), with a median of $85 per resident.[11]

The cities ranked in the top ten for a combination of acreage, access and service and investment were San Francisco, Sacramento, Boston, New York, Washington, Portland, Virginia Beach, San Diego, Seattle and Philadelphia. Cities with higher population density generally scored better on access but not necessarily on the service and investment issue. Total population was also not a predictor of park score rank. Several cities with low population density provided very large total park acreage but didn't qualify for top ranking due to access, service and investment problems. The top ranked, San Francisco, received an outstanding score for access and scored very high for investment ($291.66 per resident) and well above the median for percentage of land area dedicated to parks (17.9 percent), even though total park acreage isn't the highest.[11] Unfortunately, the Trust for Public Land doesn't distinguish undeveloped open space and habitat areas from developed parklands. Therefore, judging biodiversity capacity of the cities isn't possible. Larger expenditures per resident probably result in parklands that are better maintained and more highly programmed with activities.

Programming increases the value of existing park acreage, as demonstrated by the following research results. An analysis of 20 studies investigating the value of open space defined a forested land situation (forest size = 24,500 acres; population density = 87 people per square mile) and found that the open space value was $620 (2003) per acre per year. However, when the forest area increased above 24,500 acres, then the open space value per acre decreased, but total value did not decrease. If recreational opportunities are provided, then the open space value increases by 322 percent. This means that programmed urban parkland has higher open-space value[13] and the municipality is maximizing the benefit of its investment in parkland.

Systematic open space

A reasoned approach to open-space planning balances open-space standards with an assessment of local and regional demand for various outdoor recreation pursuits, the presence of outstanding visual character and local habitat. Comparison of existing supply with demand and existing service levels in the municipality or county would focus attention on where parks of various types are needed. Park and recreation standards, as suggested in Table 7.1, are a starting point for public participatory planning events to tailor an open-space system to local desires and conditions.

Provision of open space at Stapleton

Large subdivision projects and planned unit developments in the US are often required to provide a percentage of the site as public open space. The amount is determined through direct negotiation of housing density, commercial space and public amenities. This requirement often arises from a public participatory planning process that is absent from the consideration of small-parcel development. As the result of an extensive public planning process, the developer of Stapleton in Denver was required to dedicate 25 percent of the land area to parks, recreation and habitat restoration.

The citizen planning effort at Stapleton established a range of open-space types. The eight types are: (1) formal urban parks (about 175 acres); (2) nature parks (in this case Sandhills Prairie park at about 365 acres and the Sand Bluff Nature Area); (3) community parks (20–40 acres each); (4) neighborhood parks (up to ten acres each); (5) parkways or greenways (planted medians, vegetated street edges or landscape corridors with multiple functions, including stormwater management); (6) sports complexes (107 acres); (7) golf courses; and (8) community vegetable gardens. All of the open space shown in the master plan developed by the citizen planning group comprised about 35 percent (1,680 acres) of the land area, but has been reduced to about 25 percent or 1,200 acres.[12] This reduction had the greatest impact on habitat and biodiversity. However, compared to the 6 percent that is dedicated to parks for Denver as a whole, the case of Stapleton is a great improvement and exceeds the best performance of the 40 largest US cities. Similarly, the provision of a continuous green infrastructure that is multifunctional more efficiently delivers the variety of ecosystem services, including wildlife habitat (Figure 7.9). Residents have great access to spaces ranging from plazas, boulevards, greenways, active recreation and nature areas. Upon completion of all development at Stapleton there will be 40 acres of open space for every 1,000 people, exceeding the recommended standards by 400 percent. This also greatly exceeds the acreage provided by Seattle and Philadelphia to their citizens, but is far less than the combined park and habitat area provided by Boulder, Colorado.

Density and proximity

People value public open space more highly as population density increases. When the population density increases by 10 percent the value of open space increases by

Figure 7.9
This newly restored stream corridor at Stapleton once flowed through box culverts below airport runways. Today the corridor is valuable habitat connected to a regional preserve and other corridors. Note the new public recreation center building at the upper right.

Figure 7.10
This neighborhood park in a single-family residential neighborhood provides lawn, ornamental planting and a shade structure. All of these features are available in most of the private open space, which reduces park use except for neighborhood events.

5 percent.[13] Poorly used neighborhood parks (Figure 7.10) are often located in single-family residential areas where ample private open space reduces the demand for public space except for neighborhood celebrations or events. Small urban lots within single family, row house or townhouse neighborhoods are more acceptable to residents if parks are nearby.[14] When planning higher-density neighborhoods where multistory apartment, condominium or mixed-use buildings increase population density to above 20 people per gross acre, adjacent public open space should be prioritized to compensate for the absence of private open space and because these residents are most likely to use the provided amenities.

When the open space is close to residences it increases their value. Studies demonstrate that when considering properties an average distance (190 feet) from open space, compared to those 30 feet closer to open space, there is about 0.1 percent increase in price for the closer property. The price increase effect grows with each increment closer to the open space.[13]

Recreation facilities

In the US the National Recreation and Park Association recommends recreation facility standards just as they do for types of park acreage. From the green infrastructure point of view these facilities need to be located where they can be linked to other network resources and the residential and employment centers that might contribute users. Again the proximity of the recreation opportunities will encourage public use.

Land-use mix and destinations

Greater use of public open space results when development types are varied. When retail, employment and civic opportunities and residential areas are adjacent to each

Figure 7.11
As residential and employment density increase, so does use of public plazas, promenades and formal parks.

other and connected by pedestrian-friendly streets, then people are encouraged to walk between use areas (Figure 7.11). Some destinations are anchors within a network of pedestrian and bicycle routes and other uses. Schools, libraries, city administration, shopping districts, civic plazas, waterfronts and many other elements can function as anchors, drawing people along circulation routes. In Figure 7.12 restaurants, shops and offices surround an urban park and plaza. These attract pedestrians from apartments, condominiums, row houses and townhouses, and even regional shopping and auto services that are all visible in this small section of Stapleton. The beautiful promenade shown on the right side of the image and in Figure 7.13 inspire evening

Figure 7.12
This image shows the 29th Avenue promenade (right) leading to the Founders Park and urban plaza. The mixed-density neighborhood includes apartments, row houses, townhouses and multistory mixed-use buildings. Photo 39°45′28.94″ N 104°53′58.61″ W, September 2011 (accessed 15 March 2013), by Google Earth.

Figure 7.13
This wide median is a wonderful place to walk and is anchored by a destination – the mixed-use neighborhood center and plaza on 29th Avenue. It is Stapleton's version of the passeggiata.

strolls and daily commuting on foot. The resulting concentration of people arriving for different purposes encourages other people to come to see the activity (Figure 7.3).

Residential density

Low residential density results in lower pedestrian and bicycle activity and use of public open space. Conversely, as residential density increases, privately owned open space shrinks and the demand for public space and facilities increases. This is also true for the size of the residential living area. In Italy, for example, the evening stroll (passeggiata) is the opportunity to meet with friends, bump into playmates or eat an ice cream or a meal. There is no reason not to window shop, discuss a bit of business or study the latest fashion trends. There is no reason not to relax, get some exercise and enjoy the beauty of the city. This is all possible when the civic realm is nearby and well designed. It is possible even if the home or apartment is too small to accommodate a crowd of friends. Visitors from the US are astounded at the numbers of citizens of all ages who engage in the gregarious passeggiata, even in chilly winter months. It requires more effort, but even in the US we can find inviting urban spaces teeming with our neighbors and visitors (see Figure 7.16). Unfortunately, in the US there are fewer of these settings because the residential density is so low that the walk from the home to the public plaza is too far to become incorporated into our daily lives, unless we drive and park, which are often inconvenient.

Neighborhood civility and safety

There are often neighborhood disincentives for walking, bicycling or making other use of the public landscape. Planning and design can make public places safer, but other efforts must be brought to bear when fear of becoming a victim of crime or prejudice prevents people from using the streets, parks and trails. Tackling the problems of poverty, limited education, racism, gangs or other examples of failing community health is as important as it is difficult.

Walkability facilities and street connectivity

People walk or bicycle when the infrastructure encourages it. There is really a fundamental level of service and a more robust infrastructure that is necessary as the numbers of people walking and bicycling increase. Fundamental planning and design measures include supportive street widths, street patterns and environmental measures to reduce heat, glare and accidents, and to increase access. Streets need to connect to other streets in a legible pattern that allows direct routes to community destinations like civic buildings, open space, employment centers, schools, etc. Dead ends and cul-de-sacs should be limited or have non-vehicular routes through them. The system of roads must incorporate the needs of all users, not only those of vehicle operators. For example, short blocks (200–300 feet) encourage pedestrians, while long ones (600 feet) discourage walking because routes become too indirect. Bicycle paths need a minimum network density to allow reasonable routes through the city. Walking requires smooth surfaces and separation from cars and trucks, as well as ramps for wheelchair users and others.

When a fundamental and functional set of routes and surfaces have been provided then planning and design should concentrate on quality improvements, as well as system expansion (Figure 7.14). Walkability is as much about the satisfaction of walking as the engineering aspects of routes and surfaces. What will make walking a satisfying experience?

There are facilities and amenities that will better support a journey. Frequent places to stop for water, shade and seating improve the experience. Separation between motorized vehicles, bicycles and walkers is necessary as the density of each increases. The separation improves the experience and reduces conflicts and accidents. For bicyclists, more frequent facilities to lock and store bicycles, and frequent stations where there is air or supplies for bicycle tire maintenance and repair lead to ever more participation in non-motorized transportation. An expanded range of bicycle rental (Figure 7.15) and bicycle storage options, like covered shelters or lockers, serves an expanded group of users. Public or workplace facilities to shower or change clothes are beneficial.

Another group of pedestrian and bicycling amenities are less tangible or functional. Walking and bicycle routes should be choreographed. They are, after all, spatial-temporal environments where the experience can be punctuated, focused and enriched by a variety of design elements. Bringing the concepts of nodes, districts and thresholds to the recreation or transportation experiences of walking and bicycling offer many opportunities for creative design. Changes in color and texture of the

Figure 7.14
Special infrastructure is needed to support high levels of bicycle ridership. This applies to increased pedestrian density as well.

paving and the character of the plantings or building types can enliven and structure the experience. Manipulating the character of the enclosing edges and overhead plane also changes the spatial experience and increases the variety and sense of place in sections of the journey.

Cultural, educational or interpretive signage, sculpture and other site art add meaning and place attachment. These elements distinguish one route, city or region from another and increase the satisfaction of moving through the landscape. Cultural and natural history interpretation can be combined with local building and plant materials to create unique settings.

Traffic

High traffic speed and volume discourage use of urban sidewalks. Reducing these factors within central business districts improves the pedestrian experience and willingness to frequent local businesses. Increasing public transportation ridership and creating disincentives for driving a private vehicle has been successful in many US cities. Portland capped the number of parking lots and spaces within the city center. In fact, since this regulation was enacted the number of parking spaces has steadily declined as parking lots are converted to more profitable commercial or residential uses. This has caused the price of daily parking to increase in private and public lots and structures. Light rail and bus ridership for travel to and from the city

Figure 7.15
As bicycle and pedestrian use increases, cities need to respond with additional support facilities, such as bike storage, signage, rest areas, dedicated routes and bicycle rental programs. Additional facilities foster greater citizen participation.

Figure 7.16
An autumn afternoon in Boulder, Colorado. This civic and commercial mall is a closed street refurbished with new paving, seating, play areas, trees and outdoor cafes.

has increased steadily. Short-term rental of automobiles within the city is growing rapidly to serve the needs of commuters who have to make short trips within the city during the workday. Rentals of publicly or privately provided bicycles satisfy the same needs.

Slowing the speed of traffic on streets intended to serve pedestrians can be accomplished by narrowing travel lanes slightly, by providing on-street parallel or angled parking and by including planted medians and parkway tree plantings.

Pedestrian and bicycle safety structures

Of course, crosswalks and traffic signals need to be provided wherever pedestrian or bicycle safety is a concern, but as pedestrians and bicyclists become a greater proportion of the users of urban streets, additional safety measures can be implemented. Mid-block crosswalks are safer crossing locations for pedestrians than busy intersections, since many accidents involve turning vehicles. When the street is wide, curb extensions and a median reduce the expanse of roadway the pedestrian must cross.

Figure 7.17
Bicycle signaling to reduce conflicts with turning automobiles.

The median provides a refuge spot if the pedestrian can't cross the street in a single traffic cycle.

Copenhagen and other European cities have implemented traffic signals that allow bicycles to cross intersections before autos begin moving or turning operations (Figure 7.17). This practice and the provision of an extensive network of bicycle lanes and other amenities have dramatically increased commuting by bicycle. In addition to increased safety, bicycle traffic signals increase the speed of travel for cyclists, making them more competitive with private and public transit modes. Incidentally, preferential traffic signals and other rules for public transit also increases ridership by making it more time-competitive with the private automobile.

Vegetation

Vegetation is an open-space element that can have many benefits. Elsewhere street tree amelioration of the urban heat island effect was noted, but street trees, hedges and flowers are part of an enjoyable urban environment that encourages walking and bicycling. The beauty, shade and rain protection all contribute to the pedestrian environment (Figure 7.18), as does the real and suggested protection from nearby motorized vehicles. Capture of particulate air pollution is a more direct health benefit of urban vegetation. The presence of street trees and nearby green spaces has been shown to improve physical activity as discussed in the chapter on human health.[15,16,1]

Figure 7.18
This comfortable park in Stapleton is the focus of enclosing office and retail buildings. Its appealing vegetation offers many benefits.

References

1   D. Ding, J. F. Sallis, J. Kerr, S. Lee and D. E. Rosenberg, "Neighborhood Environment and Physical Activity Among Youth," *American Journal of Preventive Medicine*, vol. 41, no. 4, pp. 442–455, 2011.
2   L. Grant, "Multi-Functional Urban Green Infrastructure," The Chartered Institution of Water and Environmental Management, Briefing Report, 2010.
3   European Commission, "The Multifunctionality of Green Infrastructure," 2012.
4   The National Forest Company, "The National Forest Biodiversity Action Plan," 3rd edition, 2011.
5   T. Maruani and I. Amit-Cohen, "Open Space Planning Models: A Review of Approaches and Methods," *Landscape and Urban Planning*, vol. 81, no. 1–2, pp. 1–13, 2007.
6   B. Beckner, "The Conservation Imperative," Parks & Recreation, 2012.
7   R. Lancaster, "Park, Recreation and Open Space Standards and Guidelines," National Recreation and Park Association, 1983.
8   J. Mertes and J. Hall, "National Park, Recreation, Open Space and Greenway Guidelines," National Recreation and Park Association, 1995.
9   D. Taylor, E. Beard and P. Hayward, "Green Giants: Mayors Who Make Parks a Priority," Parks & Recreation, 2012.
10 City of Boulder, "Parks & Recreation Master Plan Update," 2013.
11 Trust for Public Land, "ParkScore," 2013. [Online]. Available: http://parkscore.tpl. org/methodology.php (accessed 9 February 2013).
12 City and County of Denver, Stapleton Redevelopment Foundation and Citizens Advisory Board, "The Stapleton Development Plan," 1995.
13 L. M. Brander and M. J. Koetse, "The Value of Urban Open Space: Meta-Analyses of Contingent Valuation and Hedonic Pricing Results," *Journal of Environmental Management*, vol. 92, no. 10, pp. 2763–2773, 2011.
14 D. Waugh, "Buying New Urbanism: A Study of New Urban Characteristics that Residents Most Value," Texas State University, San Marcos, 2004.
15 M. L. Booth, N. Owen, A. Bauman, O. Clavisi and E. Leslie, "Social–Cognitive and Perceived Environment Influences Associated with Physical Activity in Older Australians," *Preventive Medicine*, vol. 31, no. 1, pp. 15–22, 2000.
16 T. Takano, "Urban Residential Environments and Senior Citizens' Longevity in Mega-City Areas: The Importance of Walkable Green Space," *Journal of Epidemiology and Community Health*, vol. 56, no. 12, pp. 913–918, 2002.

CHAPTER EIGHT

Stormwater management and treatment systems

Introduction

The treatment of urban stormwater runoff by rain gardens and other landscape measures is a terrific green infrastructure opportunity. This feature can support other landscape functions, such as recreation and biodiversity. This chapter demonstrates how to size and construct high-performance stormwater facilities for management and water quality. In addition, the chapter presents techniques to maximize the secondary benefits of stormwater landscapes.

There are two classes of issues when considering the impacts of stormwater runoff. The first is generally called stormwater management. These impacts occur when land use changes from a natural condition to one with less pervious surfaces. The addition of roofs and paving to the landscape causes greater rainwater volumes to run off the surface, to run off at a higher rate and to run off at higher velocity. An increase in imperviousness of only 10 percent negatively impacts the receiving streams, lakes, rivers and oceans. The result is flooding, channelization due to erosion (Figure 8.1) and sedimentation of streams and rivers. Since the width and depth of streams and rivers were established in balance with the climate and natural retention of rainwater in vegetated, friable soil and humus, the change in hydrological conditions because of urban development overwhelms the capacity of the natural channels.

The second category of stormwater issues is water quality impacts that occur when rainwater collects pollutants from the air or, more often, from land surfaces and delivers them to the aquatic system. Toxic substances, such as heavy metals and petroleum hydrocarbons, join excess nutrients (ammonia, nitrate and phosphorus) and pathogenic bacteria to make urban stormwater a significant pollution problem. Polluted stormwater runoff can be treated in managed landscapes to remove contaminants and excess nutrients through several processes. Sequestration, filtering or biological conversion of toxins or nutrients into less harmful substances can be accomplished with managed natural systems (Figure 8.2).

Control and treatment of stormwater is increasingly regulated in developed countries. Complying with government standards by using managed natural systems is a cost-effective method that also contributes to a multifunctional green infrastructure. Therefore, the location and character of these facilities should be planned with the many other green infrastructure components within a continuous network.

Figure 8.1
This stream bank
erosion resulted from
urban development
upstream near
Springfield, MO. Over a
decade this seasonal
streambed has grown
steadily wider and
deeper as undermined
trees on the bank fell.

Figure 8.2
Bioretention Swale, in the High Point neighborhood of Seattle, WA. The check dam visible in
this photo holds a volume of stormwater for treatment and infiltration. Heavy metals,
suspended solids and hydrocarbons are effectively removed by these systems. This swale
contains a mixture of 65 percent gravely sand and 35 percent compost. The infiltration rate
is two to three times more than the two inches per hour predicted in the design phase.

Stormwater management

There is almost always more impervious surface on land that has been developed for human use compared to its predevelopment condition. State, county and city governments regulate the rate of stormwater runoff from a site proposed for development. This rate is generally limited to the runoff rate that exists in the pre-developed condition. Therefore, if the predevelopment runoff rate was 10 cubic feet per second (cfs), for example, and the postdevelopment rate is 15 cfs, then storage of some stormwater on the developed site would be required. Water may continue to drain from the site (after the storm has passed or abated) at the predevelopment rate (10 cfs) until the temporary storage basin is empty. Therefore, stormwater water is simply detained.

Of course, rainstorms occur at different intensities and durations. Therefore a "design storm" is defined in the stormwater regulation. Often this is the 10-year and 25-year storm for residential and commercial property, respectively. This means that the amount of water stored on-site and the permitted runoff rate is based on storms of an intensity expected to occur once in ten years (a 10 percent chance of occurring in any year) or once in 25 years (4 percent chance every year). Storms larger than these would result in temporary flooding. The design storm is loosely related to the value of the property being protected from flooding.

A depression that temporarily holds the stormwater on-site is called a detention basin or dry pond. The use of detention basins protects the natural aquatic system from excessive volume and velocity, but it doesn't improve water quality much. Furthermore, detention basins offer few secondary benefits to a green infrastructure since they are often deep, include steep slopes, often require fencing to protect the public from the drowning hazard and are often made of concrete (Figure 8.3). This

Figure 8.3
Detention basins are designed to control runoff rate only. Their single purpose fails to contribute significantly to a green infra-structure network.

Figure 8.4
This retention basin in High Point near Seattle is the central feature of the neighborhood park. This basin receives water that has already been treated by bioretention swales.

is really an outdated single-purpose technology that is being replaced with facilities that are more attractive, improve water quality and serve as visual and recreation amenities.

An improvement on the detention basin is the retention basin (Figure 8.4). It contains a permanent pool of water, but there is capacity to temporarily store the required volume of stormwater just as the detention basin does. These basins tend to be more attractive but don't improve water quality sufficiently. Better solutions are vegetated swales (bioswales), infiltration beds, bioretention basins (rain gardens) and constructed wetlands, which are discussed in later sections.

The rational method and the TR-55 are engineering calculation procedures that are commonly required to estimate predevelopment and postdevelopment runoff rates and storage requirements. TR-55 is a method developed by the US Natural Resource Conservation Service that includes a public software program to simplify the calculations. For more information and to download the program, see www.nrcs.usda.gov/wps/portal/nrcs/detailfull/national/water/?&cid=stelprdb1042901

Stormwater runoff characteristics

It is necessary to understand the sources and level of contaminants in urban runoff before introducing water quality improvement techniques. Some land uses contribute high concentrations of contaminants (Table 8.1). Most of the concentrations of nutrients, bacteria and metals are far above EPA standards for surface water.

Table 8.1 Stormwater runoff pollution concentration and land uses making the greatest contributions.[2] All of the land uses listed in the table contribute all of the pollutants listed, but the table displays only pollutant concentrations for the land uses contributing the highest levels

Contaminant	TSS a	E. coli b	TN a	P a	Copper c	Lead c	Zinc c
Land use							
Lawns	602		9.1	2.1			
Commercial Streets	468						
Auto Recyclers	335				103	182	520
Industrial Parking	228						
Landscaping		94,000			94	182	263
Residential Streets		37, 000		0.55			
Driveways			2.1	0.56			
Urban Highways			3	0.32	54	400	329
Rural Highways			22				
Industrial Roofs					62	43	1390
Heavy Industrial Land					148	290	1600
Water Quality Standard	30	126		0.05	13	65	120

Notes: a = mg/L, b = colony forming units per 100 mL, c = micrograms. TSS = total suspended solids, TN = total nitrogen, P = phosphorus.

The table allows the designer to concentrate on the pollutants most problematic in the drainage area. Total nitrogen includes organic nitrogen, ammonium, nitrite and nitrate. While there are no water quality standards for total nitrogen, concentrations of 0.2 mg/L (milligrams per liter) for nitrite and 1 mg/L for nitrate are generally accepted.[1]

The level of pollution in stormwater indicated in Table 8.1 is diluted when it enters streams and rivers, but research demonstrates that urban steams are highly degraded. From 2003 to 2007 data were collected for more than 20 stream watersheds near Atlanta, Georgia. The degree of watershed urbanization ranged from 69 to 93 percent. The data from the watersheds were compared to a small forest watershed and a larger, lightly developed watershed as references.[3]

The study indicates that urbanization impacts stream water quality, but this impact is highly variable. Increased alkalinity and concentrations of calcium and magnesium in urban streams were thought to be associated with the weathering of concrete. High levels of chlorine were associated with combined storm and wastewater sewer outflow treated with sodium hypochlorite, as well as drainage from swimming pools and road deicing salts ($CaCl_2$). The fecal coliform bacteria levels exceeded the EPA standard for recreation uses in more than 90 percent of the test samples taken from urban watershed streams. Nutrient levels in streams were high compared to streams in natural areas, but lower than EPA standards.[3]

The first 25 percent of stormwater runoff from impervious surfaces (the first flush) resulted in high concentrations of copper, lead and zinc. Copper and zinc in most

Figure 8.5
This image of spring
rain runoff shows the
oil contaminants in the
runoff from a parking
lot. In addition to
hydrocarbons, this
runoff is likely to
contain elevated levels
of TSS, bacteria, lead,
copper and zinc. This
level of pollution was
present on the second
day of intermittent light
rain, rather than in the
first flush.

of the streams exceeded Georgia's chronic and acute standards (chronic levels damage aquatic organisms when exposure exceeds four days, acute levels damage aquatic organisms when exposure exceeds one hour). Lead was detected at chronic levels. These metals are common in highway runoff. Vehicle tire particles and decayed metal fittings used in building construction are common sources of these metals.[3]

Species of pathogenic bacteria, in addition to *E. coli* noted in Table 8.1, are also present in high concentrations. Fecal coliform, total coliform and *E. coli* bacteria usually occur together and are associated with turbidity and suspended solids.[3]

Riparian buffers

Urban streams receive water from the landscape in several ways. Pipes discharge untreated stormwater from stormwater sewers and treated water from wastewater treatment plants. Water can also come from the groundwater (base flow), especially after storms have passed. Finally, water can drain directly from overland sheet flow or through a network of tributaries. Overland flow is contaminated by industrial, agricultural or urban land use. Vegetation buffer strips can filter and treat some of the pollutants from these areas before they enter streams and rivers (Figure 8.6). Pollutants of particular concern in the urban environment are heavy metals, hydrocarbons, nitrates, phosphorus and total suspended solids. A study in Iowa demonstrated that riparian buffers ranging in width from 42 feet to 72 feet (13–22 m) reduced nitrates from agricultural field levels of 9.3–13 mg/L to less than 0.3 mg/L.[4] Between 80 and 100 percent of the sediment in stormwater is removed by vegetated buffers 15–30 feet (4.6–9.1 m) in width. Removal of total nitrogen is more variable, but 30 feet wide buffers generally demonstrate reductions of 80 percent or greater.[5]

Figure 8.6
This restored urban stream was re-vegetated to improve water quality, habitat and as a public amenity.

Urban stream buffers, required by government agencies, range from 20 feet to 200 feet (6–61 m) depending on the jurisdiction, but the typical width (from the top of the stream bank) is 100 feet (30.5 m). The recommended minimum buffer is 100 feet and it should include three zones. The first zone is the stream ecological area (15 feet minimum on each side of the stream). Next is the buffer core area. It should be fully forested in temperate climates and express the typical riparian vegetation elsewhere. This core zone can be managed for limited timber harvest and other uses that don't adversely impact the pollution prevention and habitat functions. Finally, the buffer edge (25 feet) is the transition area for trails and other human activity. The width of the stream buffer should be increased if necessary to include the 100-year floodplain, and slopes steeper than 25 percent. For slopes above 5 percent, four feet of buffer width should be added for each 1 percent of steepness. For example, a 10 percent slope would add 40 feet to the buffer for a total of 140 feet from the stream edge. The width of the stream buffer should also increase to include all wetlands connected to the stream.[6]

The recommended widths for pollution control and stream health can be compared to the ecological corridor needs of urban birds and other species discussed earlier. Habitat, recreation and treatment of urban stormwater pollution are compatible uses of the green infrastructure along rivers and streams. These are biologically rich corridors that connect other habitat and human use areas. In some cases, especially where there has been poor planning in advance of urban development pressure, purchase of land or conservation easements may be required to establish stream corridors. Other planning accommodations to secure support for riparian buffer ordinances include density bonuses for developments adjacent to particularly wide riparian buffers.

Water quality storms

Regulatory agencies determine how much stormwater must be treated to improve water quality. Often the amount is 1–1.5 inches of water covering the entire site area. For example, a 10,000 square foot site area with 1 inch (0.083 feet) of rainfall would yield 833 cubic feet of water that would require treatment. Some agencies require treatment of the two-year, 24-hour storm or use other procedures to determine the water quality storm, but the results are similar. About 80 percent of the stormwater from a site receives treatment when 1–1.5 inches of rainfall from each storm is captured. In general, the design storm for water quality is smaller in regions characterized by gentle rainfall, but will be larger in areas with more intense storms.

Constructed wetlands for stormwater runoff treatment

Urban runoff can be effectively treated by shallow marsh wetlands (free water surface, FWS wetlands). It is correct to think of FWS wetlands as treating batches (the design storm volume) of water. One batch remains in the wetland after the storm ends and receives extensive treatment. The inflow from a new storm displaces the batch in the wetland. However, if the storm is larger than the design storm then there will be a flow-through period with very little treatment. If storms occur in rapid succession then the treatment time is also limited. The best water-quality performance will result from sizing the FWS wetland to contain the volume of more than one design storm. An FWS wetland with the capacity to hold one batch will result in pollution removal of about 20 percent while a wetland that contains six batch volumes will remove approximately 80 percent of the pollutants.[7]

Stormwater wetland case study

The example presented here shows the performance of an FWS wetland for water quality improvement, but also the potential for these facilities to provide recreation opportunities for the community. In 2007 a 11.5-acre (4.7-ha) wetland and park was constructed in Wilmington, North Carolina. The 3.4 acres (1.4 ha) of parkland around the wetland includes park buildings, picnicking areas and a 0.75-mile (1.22-km) pedestrian loop trail including a boardwalk across the wetland. The wetland (including the upland recreation area) represents less than 1 percent of its drainage area, but treats 47 percent of its potential runoff. The wetland was designed for a 1-inch (2.5-cm) water quality storm, but can contain and convey storms up to the 100-year, 24-hour rainfall (Figure 8.7).[8]

Eight storms ranging from 0.4 inches to 1.4 inches (1–3.5 cm) were monitored for six-hour durations. The wetland dramatically reduced both the rate and volume of the stormwater runoff. The wetland retained an average of 63 percent of the storm inflow. The average inflow of 15,185 ft³ (430 m³) per hour was reduced by the wetland to an outflow of 4,944 ft³ (140 m³) per hour.[8]

The primary water quality deficit in the stormwater was pathogenic bacteria. High bacteria levels had caused the closure of shellfish harvesting in the downstream tidal

Figure 8.7
The Wilmington wetland treats stormwater from a suburban watershed and dramatically improves the water quality of the receiving stream. It also provides recreation and habitat benefits to the community. Photo 34°10'39.96" N 77°52'40.43" W, 1 March 2013 (accessed 25 April 2013) by Google Earth.

stream reach. The stormwater wetland decreased the fecal coliform bacteria an average of 99 percent. In the wetland outflow, coliform bacteria was less than the 200 cfu/100mL (cfu = colony forming units) standard for human contact. When total suspended solids (TSS) concentrations were highest in the inflow, the wetland removed 98.8 percent of TSS.[8]

The Wilmington wetland removed more than 90 percent of the ammonium and orthophosphate, and 89 percent of the total phosphorus. Nitrate removal was very high, especially in the warmer months. It is important to remove nitrate from stormwater since it is toxic to aquatic organisms, causes algae blooms in lakes and the ocean and is a human health risk in drinking water. The EPA drinking water standard for nitrate is 1 mg/L, but it is harmful to newborn babies and can cause algae blooms at much smaller concentrations. Total nitrogen removal ranged from 66 to 96 percent.[8]

The excellent performance of this stormwater wetland is the result of several design factors. In Figure 8.7 the two six-foot deep forebays are visible. These are necessary to allow sediment to settle from the two stormwater inflow points. This wetland also features a weir that distributes the stormwater inflow evenly across the wetland, which is densely vegetated with a diversity of plants.[8]

Removal of bacteria pathogens in FWS and other wetland types is highly dependent on residence time and internal flow patterns. Rotifers and protozoa are microorganisms that prey on bacteria. Rotifers are abundant in the outflow of treatment wetlands. They are commonly present at 10 per milliliter. At this concentration rotifers can disinfect stormwater detained for 1.2 hours in a marsh wetland.[7]

A study of two detention basins, a retention pond, two wetlands and one bioretention basin confirmed the effectiveness of FWS wetlands for bacteria removal.

The detention basins actually increased the concentration of harmful bacteria while one wetland met EPA recommendations for primary recreation contact for *E. coli* and fecal coliform. The bioretention bed met EPA recommendations for primary recreation contact for *E. coli* and nearly met the standard for fecal coliform concentration.[9]

Stormwater wetland design

Stormwater wetlands can be designed for both managing the runoff rate and volume, as well as water quality improvements. The Wilmington wetland (Figure 8.7) illustrates the basic elements of a stormwater wetland. Water should enter the wetland at one end and flow into a sedimentation basin. These are deep basins that may normally be dry. The heaviest particles settle to the bottom of the sedimentation basin, carrying bacteria and heavy metals attached to them. The sedimentation basin or forebay must be cleaned out after a few years for continued water quality performance of the wetland.

Healthy, dense vegetation is a critical feature of a stormwater wetland. In the Wilmington case, the groundwater is high enough that it provides a minimum level of water for the wetland and low-flow channels through the wetland. The base flow of groundwater keeps the wetland vegetation healthy during the dry periods.

The stormwater must be evenly distributed across the wetland. At Wilmington this is done with notched weirs at the outlet of each sedimentation basin and along a third weir that crosses the entire wetland. The water quality storm flow must be shallow and move slowly through the wetland to receive maximum contact with the stems of the wetland plants and bottom sediment. The microorganisms and bacteria establish an ecosystem that utilizes the organic material, ammonium, nitrates, phosphorus and even complex and toxic organic compounds such as petroleum hydrocarbons. The wetland should be constructed with a flat or minimal slope (0.5–1 percent). The water flowing through the wetlands will seek preferential routes across the wetland, which decreases the treatment effectiveness. Therefore, the shape of the wetland should not be long and narrow, but roughly circular or square, as in the Wilmington example. The water depth should vary from 6 inches to 18 inches deep for the water quality storm. Sometimes deeper (4 feet) trenches are placed across the flow path to encourage mixing and redistribution of water, and to provide cooler water for fish habitat. In the Wilmington example, the sinuous route of the low-flow channel extends the length of pathway through the wetland and crosses the storm flow to encourage distributed flow through the vegetation.

There is a small pool at the outlet of the Wilmington wetland where an overflow structure controls the normal depth of water in the wetland and the depth for storms greater than the water quality storm. This structure releases water at the predevelopment rate for the larger storms (10- or 25-year storms typically). Ideally, the stormwater wetland has an area large enough to hold the volume of several water quality storms with a depth of 18 inches. The entire wetland is contained by a berm that prevents stormwater from flowing into the basin.

Mosquitoes are potentially a problem in stormwater wetlands. However, highly functioning wetland ecosystems significantly limit the population of mosquitoes.

High plant diversity leads to greater numbers and diversity of predatory insects, which reduce the number of mosquito larva in marsh wetlands compared to open water ponds without vegetation. Very shallow water and dense vegetation, such as cattail, encourage the development of larva and reduce predation by fish and insects. Mosquito fish and any other carnivorous or omnivorous small fish eat large numbers of larva. The flying range of adult mosquitoes is 100–300 feet (although wind can extend this distance, and some species have a longer flight range), so placement of the wetland in the watershed or buffers of recreation areas or upland habitat can control the impact of mosquitoes on people in residential areas.

Bioretention basins

An alternative to a stormwater wetland is a bioretention basin (rain garden, infiltration basin) (Figures 8.8 and 8.13). This was originally developed for stormwater management and water quality improvement on individual parcels (low-impact development), but it is valuable as a green infrastructure element at the neighborhood scale. The stormwater flows into a forebay and then into a shallow basin, just as with the stormwater wetland. However, the bioretention basin holds only 6–12 inches of water that completely drains away within 24 to 48 hours (less time than required for mosquito larva to become adults). Below the temporary pool is a four feet deep basin filled with sandy soil. The water quality storm is held by the forebay, temporary pool and soil reservoir.

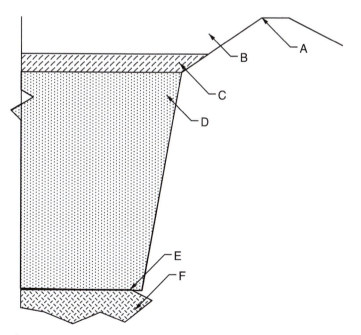

Figure 8.8
Bioretention basin section. A, earth berm with spillway or pipe overflow; B, 6–12-inch ponding depth; C, 4-inch cedar woodchips; D, sandy loam filter media; E, scarified basin bottom and sides; F, existing uncompacted subgrade with infiltration of at least 0.5 inches per hour and two feet minimum to the high water table surface.

Bioretention basins for stormwater treatment

Vertical subsurface flow (VSF) constructed wetlands developed to treat domestic sewage (see the discussion in Chapter 11) are the model for the design of bioretention basins. Bioretention basins are similar to infiltration beds, but are vegetated and deeper. Since bioretention basins treat stormwater and reduce runoff volume and delay time of concentration (peak runoff), the design of basins are complicated by a range of possible goals that can expand to reducing runoff rate, recharging groundwater, improving base flow and preventing sedimentation. Several states, such as Maryland, Pennsylvania and North Carolina, have guidelines or regulations for bioretention basins, but most do not. Some existing state design requirements do not reflect the range uses and goals or the recent research demonstrating the design and performance of bioretention basins.[10]

Design criteria

Initially, design guidelines were established based on very little research data and a limited set of goals. Monitoring of installed bioretention basins over the last 15 years provides more reliable criteria, installation requirements and performance expectations.[11]

Pretreatment

The failure of bioretention basins is most often due to construction errors and clogging of the filter media. Therefore, a sedimentation basin, swale or tank is recommended to remove as much sediment and suspended organic material as possible before water flows into the basin. It is recommended that the sedimentation pool and the temporary pool above the bioretention basin are sized to contain 70–75 percent of the water quality storm volume. A vegetated filter strip should attenuate any overland flow into a detention basin.

Basin

For initial planning and design purposes, the area of a bioretention basin is typically 5–8 percent of the catchment area, but the size varies with the pollutant load and water quality goals (Figure 8.9). Suggested maximum width for bioretention basins (25 feet) is based on the ability to excavate the basin with heavy equipment, located outside the basin to avoid compaction of the bottom soil. The width could be expanded with post-excavation measures such as ripping the soil, installing boreholes or infiltration trenches.[12] The basin includes a portion above the surface to temporarily pond 70–75 percent of the water quality storm. This can be reduced to as little as 25 percent if a sedimentation basin precedes the bioretention basin.

The maximum depth of ponding is a matter of some debate. Most states with regulations set surface pond depth between 6 inches and 18 inches. If the filter media and subsoil have a high infiltration rate or the basin has an under-drain, then a deeper surface pond is acceptable. The depth of the surface pond should drop at about 1 inch per hour due to infiltration into the subsoil.

Figure 8.9
The one-acre catchment area for the Villanova bioretention basin (blue) is about 50 percent impervious (red) and vegetated (green). Some pretreatment occurs in a vegetated swale in the parking lot. Photo base 40°02′27.79″ N, 75°20′45.25″ W, 7 October 2011 (accessed 25 April 2013) by Google Earth with overlay by author.

A 6–12-inch freeboard above the maximum water level is necessary. The surface of the basin should be covered with 3–4 inches of wood chips or other mulch. This appears to be particularly important if hydrocarbons are targeted for removal since bacteria in mulch rapidly decompose absorbed hydrocarbons, such as toluene and naphthalene.[11] The basin should be deep enough to contain 24–48 inches of sandy filter media (Figure 8.8). Underneath the filter media, a 6–16-inch depth of sand or gravel is sometimes specified to improve infiltration. However, this is probably not beneficial for a correctly designed and constructed basin. Metals and suspended solids are reduced significantly in the top eight inches (20 cm) of the media, which is where many of the pathogenic bacteria are removed also. However, removal of hydrocarbons, total nitrogen and phosphorus seems to benefit by depths of at least 30 inches.[11]

When the subsoil has an infiltration rate below 0.5 inches per hour, an under-drain in an eight-inch deep bed of coarse gravel (1–2 inches diameter) is recommended (Figure 8.10). As a transition layer to prevent media wash out, the coarse gravel should be separated from the filter media by a 2–4-inch layer of 0.25-inch diameter gravel (pea gravel). Some installations even include a coarse sand transition between the filter media and the pea gravel.[13]

A bucket with teeth should excavate the final 12 inches of the basin in order to limit compaction of the basin bottom. Research shows that infiltration into loamy sand subsoil is 2.6 inches per hour when the basin is dug with a rake bucket compared to 1.2 inches per hour for a basin dug with a flat-edged bucket. This translates into a basin drawdown of 12 hours and 27 hours for the rake and flat-edge bucket, respectively. Similarly, infiltration will be higher if the basin is dry when dug.[12]

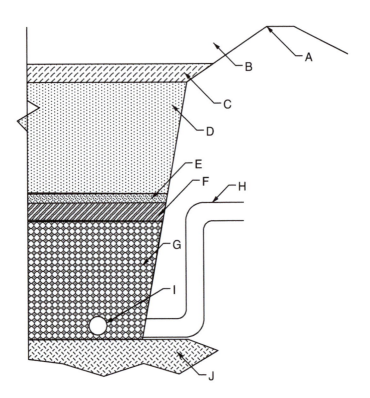

Figure 8.10
Bioretention basin with under-drain. A, earth berm with spillway or pipe overflow;
B, 6–18-inch ponding depth; C, 4-inch woodchip mulch; D, 24-inch sandy loam filter media;
E, 2-inch coarse sand layer; F, 4-inch pea gravel layer; G, 24-inch layer of 2-inch diameter
drain rock with waterproof liner; H, 4-inch diameter PVC drain; I, 4-inch diameter perforated
PVC under-drain; J, existing subsoil.

Filter media

Originally bioretention basins were planted with a mixture of shrubs, ground cover
and trees to resemble a native forest (Figure 8.11). Concern that coarse sand or
gravel, as in a vertical subsurface flow wetland, would be too infertile and dry too
quickly led to initial specifications for loam soil. This caused the bioretention basins
to clog quickly, as did the use of filter fabrics to separate the media layers in the
basin.[13] Most specifications today require 80–88 percent sand for the main filter
layer. Small amounts of shredded bark, mulch and loam soil are generally specified,
but fines (silt and clay) are limited to 7 percent. Compost should be used with caution
since it can increase the amount of nitrogen and phosphorus in the outfall.
Specifications should require that all gravel be triple-washed and that filter media
with a low phosphorus index should be used. A bioretention basin at Villanova University in Pennsylvania has been in operation for seven years with no reduction in the
infiltration rate (Figure 8.9). Its filter media is composed of 50 percent sand and 50
percent existing site soil.[14]

Subsoil

Infiltration of water treated in a bioretention basin may be desirable for groundwater recharge, to maintain base flow in the soil or to reduce stormwater runoff volumes. Where groundwater recharge is implemented, high water quality should be achieved before infiltration. Nitrates are often poorly removed from bioretention basins constructed without a water impoundment below the media (see Figure 8.10 for a section of a basin with a flooded storage zone, F and G). Nitrates are also not held in the soil and therefore are likely to drain into groundwater, especially if it is within a few feet of the surface. In this case a waterproof liner, as shown in Figure 8.10, prevents infiltration into the groundwater. Therefore, agricultural drainage areas, brownfield or current industrial land uses are poor locations for bioretention basins with infiltration due to elevated levels of nitrates or toxic chemicals.

If infiltration is desired (Figure 8.8), then the character of the soil below the bioretention basin is important. Generally, a subsoil infiltration rate of 0.5 inches per hour is required to drain the saturated basin. The saturated hydraulic conductivity of loam is 0.52 inches per hour, while for silt loam and sandy loam it is 0.27 inches per hour and 1.2 inches per hour, respectively. Hydrologic soil groups A and B, as defined by the US Natural Resources Conservation Service, are most suitable for infiltration basins, but a silt loam soil (type C) might be suitable under certain design conditions. A silt loam soil below 13 inches of ponded water in a bioretention basin will be eliminated in 48 hours, while in a loam soil this takes only 24 hours. A sandy loam soil will draw down 24 inches of ponded water in 24 hours. It is important to reduce the standing water in the bioretention basin rapidly so that there is capacity available for storms occurring at short intervals. However, an excessive infiltration

Figure 8.11
This lush planting of a bioretention swale on 2nd Avenue NW in Seattle establishes the character of the neighborhood. Bioretention swales are simply linear bioretention basins.

rate of more than three inches per hour is not desirable, since this reduces treatment time and also indicates a soil unsuitable for most plants. If 0.5–1 inch of water from every storm is infiltrated to recharge groundwater, this typically meets or exceeds preconstruction infiltration rates.[11]

Under-drains

Under-drains are used when the infiltration rate of the native soil is less than 0.5 inches per hour, or when the groundwater is seasonally within two feet of the bioretention basin bottom. When there is limited infiltration, perforated pipe in a coarse gravel drainage layer discharges the treated stormwater to the surface waters or storm sewer.

Removal of contaminants

In bioretention basins, the stormwater filters vertically through a sandy substrate, fully saturating the filter material before infiltrating into the subsoil or being drained by pipes below the basin. Bioretention basins are intended to dry (and renew their oxygen content) between storms. Therefore, treatment of pollutants occurs in an oxygen-rich (aerobic) environment.

Filtration, chemical and biological processes all contribute to the removal of contaminants in the stormwater. This full set of treatment processes makes bio-retention basins much more effective in the removal of contaminants than detention or retention stormwater basins. In fact, typical stormwater basins have little, or even a negative, water quality improvement benefit. The soil media very effectively filters suspended solids in stormwater (as high as 602 mg/L, according to Table 8.1).[17,11,9] The removal of suspended solids is important since heavy metals and pathogenic bacteria attach themselves to even very small particles. Beneficial bacteria in the soil filter are responsible for the consumption of organic material and the conversion to ammonia, nitrite and nitrate before removal as nitrogen gas. Soil bacteria are also major agents in the removal of pathogens in stormwater. The soil media high in calcium or other substances increase the removal of ammonium and phosphorus. Table 8.2 illustrates the water quality improvement data from a monitored bioretention basin in Charlotte, North Carolina.

The bioretention basin was constructed at the Hal Marshall Municipal Services Building in the City of Charlotte to treat 1 inch (25.4 mm) of rainfall (the two-year, 24-hour storm is 3.36 inches). The bioretention cell received water from a 0.92-acre (0.37 ha) parking lot. The surface of the infiltration bed was 2,480 ft² (229 m²), which represents 6 percent of the catchment area. The bed was composed of a 4 feet (1.2 m) depth of loamy sand (silt/clay = 5.7 percent) with a 6-inch diameter corru-gated under-drain. The subsoil permeability was 0.43 inches per hour and the basin was planted with a variety of water-tolerant species. The bioretention bed reduced contaminants significantly with one exception (Table 8.2). The low total nitrogen removal was due to low organic matter in the runoff.[18]

The increase in nitrite and nitrate to 0.43 mg/L indicates that the bed provides aerobic conditions for the conversion of ammonium to nitrite and nitrate. However,

Table 8.2 Charlotte Bioretention basin performance[18]

Pollutant	Removal %	Pollutant	Removal %
Total Nitrogen	32	Fecal Coliform Bacteria	69
Total Kjeldahl Nitrogen	44	E. coli	71
Ammonium	73	Zinc	77
Nitrite and Nitrate	- 5	Copper	54
Total Suspended Solids	60	Lead	31
Biological Oxygen Demand	63	Iron	330
Total Phosphorus	31		

Note: Total Kjeldahl nitrogen is organic nitrogen plus ammonia.

the removal of nitrate requires an oxygen-depleted environment that is not a feature of this design. A bioretention basin with an internal water storage feature (Figure 8.10) installed at Rocky Mount, North Carolina performed better with nitrate removal at 58 percent.[19]

A University of New Hampshire bioretention basin featured total suspended solids (TSS) removal of 99 percent and zinc removal of 99 percent, which is better performance than the basin data shown in Table 8.2.[13]

Nitrate removal

When the reduction of nitrate is an important goal, then a permanently saturated 24-inch deep layer of gravel is included below the main filter media. This creates an anaerobic zone that encourages the growth of bacteria that use carbon instead of oxygen as an energy source. In the process nitrate is converted to nitrogen gas that escapes to the atmosphere. In Figure 8.10, the elevated discharge pipe, H, will cause water to be retained in the gravel beds, F and G. Inflow from the subsequent storm causes the retained water to be discharged. Therefore, a volume of water is held for longer treatment. Within about one hour, oxygen in the retained water will be depleted by organisms, creating anaerobic conditions that are suitable for denitrification of nitrates by bacteria. This is the final step in a complex sequence including organic matter > ammonification > nitrification to nitrite and nitrate > denitrification to nitrogen gas. When nitrate reduction is an important goal, ideally the entire design storm would be contained within the basin's internal storage area.

Where organic matter, ammonium or nitrates are at high concentrations, such as in agricultural runoff, solid carbon (woodchips) in a horizontal subsurface flow bed has proven to be very effective for removal of nitrates.[15] A laboratory study demonstrated an 87 percent reduction of nitrate when carbon was added to the media of a saturated biofilter.[16]

The role of plants

Plants are an important part of the bioretention basin. They remove some nutrients from the stormwater but also transpire water, while their roots help maintain the porosity of the filter media. The soil media and the plants are important to treatment

Figure 8.12
This retention swale in Seattle illustrates the use of infiltration techniques for sloping sites.
This bioretention swale on 2nd Avenue NW reduced winter and spring runoff by 98 percent
compared to the conventional street design. Storms 0.75 inches (19 mm) and smaller are
completely retained and infiltrated. The infiltration swale reduces runoff from this
neighborhood to the local creek by 470 percent during the wet season, compared to a
conventional stormwater system.[21]

performance, as demonstrated in an Australian study. The significant difference in
the best-performing biofilter was the presence of *Carex appressa*, which is characterized by deep and fine roots. The bioretention column with the *Carex* removed
99 percent of TSS, 93 percent of ammonium, 85–96 percent of nitrite and nitrate,
71–79 percent of total nitrogen, 93–96 percent of total phosphorus and 87–98
percent of particulate phosphorus. The study demonstrated that sandy loam was the
best media and that compost or mulch in the media should be avoided, since this
increased total phosphorus in the effluent. Using plants that remove ammonia and
nitrate at accelerated rates seems to be important, but there has been little research
to identify these plants for various climate zones.[20] This study suggests that significant
improvements in water quality are possible as the design and construction of
bioretention basins are refined.

Pathogenic bacteria

Bioretention basins reduce pathogenic bacteria significantly, as demonstrated by a second study of the Charlotte bioretention basin described above. The study found that fecal coliform bacteria were reduced (89 percent) and *E. coli* bacteria were reduced (92 percent). The bioretention basin outflow met EPA recommendations for primary recreation contact for *E. coli* and nearly met the standard for fecal coliform bacteria concentration.[11] Part of the explanation for this good performance is that, in bioretention basins, the soil often dries between storms, reducing pathogenic bacteria. Since drainage through the soil media is rapid, high oxygen levels return to the soil volume quickly and drying is due to evaporation and transpiration in addition to infiltration into the subsoil of the bioretention basin.[22]

Phosphorus removal

Phosphorus removal in bioretention basins is highly variable due to differences in the filter media. Some basins removed only 5–30 percent of the phosphorous. Mulch and sand high in phosphorus in the filter media cause low removal rates, or sometimes an increase in phosphorus in the outflow. Sedimentation and adsorption are the primary removal mechanisms for phosphorus. Therefore, using media with high levels of calcium or magnesium results in good removal of phosphorus. Even with the correct filter media, the adsorption sites will be filled eventually and removal rates will drop, but this can take decades. Reducing the source of the phosphorus, such as artificial fertilizers with high phosphorous content, is perhaps more effective than treating highly polluted water.

Other contaminants

There are a host of toxic substances that find their way into urban stormwater runoff. Wetlands and bioretention basins also reduce many of these. A laboratory-scale study demonstrated 84–100 percent removal of the common pesticide atrazine in bioretention systems with and without an anaerobic stage.[16] The New Hampshire basin, noted above, achieved total hydrocarbon removal of nearly 60 percent for a 30-inch deep filter bed and 99 percent for a 48-inch deep bed.[13]

Stormwater management with bioretention basins

The Charlotte, North Carolina bioretention basin, described above, was designed to capture storms of 1 inch or less. However, for storm volumes of 1.65 inches (42 mm) the peak storm outflow was decreased by 96 percent, even though the entire catchment area was impervious.[18] This performance is confirmed by a study of a bioretention basin constructed at Villanova University in Pennsylvania (Figure 8.9). Its catchment area is 50,000 square feet and is 52 percent impervious. The 4-feet deep infiltration basin consistently removes 50–60 percent of the storm runoff. In fact, for storms 1.95 inches and under there was rarely any outflow from the basin at all. This is partly because there is infiltration into the subsoil during the entire storm. Even during a 6-inch storm the retention basin reduced the storm peak.[14]

Figure 8.13
Like the Villanova example, this attractive infiltration basin at the Mt. Tabor School in Portland, Oregon receives water from the adjacent parking lot.

A University of New Hampshire bioretention basin, comprising a 30-inch depth of sandy media and a 16-inch depth of gravel below the media, achieved an 82 percent reduction in peak stormwater flow and a 92-minute delay in the storm peak.[13]

Base flow and groundwater

Interest in the recharge of groundwater by local agencies may add requirements that some postdevelopment runoff is to be infiltrated to meet predevelopment conditions. Bioretention basins respond to this concern. For example, a wooded site slated for low-density residential development might typically have a predevelopment curve number of 55. Runoff curve numbers are based on the US Natural Resources Conservation Service method of estimating the percentage of stormwater runoff and are influenced by soil type, land use, vegetation and land management practices. If, after development, the wooded site had a curve number of 70, then 15 percent more water is expected to runoff. An infiltration of 0.22 inches of runoff volume from the developed site would be required to match predevelopment conditions for a storm with a 2-inch rainfall depth. Over a half-acre site this would equal approximately 400 cubic feet for a 2-inch storm and could be accommodated in a 20 × 20 feet bioretention basin.[23]

Secondary benefits

Even higher stormwater treatment performance might be achieved if a sequence of treatment stages is implemented.[24] For example, bioswales within ecological corridors might collect runoff from residential housing and streets and feed water to bioretention basins for attenuation of storm volumes and reduction of heavy metals, hydrocarbons, phosphorus and nitrates. The bioretention basins could in turn feed water to stormwater wetlands for additional treatment and habitat enhancements.

Multiple functions

Lenexa, Kansas in an example of a city (population of 45,000) that developed a regional stormwater management plan to reduce flooding, improve water quality and provide environmental, open space, recreation and education benefits (Figures 8.14 and 8.15). They made stormwater lakes the central feature of their park system, but the lakes are intended to receive pretreated water from stormwater management techniques like bioretention basins and pervious paving.

The multiple-use design of the stormwater landscape enhanced the park. Instead of focusing only on engineering functions, the stormwater basin design includes aesthetic treatment of the basin edges and dam. The adjacent recreation facilities encourage fishing, boating and many other kinds of recreation. The use of the lake and adjacent landscape for civic celebrations and festivals indicates that this space engenders a sense of place and civic pride. These social values are rarely associated

Figure 8.14
Lake Lenexa is the 35-acre focus of community festivals and daily recreation. This stormwater basin features an elaborate dam (right), which includes cascading pools and a fountain. The park is 240-acres and includes three wetlands, trails, docks, a boat ramp, picnic areas and boardwalks. Photo 38°57′53.18″ N, 94°50′19.08″ W, 2 September 2012, (accessed 15 April 2013) by Google Earth.

Figure 8.15
Lake Lenexa and park during the 2011 Spinach Festival. Photo by Leonard Rosen, city of Lenexa.

with stormwater infrastructure, but they demonstrate the value of creating a green infrastructure that serves many purposes simultaneously (Figure 8.16).

Lenexa found that a landscape approach to treating stormwater costs about 25 percent less than traditional storm sewer infrastructure. Nevertheless, the cost of municipal treatment of stormwater was estimated to be $0.504 per square foot of impervious surface of new development. To recover a portion of this cost the city charges an impact fee of $850 per dwelling unit for new construction. Developers can reduce this fee by implementing on-site measures to reduce runoff, such as

Figure 8.16
Bioretention basin planting design in the High Point neighborhood of Seattle. This stormwater facility reduces stormwater runoff and improves its water quality while creating a beautiful park setting.

reducing the amount of impervious surfaces, or treating the stormwater in infiltration swales or bioretention basins. The city found that there was little or no reduction in the development area as a consequence of the landscape stormwater requirements it implemented. The costs to the developer were the same or less to install the landscape approaches compared to conventional development and the fiscal impact on the taxpayer was neutral.

References

1 H. Li, "Water Quality Improvement Through Reductions of Pollutant Loads Using Bioretention," *Journal of Environmental Engineering*, vol. 135, no. 8, pp. 567–576, 2009.

2 R. H. Kadlec, "Comparison of Free Water and Horizontal Subsurface Treatment Wetlands," *Ecological Engineering*, vol. 35, no. 2, pp. 159–174, 2009.

3 N. E. Peters, "Effects of Urbanization on Stream Water Quality in the City of Atlanta, Georgia, USA," *Hydrological Processes*, vol. 23, no. 20, pp. 2860–2878, 2009.

4 D. Jaynes and T. Isenhart, "Re-Saturating Riparian Buffers in Tile Drained Landscapes," presented at the IA–MN–SD Drainage Research Forum, Okoboji, Iowa, 2011.

5 US Environmental Protection Agency (EPA), "Guidance for Federal Land Managers in the Chesapeake Bay Watershed," EPA 841-R-10–002, 2010.

6 Federal Interagency Stream Restoration Working Group (US), *Stream Corridor Restoration: Principles, Processes, and Practices*, Washington, DC: Federal Interagency Stream Restoration Working Group, 1998.

7 R. H. Kadlec, *Treatment Wetlands*, Boca Raton, FL: CRC Press, 2009.

8 M. A. Mallin, J. A. McAuliffe, M. R. McIver, D. Mayes and M. A. Hanson, "High Pollutant Removal Efficacy of a Large Constructed Wetland Leads to Receiving Stream Improvements," *Journal of Environment Quality*, vol. 41, no. 6, p. 2046, 2012.

9 J. Hathaway, "Indicator Bacteria Removal in Storm-Water Best Management Practices in Charlotte, North Carolina," *Journal of Environmental Engineering*, vol. 135, no. 12, pp. 1275–1285, 2009.

10 Idaho Department of Environmental Quality, "Storm Water Best Management Practices Catalog," 2005.

11 A. Davis, W. Hunt, R. Traver and M. Clar, "Bioretention Technology: Overview of Current Practice and Future Needs," *Journal of Environmental Engineering*, vol. 135, pp. 109–117, 2009.

12 R. Brown, "Impacts of Construction Activity on Bioretention Performance," *Journal of Hydrologic Engineering*, vol. 15, pp. 386–394, 2010.

13 University of New Hampshire, "Annual Report," 2007.

14 National Research Council, *Urban Stormwater Management in the United States*. Washington, DC: National Academies Press, 2009.

15 L. A. Schipper, W. D. Robertson, A. J. Gold, D. B. Jaynes and S. C. Cameron, "Denitrifying Bioreactors: An Approach for Reducing Nitrate Loads to Receiving Waters," *Ecological Engineering*, vol. 36, no. 11, pp. 1532–1543, 2010.

16 H. Yang, "Dissolved Nutrients and Atrazine Removal by Column-Scale Monophasic and Biphasic Rain Garden Model Systems," *Chemosphere*, vol. 80, pp. 929–934, 2010.

17 M. Mallin, "Pollutant Removal Efficacy of Three Wet Detention Ponds," *Journal of Environmental Quality*, vol. 3, pp. 654–660, 2002.

18 W. Hunt, "Pollutant and Peak Flow Mitigation by a Bio Retention Cell in Urban Charlotte, N. C.," *Journal of Environmental Engineering*, vol. 135, no. 5, pp. 403–408, 2008.

19 R. A. Brown and W. F. Hunt, "Evaluating Media Depth, Surface Storage Volume, and Presence of an Internal Water Storage Zone on Four Sets of Bioretention Cells in North Carolina," World Environmental and Water Resources Congress, pp. 405–414, 2011.

20 K. Bratieres, T. D. Fletcher, A. Deletic and Y. Zinger, "Nutrient and Sediment Removal by Stormwater Biofilters: A Large-Scale Design Optimization Study," *Water Research*, vol. 42, no. 14, pp. 3930–3940, 2008.

21 R. Horner, Heungkook Lim and Stephen J. Burges, "Hydrologic Monitoring of the Seattle Ultra-Urban Stormwater Management Projects," Department of Civil and Environmental Engineering, University of Washington, Seattle, WA, Technical Report 170, 2002.

22 W. Hunt and A. Jarret, "Evaluating Bioretention Areas from Two Field Sites in North Carolina," in *BMP Technology in Urban Watersheds*, Reston, VA: American Society of Civil Engineers, 2006, pp. 209–218.

23 Department of Environmental Resources, "Bioretention Manual," Environmental Services Division, Prince George's County, MD, 2007.

24 K. L. Guenter Langergraber and R. H. Roland Rohrhofer, "High-Rate Nitrogen Removal in a Two-Stage Subsurface Vertical Flow Constructed Wetland," *Desalination*, vol. 246, pp. 55–68, 2009.

CHAPTER NINE

Green roofs

Introduction

When green roofs are located in, or adjacent to, open space they can contribute significantly to a green infrastructure network. The Academy of Sciences building in San Francisco, designed by architect Renzo Piano, was completed in 2008 and features a 2.5-acre green roof. The roof includes several distinctive mounds and undulations (Figure 9.1). It is an example of a landscape that does contribute to the broader landscape since it is located in a large park. Generally, green roofs are marginally part of the green infrastructure, as defined in this book, since they are disconnected from each other and often from the larger landscape. Subsurface drainage pipes usually connect them with the adjacent landscape only tenuously. However, sometimes green roofs do connect to a green infrastructure through ground-level landscaping and surface drainage, or they are close enough together that they are functionally connected habitat patches.

Types of green roofs

Green roofs are generally divided into two categories. The extensive green roof has a soil depth of less than three inches (150 mm) and is entirely vegetated with herbaceous and other low-growing plants (Figure 9.2). These roofs are intended to function primarily as stormwater and energy management systems. Their advantage is that the structural demand on the building roof is low. Therefore, they are often selected when retrofitting conventional roofs.

In contrast, people use intensive green roofs as an amenity. A portion of the roof is paved and the soil in the planting areas is more than three inches deep. Shrubs and trees are often planted in addition to herbaceous plants, as they would be in a garden, park or plaza (Figure 9.3). Intensive roofs are more expensive than conventional roofs but compensate for their higher cost over time with reduced energy costs for building heating and cooling. They also provide valuable use area. For new construction, extensive green roofs are somewhat less expensive to build than intensive ones. Steel and concrete buildings are best suited for intensive rooftop gardens because they can support up to 250–300 pounds per square foot of weight. When planning a new green roof or retrofitting an existing building for an extensive roof, a structural engineer should provide the landscape architect with the load-bearing

Figure 9.1
The extensive green roof of this natural history museum is part of the green infrastructure due to its location and the habitat connection to adjacent forest and meadow areas.

Figure 9.2
Autumn weather causes the *Sedum* on this steeply sloping roof in Copenhagen to blaze with color. Steep (slope ratios greater than 2 vertical to 12 horizontal) green roofs require special engineering to anchor the soil and plants.

capacity as a landscape design limitation. The location of structural columns is also necessary, since these are locations where heavier elements, such as trees, can be located. Extensive green roofs can be designed for roofs with a structural capacity as low as 25 pounds per square foot, but 35 pounds per square foot is preferred. Typically, wet soil media used for green roofs weighs about 7.5 pounds per square foot for a one-inch depth.[1]

Figure 9.3
This multiple-level roof garden is on the public library in Salt Lake City.

Roof construction

The green roof of the Academy of Sciences building includes a small observation deck and interpretive area, but the roof is essentially of the extensive type since people can't walk among the plants. This roof is built of several layers. A 6–8-inch thick concrete roof is covered with four layers of roofing materials. This roof thickness is greater than the typical 2.5–4-inch slab on most roofs.

Figure 9.4 shows the next layers of the green roof. The light blue material is rigid foam insulation that protects the roof membranes and insulates the roof. The next layer is a thin waterproof membrane followed by a corrugated polypropylene drain

Figure 9.4
This model illustrates
the layers of materials
that compose the
Academy of Science
green roof.

mat (Figure 9.5). The next layer is a filter fabric that separates the three-inch soil layer (represented by the brown cork) from the drain mat. At the top of the stack is a wooden tray covered in coconut fiber that holds three inches of soil and the plants. The soil used for green roofs is engineered to be lightweight. It often includes pumice, vermiculite and expanded shale or other lightweight and inert components. The soil often provides few nutrients to the plants. Fertilization of the plants must be done carefully (preferably with time-released material) to avoid runoff polluted with ammonia, nitrates and phosphorus.

Figure 9.5 is a close-up of the drain mat. The holes in the top of the egg-crate-like mat are visible. These are the overflow outlets. This structure holds about 1.5 inches of water in the tray after a rainstorm for later use by the plants. This storage capacity is the reason that this green roof is able to retain all of the rainwater with the exception of some of the rain from most intense storms.

The soil and vegetation extend the life of the building roof. Green roofs last 45 years or more, compared to conventional roofs which last about 20 years. In fact, the green roof of a wastewater treatment plant in Zurich, installed in 1914, was

Figure 9.5
Water reservoir and
drain mat.

repaired for the first time in 2005. The protection of the roof membranes from ultraviolet light and rapid changes in temperature accounts for this difference. Temperature fluctuations of conventional roofs can be as wide as 81°F (45°C) and reach maximum temperatures of over 150°F. The expansion and contraction caused by this temperature fluctuation leads to premature failure of the membranes. Old roofing is generally disposed of in landfills, adding to the solid waste stream and leachate treatment costs.[2]

The costs of green roofs are about $10 and $25 per square foot for intensive and extensive types, respectively. The cost of the intensive roof is about twice the cost of a conventional roof.[3]

Green roof plants

Landscaped roofs present plants with a set of very difficult growing conditions. Green roof plants are exposed to high wind velocities and maximum solar radiation. If the roofs slope steeply, the water runs off more quickly, increasing drought stress. Finally, the limited soil depth, especially on extensive green roofs, and its lightweight character reduce the water-holding capacity. *Sedum* species are widely used to vegetate green roofs since they are hardy and tolerate drought conditions. Species effective on extensive roofs include *Sedum album*, *S. reflexum*, *S. spurium* (Figure 9.6) and

Figure 9.6
Sedum spurium
tolerates the difficult
growing conditions
presented by intensive
green roofs.

Figure 9.6
Sedum spurium tolerates the difficult growing conditions presented by intensive green roofs.

S. sexangulare, but many other native and non-native species are suitable. Many more plant choices are available for intensive roofs since the soil is deeper, but *Rhus copallina* (flame sumac), *Rhus aromatica* (smooth sumac), *Campsis radicans* (trumpet vine), *Eragrostis spectabilis* (purple lovegrass), *Allium ceruum* (nodding onion), *Coreposis verticillata* (thread leaved tick seed), *Asclepia tuberose* (butterfly milkweed) and *Rosa carolina* (pasture rose) perform well.[4] The testing and use of native plants is valuable for better habitat value. A Canadian study successfully cultivated ten native plants that performed as well or better than the standard *Sedum*s for various green roof functions such as temperature and albedo.[5]

The Academy of Sciences roof was planted with perennial and native species based on research and testing of 35 species for tolerance of the difficult conditions (Table 9.1). The 1.7 million plants are contained in 50,000 plant trays. The trays were necessary to support the plants until they were established on the areas of 60-degree roof slopes. The wood and fiber trays will decompose within about five years, but by then the plant roots will have knitted the soil together to control soil erosion and stabilize the slopes. The vegetation is irrigated to maintain the high aesthetic expectations of the millions of annual visitors. The irrigation tends to favor some plants, causing the perennial self heal to compete more effectively than other species (Figure 9.7).[6]

The use of irrigation on a green roof seems, at first glance, to contradict other sustainability benefits. However, irrigation water increases evapotranspiration from the roof, thereby cooling it. This reduces the demand and energy used to cool the building interior. From a cost perspective, using irrigation as a cooling mechanism is about 40–90 times less expensive than using electricity to cool the building. The use of non-potable water for irrigation could increase the sustainability of this practice even more.[2]

Table 9.1 Plant list for the Academy of Sciences green roof

Common Name	Botanic Name
Self heal	*Prunella vulgaris*
Sea pink	*Armeria maritima*
Stonecrop	*Sedum spathulifolium*
Miniature lupine	*Lupinus bicolor*
Goldfield	*Lasthenia californica*
Tidy tips	*Layia platyglossa*
California poppy	*Eschscholzia californica*
California plantain	*Plantago erecta*

Figure 9.7
Prunella vulgaris (self heal) has expanded in response to artificial irrigation to dominate the Academy of Sciences roof.

Stormwater management

Rainfall captured by vegetation and soil on a green roof is evaporated and transpired after the storm ends. This reduces the runoff volume and runoff rate. Both of these reductions are especially important in intensively developed urban areas that are usually characterized by a very high proportion of impervious surfaces. Reductions in rate and volume are critical in older cities where stormwater and sanitary sewers are combined. In this case stormwater overwhelms the capacity of the wastewater treatment plant and water is discharged into the environment before receiving proper treatment. Since much larger volumes of water flow off of urban districts because there is little green space in high-density commercial and residential districts, the potential contributions of green roofs for stormwater runoff reduction are higher in these areas.

Building roofs often comprise 40–50 percent of the impervious area of a city center.[2] The percentage of rainwater captured by green roofs depends, in part, on storm intensity, duration and frequency. These factors vary by region and season. The construction techniques and materials for green roofs vary and also influence the stormwater performance of the roofs. This makes comparisons of different green roofs somewhat difficult.

Runoff volume reduction

Intensive roofs typically reduce stormwater runoff by 75 percent when soil depth is six inches (150 mm) or more. This conclusion is based on the performance of 11 roof gardens. A review of 121 extensive green roofs with a typical soil depth of four inches (100 mm) revealed a 45 percent reduction in the annual stormwater runoff.[7]

Another more recent study showed a somewhat better performance for extensive roofs. This Auckland, New Zealand study of four extensive green roofs demonstrated that, compared to conventional roofs, up to 56 percent of the cumulative stormwater was captured and then evaporated or transpired. On the green roofs in the study, the vegetative cover was more than 80 percent and the soil depths were two, three, four and six inches (50 mm, 70 mm, 100 mm and 150 mm) for the four roofs studied. In this study the soil depth didn't impact the amount of stormwater mitigation. The soils were about 80 percent lightweight aggregate and 20 percent organic material supporting *Sedum* species and native plants.[8] In general, each inch of soil depth retains 0.3 inches of rainfall.[1]

Since summer temperatures, evaporation and plant transpiration rates are higher than in other seasons, all green roofs are more effective in managing summer stormwater runoff. The summer evapotranspiration more quickly depletes soil moisture, making storage capacity more quickly available for the next storm.[7]

Runoff rate reduction

As with runoff volume, impervious roofs increase the rate of stormwater runoff. Green roofs can delay the time of peak runoff and reduce runoff velocity. This is important if receiving streams are being eroded by urban runoff. However, several factors can limit the effectiveness of green roofs. In areas with frequent high-intensity storms the capacity of the green roof to store water and slow runoff is limited, especially in winter. Deeper soils or other measures to slow the runoff increase the ability of green roofs to delay storm peaks.

A curve number has been established for extensive roofs for use in stormwater modeling using the TR-55 software provided by the Natural Resource Conservation Service of the US government. The green roof used to establish the curve number was composed of a three-inch (7.62 cm) deep soil (55 percent expanded slate, 30 percent sand and 15 percent organic matter). The soil had a total porosity of

50.6 percent. It was planted with three *Sedum* and two *Delosperma* species at a density of 50 plants per square meter.[9] The green roof curve number of 86 can be compared to the curve number of 98 for impervious roofs, indicating a 12 percent reduction in runoff. The development of the curve number allows more accurate calculation of runoff peak time, rate and volume. This is important for planning stormwater management for new construction of buildings with green roofs and for determining the benefit of retrofitting a building with an extensive green roof.

Air pollution reduction

Pollutants deposited on green roofs are effectively retained. The percentage of lead, cadmium, nitrates and phosphorus retained by green roofs is 95, 88, 80 and 67, respectively, according to one study.[2] Since ammonia, nitrate and phosphorus are components of artificial fertilizer, minimum applications of time-release fertilizer are necessary, just as for any other landscape, to avoid migration of excess nutrients into the aquatic system.

Particulates and other pollutants

The removal of particulates and other pollutants is an ecosystem service with economic value. A 2,000 square foot green roof is estimated to provide $895–3,392 of annual economic benefit for the removal of nitrogen oxide pollutants. About 75 pounds per acre (85 kg per hectare) of air pollutants are removed annually by 2,000 square foot of green roof. Slightly more than half of this is ozone, nearly one-third is nitrogen oxides, and particulates (PM10) and sulfur dioxide represent 14 and 7 percent, respectively. *Sedum* species are not the most effective plants for removal of pollutants. Grasses, shrubs and trees are more effective. The air pollution removal benefits of green roofs are too expensive to justify their construction for this purpose alone. Slightly more than 200 square feet (19 m²) of green roof is required to remove as much air pollution as a medium-sized tree, and the cost is far higher.[2] Nevertheless, the air quality benefit is a welcome secondary outcome, especially if landscaping at ground level is limited.

Carbon sequestration

Sequestration of carbon by extensive green roofs is not very significant. Intensive roofs perform better since the soil is deeper and the vegetation often includes shrubs and trees. In fact, the amount of carbon sequestered would not be significant compared to the amount of carbon expended in the materials and construction of the green roof. But the impact on the carbon cycle of both types of green roofs is significant. The explanation of this paradox is that green roofs reduce the amount of energy required to heat and cool the building. This is important since buildings are responsible for a large portion of carbon dioxide emissions (38 percent). Green roofs reduce the building's use of electricity by 2 percent and natural gas use by 9–11 percent. Therefore, green roofs have a positive impact on carbon dioxide emissions.[2]

Habitat value

The habitat value of green roofs is limited by their size and typical use of non-native plants. However, a number of green roofs in a small area and planted with native plants could offer biodiversity benefits for insects and birds. Green roofs might be of particular value to pollinators. A green roof designed to contain many microhabitats fosters biodiversity. A green roof of this type in Germany supports a total of 119 species of beetles and spiders, 20 of which are endangered. The 2.5-acre landscape of native vegetation on the roof of the California Academy of Sciences in Golden Gate Park is the city's largest patch of native plants. Birds, bees and other pollinators, including a threatened butterfly (the bay checkerspot), use this habitat fragment.[10] The roof includes a honeybee hive in two rooftop locations.

Energy benefits

The American Society of Landscape Architects (ASLA) constructed a green roof on their headquarters building. The green roof is as much as 32°F cooler than conventional black roofs.[4] Generally, green roofs provide a 15–25 percent saving in energy cost. The heating and cooling requirements of the Academy of Sciences building are reduced by 35 percent by its green roof. Energy cost saving due to the green roof on the Chicago City Hall is $3,600 per year.[3]

Figure 9.8
Green roofs provide energy conservation, stormwater management and cultural benefits.

References

1   Penn State Center for Green Roof Research, "Green Roof Brochure," Pennsylvania State University, n.d.

2   D. B. Rowe, "Green Roofs as a Means of Pollution Abatement," *Environmental Pollution*, vol. 159, no. 8–9, pp. 2100–2110, 2011.

3   US Environmental Protection Agency (EPA), "Reducing Urban Heat Islands: Compendium of Strategies," 2008.

4   American Society of Landscape Architects, "ASLA Green Roof Monitoring Results," 2007.

5   J. S. MacIvor and J. Lundholm, "Performance Evaluation of Native Plants Suited to Extensive Green Roof Conditions in a Maritime Climate," *Ecological Engineering*, vol. 37, no. 3, pp. 407–417, 2011.

6   L. McIntyre, "High-Maintenance Superstar: The Green Roof on the California Academy of Sciences," *Landscape Architecture*, vol. 99, no. 8, pp. 64–66, 68–72, 74–77, 2009.

7   J. Mentens, D. Raes and M. Hermy, "Green Roofs as a Tool for Solving the Rainwater Runoff Problem in the Urbanized 21st Century?" *Landscape and Urban Planning*, vol. 77, no. 3, pp. 217–226, 2006.

8   E. Fassman-Beck, E. Voyde, R. Simcock and Y. S. Hong, "4 Living Roofs in 3 Locations: Does Configuration Affect Runoff Mitigation?" *Journal of Hydrology*, vol. 490, pp. 11–20, 2013.

9   T. Carter and C. R. Jackson, "Vegetated Roofs for Stormwater Management at Multiple Spatial Scales," *Landscape and Urban Planning*, vol. 80, no. 1–2, pp. 84–94, 2007.

10 G. R. Aleta, "Greening a Higher Ground," *Smithsonian*, vol. 39, no. 8, n.p., 2008.

CHAPTER TEN

Integrating community agriculture into green infrastructure

Introduction

This chapter demonstrates the economic and social advantages of locally produced food. To secure these benefits, community agricultural business need to be fostered by regulations and planning to place them within the municipal and county green infrastructure network, where they contribute to the open space and where their waste products can be treated by infiltration beds or with other techniques, as discussed in Chapter 8.

To an even greater degree than open space, community gardens are typically the product of opportunistic planning, and community agriculture is rarely planned for at all. Community gardens are a collection of plots, provided by city government or non-profit organizations, and cultivated by citizens. In contrast to growing produce for home use, community agriculture is small-scale farming as a commercial enterprise. Community agriculture usually involves high-value vegetable and berry crops but includes bee-keeping and aquaculture. Distribution of the products is through farmers' markets, farm-to-school programs and other direct-sale arrangements. Civic organizations sometimes manage extensive production operations and distribute the food through food banks and meal programs. When they are located carefully, both community gardens and agriculture contribute to a municipal green infrastructure network.

Demand for local food

Opportunities for new farmers to sell locally grown foods is increasing rapidly. The number of shareholders in existing community supported agriculture (CSA) farms grew 50 percent between 2007 and 2009. In the CSA model the producer connects directly with consumers rather than through wholesalers and retailers. Customers subscribe or purchase shares in the farmer's crop. CSA farms in the US are projected to increase from 3,000 to over 18,000 by 2020.[2]

CSA is only one type of direct-sale option for community agriculture. In fact, farmers' markets are the primary direct-sale opportunity. Between 1998 and 2009 there was a 92 percent increase in the number of farmers' markets in the US (Figure 10.1)[1] and direct sales of agricultural products increased 49 percent between 2002 and 2007. Similarly, locally grown food sold to intermediaries, like grocery stores, is

Figure 10.1
Direct sale of organic produce provides farmers with viable businesses and customers with fresh, local food.

increasing,[1] and farm-to-school programs are also a growing segment of the local foods market. Sweet corn, cucumbers, asparagus, bell pepper, broccoli, carrots, salad greens and herbs are among the many high-value crops undersupplied by the conventional agricultural system for the local market. Another factor adding to the demand for local produce is the increased consumption of vegetables and melons, which rose 5.5 percent between 2002 and 2007.[3]

Geography and demographics

The greatest numbers of CSA farms occur in the northeastern region of the US, but there are concentrations in the upper midwest, Colorado, northern New Mexico and the northwest. Most CSA operations are where farmers can access relatively affluent, well-educated and urban dwellers. College towns tend to generate many CSA farms, but they are often absent from rural areas and areas with high poverty rates.[4]

The typical community farm is 18 acres, although an average of only three acres is dedicated to CSA operations. The majority of CSA farms have 100 or fewer shareholders.[2] Most CSA farmers don't generate produce exclusively for their shareholders, but also sell at farmers' markets and to restaurants.[4] The farmers generally adopt organic or sustainable growing standards. Farms involved in direct-to-consumer sales tend to be more successful if they engage in organic farming and agricultural tourism, adopt a CSA model or engage in other activities to add value to their products (Figure 10.1).[1] The farmer involved in community agriculture has a different set of interests and motivations than the commodity farmer. Direct contact with customers and engagement with the local economic, health and environmental issues inspires new methods and provides new meaning.

Economic benefits

State-level benefits

Billions of dollars are lost from states that concentrate on commodity agriculture that markets crops and livestock globally and nationally, but ignores production and sale in the local market.[5] Increasing community agriculture improves municipal, community and state economies due to multiplier effects from direct sales of locally produced goods.[6] Currently, limited local supply and high demand for local produce establishes an environment where new businesses can flourish, especially in metropolitan counties and rural counties located nearby.[1]

Governmental policies, programs and planning initiatives can foster community agriculture so that it makes sustained contributions economically, socially and environmentally. In order to succeed, community agriculture needs the support of proactive urban planning policies and physical planning to locate productive lands where they create positive relationships with other urban uses and the natural environment.

Community economic benefits

In the US almost all food consumed locally is imported,[7,5] even in rural states and towns. Therefore, local communities are foregoing economic development and tax revenue opportunities. Local farmers purchase materials, equipment and financial services, stimulating the local economy and providing an indirect benefit. Their locally produced food and payments for labor directly benefit the community. When employees and local suppliers purchase services and goods, money re-circulates through the local economy (accrued benefits).

These direct, indirect and accrued benefits create a multiplier effect, where one dollar spent generates more than one dollar of economic benefit.[1] Local agriculture multipliers are higher for local food (29 percent), labor income (17 percent) and local agricultural jobs (27 percent) than they are for commodity agriculture.[6] This demonstrates that the impact of new local foods businesses is surprisingly large. For example, if residents bought 15 percent (instead of the current 2 percent) of their food from producers within the two counties comprising metropolitan Boise, Idaho, then local farmers would earn $18,000,000 annually in new income.[8] Government agencies, including school districts and colleges, can dramatically increase the market for local products by requiring that a minimum portion of the food catered or served by them are from local sources. The Woodbury County Board of Supervisors in Iowa took this action and created an annual market worth nearly $300,000.[9]

Planning for community agriculture

Communities can begin to increase their local food production through proactive land-use planning. This effort can be initiated at any level by creating a land inventory that maps fertile soils, slopes, aspect, early frost microclimates, vacant parcels, urban development, vehicular and pedestrian access, schools, public land and community centers. The inventory maps are the bases for gaining the public's input (often via public planning charrettes). Overlaying the suitability factors identified in the inventory will yield desirable urban agriculture parcels.

Simultaneous planning of recreation facilities, trails, ecological corridors and even utility easements would incorporate the location of most suitable community agricultural lands into the comprehensive green infrastructure plan. In this way, agricultural parcels are linked to other community resources and can support them in positive ways. The most suitable agricultural parcels near the city or neighborhood should be designated as permanent uses on future and existing land-use and zoning maps. Dave Swenson at Iowa State University has developed a system to match metropolitan demand for local agricultural products to the land needed to satisfy those demands.[10]

Currently, an "agricultural" land-use designation is usually treated as transitional land intended for future urban development. This immediately increases the value of the land, its taxes and infrastructure expectations. Since proximity is important, agriculture within the city should be permitted by right, instead of as a conditional use (Figure 10.2). Furthermore, implementing a program to transfer development rights from agriculture parcels to development parcels will preserve local food capacity

Figure 10.2
Community agriculture is compatible with housing for owners, workers and others. This photo simulation features multi-family housing around a 3.6-acre organic farm. The arrangement provides open space for high-density urban dwellers. Photo simulation by author over a Google Earth base, 47°41′29.36″ N 122°20′29.36″ W.

by protecting the land from real-estate speculation and tax increases that would eventually eliminate all local farming from within or near the city. There are many other planning measures that can be adopted by communities that encourage local food businesses, including discounted water rates, permitting rooftop greenhouses, increasing the number of hens allowed within city limits, mixing community agriculture into all zones with regulations controlling the use of pesticides, noise, dust and storm-water.

Density or other development benefits should be awarded for the provision of urban farms operated by a homeowners association of a proposed subdivision. New buildings should receive development benefits, such as allowances for additional floors, for providing community gardens or beehives on green roofs. Urban renewal districts should include community gardens or for-profit farms as part of the publicly funded infrastructure, just as other utilities are subsidized in these districts. This list of planning devices is not exhaustive, but illustrates that community agriculture can be located and sustained within and adjacent to cities.

Farmers' markets

Direct sales at farmers' markets are critical for most local-food growers. These markets benefit the local economy since they create positive multipliers (indirect = 1.58; accrued = 1.47; jobs = 1.47).[11] Governments or non-governmental organizations should plan the infrastructure necessary for local farmers and customers to interact as part of the municipal green infrastructure. Pedestrian, bicycle and public transportation should be prioritized. Event space for musical performances, art shows, children's recreation space and equipment and parkland contribute to the experience of the farmers' market to expand it from a commercial activity into a community social celebration.

Waste management

Communities considering permitting community agriculture need to consider the treatment of stormwater runoff and solid wastes to avoid conflicts with neighbors and to maintain a clean environment. Effective treatment in vegetated swales or infiltration basins removes nitrogen and bacteria from water, allowing limited reuse. Similarly, composting of organic waste and reuse leads to efficiency and lower input costs. Since local agriculture is highly visible, permanent plantings to form screens and buffers need to be required by ordinance to contribute to the open space system, wildlife biodiversity and aesthetics of the city.

Spatial distribution

The number of local farms are rapidly increasing. Fifty percent of these are in metropolitan counties, while 30 percent are in rural counties. A surprisingly small acreage is required to establish viable community agricultural businesses.[13] For example, Ms. Elizabeth Taylor is the sole proprietor of her one-acre organic farm where she produces 45 varieties of organic vegetables and salad greens for direct sale to restaurants and at a farmers' market (Figure 10.3).[12]

Figure 10.3
This verdant crop of basil is one of 45 products nurtured on this one-acre organic farm. It has been a viable business operation for 20 years.

The location of community agriculture need not compete with urban development for space. Most towns own land that remains undeveloped for many years, and other government agencies have lands that can be managed for multiple uses. These properties can be leased to farmers or provided as a farming incubator to establish businesses and test crops or horticultural methods. Figure 10.4 illustrates that flood plains can be used, especially for organic agriculture. If excess nutrients and sediment are prevented from entering the river and wildlife can pass along the river edge, then organic agriculture can be a positive land use.

There are many examples of residential or mixed-use developments where the residents or their homeowners association manages community agricultural land for the production of food for the residents. A 60-acre development, Village Homes, in Davis, California is an example of a 242-home neighborhood that includes orchards, vineyards and community gardens (Figure 10.5). Residents produce about 25 percent of their fruits and vegetables. The 300-tree almond orchard produces nuts for the residents and for sale to commercial processors. Although the residents of Village Homes manage their own production, some homeowners associations hire a pro-fessional farmer to manage the agricultural production.

Along the community growth limit line (area of impact line) community agriculture provides a buffer between urban development and commodity agriculture in the county. This planning scheme can help defend the town from suburban and exurban sprawl that consumes prime agricultural land and sensitive habitat. It also buffers

Figure 10.4
Local organic farming with runoff treatment within the flood plain can be supported on public land. Since buildings are not permitted in the flood zone (mobile home and recreational vehicles are shown in this image) this use does not compete with urban development and connects to the ecological corridor flanking the river. Photo simulation by author, 2011, on a photo base 44°31'18.48" N 116°02'19.48" W.

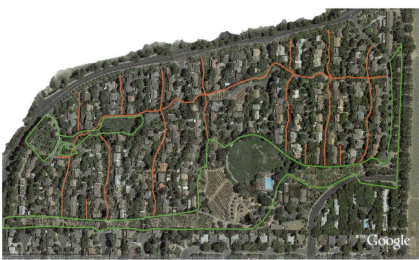

Figure 10.5
Village Homes features a continuous green infrastructure. The areas outlined in green are the open-space system and the red lines locate the pedestrian paths and surface stormwater collection areas. The residential cul-de-sacs are located between the pedestrian paths. The orchard and extensive community gardens are prominent features. Graphic by author over a Google Earth base. Photo 38°32'58.93" N 121°46'50.89" W, 1 September 2012 (accessed 25 April 2013) by Google Earth.

the town from the dust and noise generated by large-scale equipment used in commodity agriculture.

Residential development typically doesn't offer direct access to large, open spaces. Figure 10.6 illustrates a number of ecosystem services that benefit the neighborhood and especially residents living in multi-family housing. Planning for community agriculture should focus on the town–county interface where 1–10-acre parcels are available. However, farms surrounded by mixed-density housing occupied by the farmers and their employees (Figure 10.2) integrate uses positively, particularly when restored brownfield sites, such as sawmills or landfills, can be repurposed.

Figure 10.6
Community agriculture provides scenic open space. This image suggests orchard or nut trees flanking a community garden (foreground) and market agriculture. High-density development benefits from positive views, space for privacy and immediate access to recreation and community gardening. The community agriculture and citizen gardens can extend as fingers from the community perimeter into the city.

Figure 10.7
Community gardens support habitat and ecological corridors when they are sited to provide a buffer between urban or suburban development and more natural areas.

Figure 10.8
This amazing community garden is in the High Point neighborhood of Seattle. It is adjacent
to a vegetated infiltration swale, along the route to the neighborhood park and embedded
in the neighborhood. Although not visible in this image, there is a small greenhouse and a
storage building with a deck covered with a green roof. These facilities support the
gardeners and encourage social gatherings and sharing of gardening information.

Figure 10.9
The design of structures and the use of unifying vegetation such as hedges and vines can
transform unattractive community gardens into community assets. This community garden is
on the campus of the University of British Columbia.

Urban agriculture can be partnered with adjacent stormwater management facilities where water can be captured for reuse. Similarly, associations with willow or poplar tree plantations and other urban forestry are beneficial in windy or semiarid climates or to produce woody biomass for fuel or other products. Agriculture can also serve as a buffer for wildlife corridors or habitat, sports fields and trails.

Community gardens

While community agriculture is optimally located as a transition between urban development and an ecological corridor or habitat at the edge of the city or neighborhood growth limit boundary, or as fingers extending into the city (Figure 10.6), community gardens need to be distributed evenly within neighborhoods (Figure 10.8). The green infrastructure should connect these gardens with pedestrian and bicycle paths. Key locations are adjacent to schools, community and senior centers, adjacent to community agriculture and ecological corridors. In the winter, community gardens can be visually unappealing. This can be easily mitigated with permanent evergreen hedges and borders, low fencing or architectural elements (Figure 10.9). Seasonal coverage of the garden plots with straw, mulch or a cover crop also improves winter aesthetics. Well-designed community gardens are visual resources in winter and joyful riots of color and texture during the growing season.

Conclusion

Elected officials and economic development officers in rural towns can foster new agriculture businesses through planning changes. Planning should incorporate community agriculture and community gardens into the green infrastructure network. Citizens can do their part by being advocates for local food production and supporting new businesses with their patronage. Local production and sale of food increases food security and social capacity, improves nutrition, reduces energy use and even provides educational opportunities. For these, and the clear economic benefits, community agriculture should be a vigorously promoted diversification strategy near metropolitan cities.

References

1   S. Martinez, M. Hand, M. Da Pra, S. Pollack, K. Ralston, T. Smith, S. Vogel, S. Clark, L. Lohr, S. Low and C. Newman, *Local Food Systems: Concepts, Impacts, and Issues*, Washington, DC: US Department of Agriculture, 2010.
2   "Local Harvest," 2012. [Online]. Available: www.localharvest.org (accessed 15 April 2013).
3   USDA (US Department of Agriculture), "Census of Agriculture," 2007. [Online]. Available: www.agcensus.usda.gov/Publications/2007/Full_Report/Volume_1,_Chapter_1_State_Level/Idaho/index.asp (accessed 21 February 2012).
4   S. M. Schnell, "Food with a Farmer's Face: Community-Supported Agriculture in the United States," *Geography Review*, vol. 97, no. 4, pp. 550–564, 2010.
5   K. Meter, *Ohio's Food Systems*, Minneapolis, MN: Crossroads Resource Center, 2011.
6   K. Enshayan, *Community Economic Impact Assessment for a Multi-County Local Food System in Northeast Iowa*, Ames, IA: Leopold Center for Sustainable Agriculture, 2008.

7   K. Meter, *Greater Treasure Valley Region Local Farm & Food Economy*, Minneapolis, MN: Crossroads Resource Center, 2010.

8   TVAC, "TVAC (Treasure Valley Food Coalition)," 2010. [Online]. Available: http://treasurevalleyfoodcoalition.org (accessed 3 February 2011).

9   APA (American Planning Association), "Policy Guide on Community and Regional Food Planning," 2007. [Online]. Available: www.planning.org/policy/guides/adopted/food.htm (accessed 22 February 2012).

10 D. Swenson, *Measuring the Economic Impacts of Increased Fresh Fruit and Vegetable Production in Iowa Considering Metropolitan Demand*, Ames, IA: Leopold Center for Sustainable Agriculture, 2011.

11 D. Otto, "Consumers, Vendors, and the Economic Importance of Iowa Farmers' Markets: An Economic Impact Survey Analysis," Iowa State University, 2005.

12 E. Taylor, "Community Agriculture," personal interview, 1 September 2011.

13 T. Woods, M. Ernst, S. Ernst and N. Wright, "2009 Survey of Community Supported Agriculture Producers," University of Kentucky Department of Forestry, 2009.

CHAPTER ELEVEN

Wastewater treatment wetlands

Introduction

One of the great benefits of a green infrastructure system is its multifunctional performance. A new function that can be added is the below-ground treatment of wastewater. Replacing conventional wastewater treatment with biological treatment in the public landscape secures a host of secondary benefits. This book proposes a decentralized sequence of treatment wetlands followed by free water surface marshes (Figure 11.1) within public open space to add new value and enhance green infrastructure.

Research, construction and monitoring of thousands of these systems confirm that biological treatment of wastewater is safe, reliable and economically advantageous. Treatment wetlands can effectively meet secondary treatment standards for total suspended solids (TSS) and biological oxygen demand (BOD). Sequences of treatment wetlands achieve tertiary quality for ammonia, nitrates and pathogenic bacteria. Among the many valuable secondary benefits are diverse habitats leading to species abundance and variety through the cascade of vegetation, macroinvertebrate, fish, bird and mammal diversity. In addition, treatment wetlands provide pure water, regulation of climate, nutrient and water cycling, and cultural amenities, such as recreation, education and aesthetics. This chapter explains the biological and chemical processes involved in treatment wetlands. The performance of three wetland types is presented to demonstrate their effectiveness and reliability. Finally, there is an exploration of the secondary benefits that support other green infrastructure goals.

Conventional wastewater treatment plants

There are a host of disadvantages to conventional wastewater treatment plants as elements of the public green infrastructure. There are obvious odor, exposure and equipment hazards, but the usual location (as far downstream as possible) and centralized operation limit potential secondary benefits. In fact, secondary benefits are rarely considered in their design. The single purpose of the industrial scale and processes is treatment of large volumes of water on small land parcels. This is possible due to the application of chemicals and energy for pumping, agitating and aerating. The cost of these operations can be substantial. For example, it costs the 1,000 residents of an Idaho town $70,000 per year for only the electricity to operate their new wastewater treatment plant.[2]

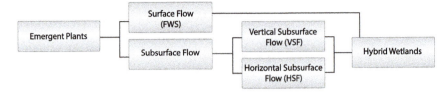

Figure 11.1
Constructed wetlands are differentiated by vegetation type and flow regime. This book considers only emergent plant wetlands for wastewater treatment. There are two types of subsurface flow wetlands and one type with surface flow that can be combined to create hybrid systems. Adapted from Vymazal 2007.[1]

Treatment wetlands and green infrastructure

In contrast to conventional plants, treatment wetlands are scaled to the neighborhood and can be distributed throughout the watershed. Wetlands constructed at higher elevations provide space and habitat that serve the neighborhood while treated water can be reused at lower elevations without the cost of pumping. The distributed character allows the wetlands to be limited in size and to contribute to a landscape network. The space and the byproducts (high-carbon sludge, excess nitrogen, phosphorus and water) can be used to augment a sustainable landscape. Since wildlife habitat is created by wetlands and related land-farming techniques (Figure 11.2), they contribute to species and habitat diversity, as discussed in detail later. Constructed treatment wetlands help restore the historic wetland loss due to extensive drainage and land-use change.

Treatment sequence

As part of green infrastructure a sequence of three wetland types is necessary. The treatment sequence begins with sewage pretreated in a below-ground two-chamber septic tank with an effluent filter. The tank removes solids and significantly improves initial water quality.[3]

After pretreatment, the wastewater flows through at least two subsurface beds of sand or gravel planted with wetland vegetation. Since the water is held underground people are protected from odors and health hazards. The subsurface treatment allows the system to be placed unfenced within the public landscape.

The horizontal subsurface flow (HSF) wetland and the vertical subsurface flow (VSF) wetland are the two options for the below-ground treatment stages. Hybrid systems composed of both HSF and VSF wetlands are explicitly designed to treat domestic sewage (Figure 11.3) to achieve very high water quality. After the subsurface stages have improved the water quality, open-water marshes (FWS wetlands) are recommended additions to the treatment sequence (Figure 11.4). In this model for green infrastructure, the primary purpose of the FWS stage shifts to habitat creation, recreation and aesthetic benefit, although further water quality improvements occur. The technology and research support for the treatment stages and sequence is presented below before returning to the topic of hybrid wetlands.

Figure 11.2
Effluent from a conventional treatment plant in Roseburg, Oregon is treated by this constructed wetland and then applied to slopes that drain to a restored wetland. The primary treatment purpose is to remove excess phosphorus, but the 340-acre parcel provides outstanding and diverse wildlife habitat. This project cost $10 million but saved $90 million compared to upgrading the conventional wastewater treatment plant.

Wastewater characteristics

Domestic sewage contains high levels of carbon, ammonia, nitrogen, phosphorus, suspended solids and bacteria. Americans generate 40–60 gallons of sewage per person per day.[4] The effluent from the septic tank contains concentrations of 180 mg/L (milligrams per liter) of biological oxygen demand (BOD) and 80 mg/L of TSS. The US Environmental Protection Agency (EPA) secondary treatment standard for BOD and TSS is 30 mg/L, while the standard for fecal coliform bacteria in streams and lakes is 100 cfu/100 mL (colony forming units per 100 milliliters) for primary recreational contact. The standard for *E. coli* is 126 cfu/100 mL for primary recreational contact (swimming) and 1030 cfu/100 mL for secondary contact.[5]

BOD measures the amount of oxygen required by microorganisms to consume organic material in water. TSS is a measure of the organic and inorganic particles suspended in water. Both parameters are indirect measures of water pollution.

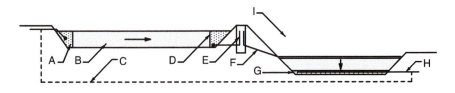

Figure 11.3
HSF wetland (left), VSF wetland (right). A, inlet from septic tank; B, horizontal flow through gravel; C, recirculate 50 percent of flow from VSF to HSF wetland for denitrification; D, collection zone; E, water-level control; F, periodic dosing of VSF; G, water drains vertically through gravel to bottom drain; H, outflow to FWS wetland; I, dense planting. See Figure 11.4 for a plan view.

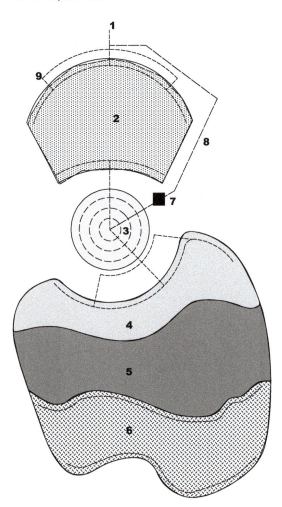

Figure 11.4
This plan view is a schematic of the three wetland types combined for high water-quality improvement and habitat value in a green infrastructure. 1, inflow from septic tank; 2, HSF wetland; 3, VSF wetland; 4, FWS wetland cell 1 (shallow marsh); 5, FWS wetland cell 2 (open water); 6, FWS wetland cell 3 (shallow marsh); 7, recirculating pump; 8, distribution piping; 9, uniform inflow distribution.

Horizontal subsurface flow wetlands

The German scientist, Dr. Kathe Seidel, working in the 1950s, was the first researcher to conduct experiments of wastewater treatment wetlands including vegetation. The subsurface wetland models that she developed were widely implemented in Europe. Beginning in the 1990s, the need for advanced treatment of wastewater inspired hybrid systems that combined horizontal subsurface flow (HSF) and vertical subsurface flow (VSF) wetlands (Figure 11.3) based on the models developed by Dr. Seidel.[6]

Subsurface flow wetlands are common in Europe, where tens of thousands exist (Figure 11.5).[7] All treatment wetlands are sized by determining the rate at which biological and chemical processes transform organic and inorganic substances. This process is influenced by temperature and the amount of material and water delivered to the wetland.[8] However, in many countries the construction and monitoring of HSF wetlands treating wastewater with a range of flow, BOD and TSS inputs has yielded simple sizing guidelines that planners and landscape architects can use for initial planning and design. About 50 ft^2 (4.5 m^2) of HSF wetland area per person served is required to meet EPA secondary effluent standards in summer and winter.[9] Winter performance, meeting EPA standards, is demonstrated by a Minnesota HSF wetland that is insulated with six inches (15 cm) of mulch to protect it from freezing at temperatures as low as −45°F.[10] In Norway, HSF systems preceded by a buried biological filter have proven to be very effective.[11]

In a HSF wetland (Figure 11.5, 11.3 left) there is no surface water, but the bed is densely planted, making it a landscape feature. Several factors are critical to the effectiveness of HSF wetlands, including gravel size, uniform water distribution and density of plants. Pre-treated wastewater must be evenly distributed through the

Figure 11.5
This attractive HSF treatment wetland serves a small town in the Czech Republic.

gravel bed. This is initiated by filling a coarse gravel inlet trench from a perforated pipe. Most HSF wetlands consist of a six-feet wide inlet and outlet zone (A and D in Figure 11.3) composed of 1.5–3-inch diameter (40–80 mm) gravel. The treatment bed is 24–30 inches (0.6–0.8 m) deep (B in Figure 11.3) and composed of gravel 0.8–1.2 inches (20–30 mm) in size. The gravel provides a surface for biofilm growth and the large pore spaces limit clogging, which was a problem in the first-generation designs. The water flows continuously through the gravel due to a hydraulic gradient, so there is no longitudinal slope required on the bottom or the top of the bed.[4,12]

Beneficial bacteria growing on the gravel and roots transform organic matter and many contaminants in the water. The plant roots must reach to the bottom of the bed in order to maintain porosity of the bed and maximize nitrogen removal.[9] HSF wetlands effectively convert organic material to ammonia, and nitrates to nitrogen gas, but they do not sufficiently convert ammonia to nitrate or remove much phosphorus unless a special media is used.[13]

The HSF example provided here demonstrates the long-term performance of the technology in achieving secondary effluent (BOD and TSS <30 mg/L) as well as removal of nitrate. The town of Ondrejov, Czech Republic built a HSF wetland to serve 362 people. Monitored for 13 years, this wetland achieved an average BOD of 18.3 mg/L and TSS of 8.3 mg/L. Removal of ammonium was only 14.8 percent, but nitrate removal was better at 41 percent.[7] However, ammonia and nitrate are not regulated for secondary treatment except when receiving waters are sensitive or degraded. The performance of a second HSF wetland serving 1,400 people was slightly better.[7] These examples show that treatment wetlands can be in neighborhood parkland and sized to serve subdivisions of hundreds of homes or groups of just a few.

These wetlands featured a single HSF cell (Figure 11.5), while in Little Stretton, UK, a treatment system built to serve 40 people featured eight subsurface beds stepping down a slope. Although BOD and TSS concentrations were low in the outflow, there was a much better reduction of ammonia (85.1 percent) since there was better oxygen transfer between the beds due to water aeration as it moved between beds, down the slope. Conversely, only 16.4 percent of the nitrate and nitrite concentration was removed since that requires the anaerobic environment normally provided in a HSF wetland.[12]

Vertical subsurface flow wetlands

Vertical subsurface flow with bottom drain

As with the HSF wetland, pretreated water in VSF wetlands can be held below the surface. VSF wetlands are flooded periodically just below a surface layer of gravel (Figure 11.3, right, Figures 11.6 and 11.7). The water then flows down through a sand bed and exits the wetland through bottom drains. Air replaces water in the pore spaces between the sand particles after the water flows through. This system creates an oxygen-rich environment where BOD, TSS and ammonia are effectively reduced. VSF wetlands require only 21.5 ft^2 (2 m^2) per person, but sometimes require energy from small pumps, and more regular attention from an operator than the HSF system.[14]

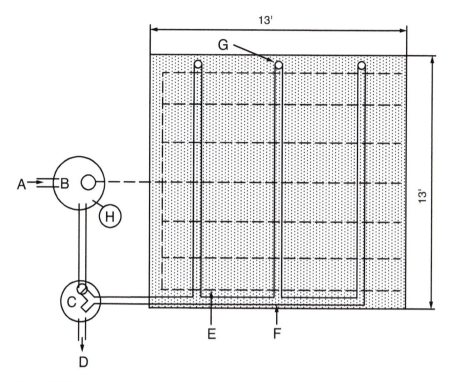

Figure 11.6
Vertical subsurface flow wetland, plan. A, inflow; B, septic tank; C, recycling tank with V-notch weirs; D, effluent; E, 1.5-inch perforated PVC distribution piping, capped, three-feet spacing; F, four-inch perforated PVC drainage piping, three-feet spacing; G, aeration pipes connected to bottom drain; H, aluminum polychloride dosing chamber with air-lift pump in septic tank, for phosphorus removal. Adapted from Brix and Arias, 2005.[3]

Vertical subsurface flow with impoundment

An Austrian demonstration wetland featured two VSF stages operated in series. The performance of this system illustrates that, like HSF wetlands, VSF wetlands achieve secondary effluent. The VSF wetland also provides advanced removal of ammonia. Each VSF cell was 108 ft² (10 m²) and was planted with common reed, *Phragmites*. The first cell included a 20-inch (50 cm) deep bed of sand ranging in size from 0.08 inches to 0.12 inches (2–3.2 mm) and a flooded sub-basin of water below the filtration bed. The second stage included a 0.002–0.16-inch (0.06–4 mm) sand layer above a coarse aggregate drainage layer. Wastewater from a septic tank flooded the top of the wetland to a depth of 0.64 inches (16.2 mm) every three hours. The wetland was monitored for 19 months. BOD in the effluent was very low at 4 mg/L in summer and 12 mg/L in winter.[15]

The average ammonia concentration in the effluent from the second wetland cell was 0.29 mg/L in summer (a 99.5 percent reduction) and 17.5 mg/L in winter (a 64 percent reduction). This wetland removed 46 percent more of the ammonia than a single-cell VSF wetland with no flooded sub-basin.[15] The EPA does not generally

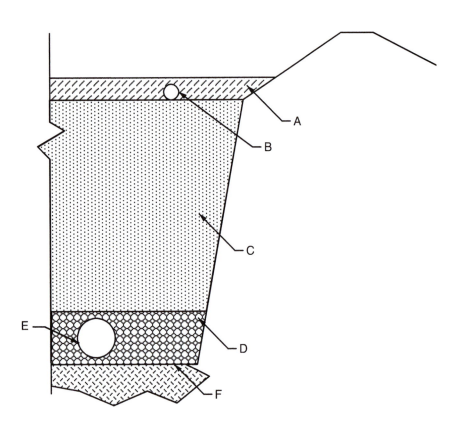

Figure 11.7
VSF wetland, section. A, wood chips; B, 1.5-inch PVC distribution pipes, space three-feet max.; C, 42-inch (1.2 m) depth of uncompacted filter sand, 0.125–4 mm with clay and silt <0.5 percent; D, six-inch (0.2 m) depth of 0.5-inch drain rock; E, four-inch perforated PVC, space three-feet max., at one end connected to aeration pipes that extend above the surface; F, 0.5 mm waterproof membrane between two geotextile layers. Adapted from Brix and Arias 2005.[3]

regulate ammonia, but aquatic organisms are sensitive to constant levels in excess of 1.8 mg/L at pH8 and 25°C.[16]

The concentration of nitrates entering the two-stage wetland averaged 0.37 mg/L in summer and 0.30 mg/L in winter. Nitrates in the effluent were 30.9 mg/L in summer and 21.1 mg/L in winter. This large increase indicates complete conversion of ammonia,[15] but low removal of nitrate.

Elimination of total nitrogen was 53.2 percent in summer and 37.1 percent in winter. This high performance is attributed to the nitrification of about 80 percent of the ammonia in the first-stage wetland with the flooded sub-basin, but with enough carbon remaining to allow conversion of some of the nitrate to nitrogen gas in the flooded sub-basin, although not all nitrate was removed.[15] This improved system performance is attributed to alternating high and low oxygen zones supporting increased nitrification (ammonia conversion) and denitrification, respectively.

Figure 11.8
This vertical flow constructed wetland treats wastewater for 6,000 residents to high water quality standards.

Removal of pathogens

The two-stage VSF wetland removed about 99 percent of the pathogenic bacteria. However, the remaining number of *E. coli*, for example, was 1,585 cfu/100 mL,[15] which is still higher than the 126 cfu/100 mL standard for primary contact (swimming). Additional treatment in another wetland stage or ultraviolet light disinfection would be required before this effluent could be used for swimming.

Facilitating the use of treatment wetlands

Expensive engineering and permitting costs discourage widespread adoption of any new wastewater treatment technology. Once systems have been monitored under a range of conditions, then standard sizing, materials and construction details can be included in development standards. This has been done in Austria, France and Denmark for subsurface flow treatment wetlands serving individual or groups of homes.[3] Standard sizing and construction details would need to be developed in the US for subdivision-scale applications.

Hybrid treatment wetlands

The examples of HSF and VSF wetlands presented above show that either easily meet EPA standards for secondary effluent. When they are used together they take advantage of efficient reduction of ammonia (VSF) and high reduction of nitrate (HSF) to achieve exceptional water quality. Treatment wetlands that combine at least two of the wetland types (HSF, VSF, FWS) are called hybrid wetlands. Figure 11.3 illustrates HSF and VSF used in sequence to achieve secondary effluent, and reduced ammonia, nitrate and pathogenic bacteria.

Table 11.1 Water quality performance of a VSF > HSF > FWS sequence of wetland. All units are mg/L[17]

Contaminant	Influent	Imhoff (pretreatment)	VSF	HSF	FWS
Total Suspended Solids	287	98	8	8	6
Biological Oxygen Demand	393	204	10	5	7
Total Nitrogen	54.6	52.7	17.6	8.2	7.9
Ammonia	42.1	43.1	10.4	5.5	2.3
Nitrate and Nitrite	0.9	0.08	3.1	0.7	0.9
Total Phosphorus	8.1	6.8	5.7	4.7	5.3
Phosphate	5.4	4.8	4.8	3.7	4.7

A recent study in Spain monitored the performance of a treatment wetland with a VSF > HSF > FWS sequence of wetlands for 18 months. The sewage was pretreated in an Imhoff tank, which is a type of septic tank. After the VSF stage, BOD and TSS had been reduced by 94 and 90 percent, respectively, and were well below the EPA standard for secondary effluent (Table 11.1). Therefore, the HSF and FWS stages provided advanced (tertiary) treatment. The VSF wetland removed 74 percent of the ammonia and 66 percent of the total nitrogen. More modest but continued reductions of ammonia were achieved by the HSF and FWS stages. Nitrate removal was also excellent, resulting in less than 1 mg/L.[17]

The VSF and HSF wetlands made dramatic reductions in the number of *E. coli*, but the FWS wetland contributed *E. coli*, probably from bird use of the wetland.[17] Therefore, the wetland sequence did not produce water clean enough for swimming, but it did meet the standards for boating, fishing and irrigation (secondary contact, 1030 cfu/100 mL). Removal of phosphorus was low at 22 percent. Using calcium-rich gravel and sand in the subsurface wetlands would improve phosphorus removal significantly.[13]

The Oaklands Park wetland in the UK is much older than the system described above, but featured the same sequence of stages (VSF > HSF > FWS). Its perform-ance was similar, but *E. coli* was removed to below the standard for swimming and 58 percent of the phosphorus was removed.[18,19]

New research is testing the capacity of subsurface wetlands to remove a range of pain, anti-inflammatory and estrogen drugs. VSF and HSF wetlands remove 97–99 percent of these substances.[20, 21]

Neither of the hybrid wetlands described above requires artificial energy, but the system illustrated in Figures 11.3 and 11.4 includes a small pump to return water to the HSF wetland to improve denitrification. In this design the HSF wetland is placed before the VSF wetland and would result in incomplete denitrification without the recirculation step.[22]

A recent demonstration project confirms the benefit of hybrid wetlands. A three-stage wetland was constructed with a fully saturated VSF cell followed by a free-draining VSF cell. The third cell was a HSF bed. Fifty percent of the effluent from stage two was pumped to stage one for denitrification. The average removal rates were: BOD 94.5 percent (10 mg/L); TSS 88.5 percent (9.2 mg/L); ammonia 78.3

percent (6.5 mg/L); phosphorus 65.4 percent (1.8 mg/L). The concentration of nitrates in the outflow was only 1.1 mg/L.[23]

Resilience

Studies show that biological treatment systems are stable and resilient, especially when a recirculation feature is included as in the system described above and in Figure 11.3. Shocks to an experimental wetland were induced by inputs of high and low pH, high amounts of organic material, high detergent content, high bleach content and high *E. coli* bacteria contamination. The impact of pump failure (no recirculation for two days) was also tested. The system recovered from these impacts within 24 hours to perform at levels similar to a control wetland. The main impact of no circulation was an increase of *E. coli*. After pumping resumed most parameters were similar to the control wetland within 24 hours. The resilience is thought to be due primarily to the buffering capacity of the bed materials and the recirculation feature of this wetland, which reduced clogging and mixed septic tank effluent with partially treated water.[24]

Increasing ecosystem service benefits

With the exception of Oaklands Park, the treatment wetland studies cited above illustrate systems that included only treatment functions, but many aesthetic, cultural and biodiversity elements can be added to the subsurface stages and especially to the FWS marshes. Attracting both aquatic and terrestrial wildlife to the FWS wetland enhances the ecosystem opportunities. The design of open water, shallow and deep marshes (Figure 11.4) and even seasonally exposed mud can be undertaken for continued water treatment, habitat, educational and biodiversity benefits.

Diversity of plants in subsurface wetlands

Most of the wetlands reviewed above featured a single wetland plant species, but a diverse planting plan, dominated by native species, would improve the habitat quality. Staging seeding and container planting is likely to lead to higher and sustained plant diversity. Manipulating water depths and flooding the surface during the wetland establishment period and before wastewater treatment begins would yield the best results. Weeding to remove invasive plants would help establish secondary species.[25] There are great opportunities for landscape architects to improve bio-diversity, aesthetics and reuse of resources by developing grading and planting concepts for the zone around treatment wetlands.

Although environmental engineers generally ignore plant biodiversity in the treatment system design, a few studies have tested the benefits of plant communities. In southeast China, a VSF wetland was divided into plots that were planted with monocultures and various associations of species. The plots with the highest diversity produced more biomass. Similarly, high-diversity plots caused significantly more nitrate and ammonia to be held in the gravel substrate.[26]

Macroinvertebrate diversity

The planting design and installation techniques described above would result in higher biodiversity of plants, but the value of subsurface treatment wetlands on the diversity of other species has only recently been researched. A recent British study of six HSF wetlands used macroinvertebrates as a general biodiversity indicator. The investigation found even more species of terrestrial macroinvertebrates than in a natural reed ecosystem.[27]

Similarly, in FWS wetlands, when macroinvertebrates are used as an indicator of overall biodiversity, plant variety is key. For example, more species of dragonflies, damselflies and other *Odonate* species are present when there is vegetation diversity compared to monocultures of reed canary grass (*Phalaris arundinacea*) or cattail. One study showed that when vegetation diversity is high, four times more uncommon and threatened *Odonate* species are present.[28] This finding is supported by a survey of 20 FWS constructed wetlands for treatment of stormwater in North Carolina.[25]

Free water surface treatment benefits

Shallow marshes effectively improve water quality through many of the same mechanisms apparent in subsurface flow wetlands (Figure 11.9). A different one is that ultraviolet light penetrating clear, shallow water kills pathogenic bacteria. A diversity of plants in an FWS wetland also improves the treatment outcome. A study comparing performance of monocultures of bulrush (*Scirpus* spp.) and cattail with plantings that mixed these species and others, including grasses and smartweed (*Polygonum*), found that the mixed vegetation removed more than three times the nitrate compared to the single-species stands. This is thought to be due to a greater and more well-distributed supply of carbon (detritus) to denitrifying bacteria in the

Figure 11.9
This free water surface wetland in Columbia, Missouri treats municipal wastewater that meets secondary standards for advanced water quality.

wetland sediment.[29] Normally, plants in treatment wetlands are not harvested because they take up less than 10 percent of the nitrates and other nutrients in the wastewater, but this reduction could be significant to amphibians sensitive to even low levels of ammonia and nitrate.[14]

Free water surface wetland habitat values

To optimize the biodiversity benefits of FWS wetlands, the landscape architect should create habitat targeted at each terrestrial and aquatic taxonomic group.[30] Generally, greater habitat diversity leads to greater species diversity, especially if food sources in each season, vegetation structure (horizontal and vertical), shelter and distance from human activity are planned effectively. For example, a ten-year study showed that blackbirds, coots, dabbling ducks and diving ducks did not prefer the dense stands of emergent vegetation and a water depth of one foot to three feet (0.3–1 m) (see Figure 11.14). This situation is the common model for FWS wetlands. Vegetation cover equal to open water in a mosaic creates higher biodiversity and continues the denitrification activity of the subsurface wetlands. For many wetland bird species, habitat preferences vary by season. Drawing down the water level in constructed marshes seasonally or even daily to expose mud adds to the value of the habitat.[31]

Diversity of birds

The example of an FWS wetland provided here illustrates the habitat values that can be added to green infrastructure, especially when previous habitat has been destroyed. In 1991 a 450-acre tract with four FWS wetlands and four ponds was constructed

Figure 11.10
This constructed, free-water surface wetland has a diversity of plants including bulrush, sedge, reed canarygrass, cattail, willow, marsh marigold and duck weed.

in Illinois for intensive study of biodiversity benefits. The watershed is 80 percent agricultural and 20 percent suburban.[32]

Biodiversity improvements were documented, using birds as the indicator. Before construction, no endangered species were found on the site. Compared to a census before construction, the number of nesting bird species increased by 30 percent, while wetland species increased 100 percent within two years. The number of waterfowl individuals using the site during migration increased 4,000 percent and the species diversity increased 400 percent. The 167 species using the site two years after construction had increased to 195 species by 2002. Of these, 13 species were endangered and eight were threatened within the state. There are five new nesting species that are on the state endangered list, including the sandhill crane (*Grus canadensis*) (Figure 11.11). The constructed wetlands have become important sites for migrating as well as resident birds.[33]

These wetlands are in a suburban and agricultural context, but urban wetlands are also refuges of biodiversity. The sizes of natural wetlands decrease as urbanization increases, according to a study in New England. The remaining urban wetlands, and newly created ones, contain a much greater abundance and richness of bird species normally associated with wetlands, and other bird species typically found in other habitat types. Terrestrial birds use wetland habitat when their preferred habitat is limited or of low quality. They are attracted by the presence of water, a range of food sources and the presence of shrub vegetation.[34] This suggests that landscape architects can support biodiversity of terrestrial species by creating a mosaic of habitats at the margin of the treatment wetland.

Small urban wetlands, like other habitat fragments in the city, are dominated by species tolerant of humans. To increase urban biodiversity to include many native species, habitat patches five acres and larger that are connected by ecological corridors

Figure 11.11
Sandhill cranes in flight above a free-water surface wetland.

are necessary.[35] This habitat would be easier and less expensive to assemble if it served multiple functions, served more than one community interest group or was subsidized because of its ecosystem service benefits. Subsurface treatment wetlands, marsh habitat, stormwater treatment and urban forestry comprise one of many possible sets of primary use areas that would provide far greater benefits at lower costs when organized into a green infrastructure than they would as isolated single uses.

Ecosystem disservice

In addition to the significant ecosystem services, treatment wetlands sometimes produce ecosystem disservices. Mosquitoes are a concern in areas with surface water. However, highly functioning wetland ecosystems significantly limit the population of mosquitoes. High plant diversity leads to greater numbers and diversity of predatory insects which reduce the number of mosquito larva in marsh wetlands compared to open-water ponds without vegetation.[25]

Unfortunately, constructed wetlands contribute to anthropogenic greenhouse gas emissions through the production of methane. Sweden is creating 30,000 acres (12,140 ha) of constructed wetlands, which will increase methane emission 0.04 percent, but remove nitrates from farm stormwater runoff. This small increase is justifiable compared to the substantial ecosystem benefit of nitrate reduction. Furthermore, planting dense emergent and floating leaf vegetation in wetlands limits the amount of methane produced.[36] Methane emissions by wetlands are also mitigated by their carbon sequestration, which is a positive contribution to climate regulation. The annual accumulation of carbon is higher in wetlands than for managed turf grass and regenerating forest.[25]

Another potential disservice of treatment wetlands is compromised health of aquatic systems or organisms due to insufficient removal of ammonia and pharmaceuticals. These substances in secondary effluent from conventional treatment plants have been shown to create abnormalities in amphibians.[37]

Design and management of FWS wetlands to reduce ecosystem disservices allows people and wildlife to benefit from a number of positive contributions to the cultural and natural landscape. The Eagle Bluffs Conservation Area in Missouri is one of many examples of wildlife refuges where water is provided by an FWS wetland (Figure 11.9) that is fed by a conventional treatment plant.[38]

Cultural ecosystem services

Treatment wetlands serve people by providing an engineering function, economic benefits and cultural benefits, such as scenic beauty, recreation and education. Physical activities (Figure 11.12), nature study, social gathering and even simple retreat from the urban environment into scenic landscapes are important urban activities that wetlands in a green infrastructure can foster. Wetlands that include open water are attractive and interesting. A comparison of constructed wetlands and ponds found that trails and wildlife viewing areas and education programs were much more often associated with wetlands.[25]

Figure 11.12
The Columbia, Missouri
constructed wetlands
provide opportunities to
secure secondary
benefits of recreation
and restoration of
biodiversity.

Once the technical requirements are discharged, then treatment wetlands can be fashioned to better serve people. HSF beds do require fairly rectangular shapes to achieve uniform water flow, but the margins beyond the beds can be designed with various elevation, hydrologic and soil parameters to generate habitat and aesthetic results. VSF beds can be virtually any shape without compromising their performance. The shape requirements of FWS wetlands fall between the extremes of HSF and VSF beds. Manipulating the physical and visual aspects of treatment wetland stages can produce creative landscapes (see Figure 11.13).

Capital and operating costs

When treatment wetlands are compared to conventional plants, it is apparent that costs and benefits are distributed differently. Treatment wetlands require more land area to treat the same volume of water. Therefore, expenditures for land and the availability of land are impediments in existing urban areas and where planning in advance of development has been inadequate. In contrast, the cost of construction is comparable, or lower, and operating costs for treatment wetlands are much lower, since sunlight, gravity and biological processes power them.[39] In treatment wetlands, pumping or artificial aeration are rarely necessary and much less demanding when they are required, but the cost of water quality testing might be higher in a distributed treatment model.

Although treatment wetlands become less competitive with conventional systems as their size increases, they have been constructed to serve as many as 6,000 residents

(Figure 11.8).[40] Often ignored in cost–benefit comparisons are the values of secondary benefits. When treatment wetlands simultaneously provide habitat that would need to be purchased or restored elsewhere, then there is a significant economic benefit. Similarly, recreation, alternative transportation, space for underground utilities, water reuse and space separating high-density buildings have economic value. This more holistic assessment would demonstrate the true value of treatment wetlands.[41]

Figure 11.13
Koh Phi Phi Multifunctional Community Garden. In this image the collection and distribution building is at the far left. The wedge-shaped VSF are at the left, while the long arcs of the HSF are in the center. The FWS areas are in the foreground and the polishing pool is the long canal (center).

Koh Phi Phi Island case study

The wetland on Koh Phi Phi Island, Thailand is a wonderful example of multifunctional landscape design (Figure 11.13). This landscape includes wastewater treatment and a city park on a 1.5-acre (6,000 m²) parcel in the center of the town. The park amenities, including a pavilion, panels of turf and flowering plants, seating and strolling areas and sports field, are fully integrated with the treatment wetlands.[42]

The island is occupied by 3,000 residents, but one million tourists visit annually. After the island was devastated by a tsunami in 2005, the Danish government provided funds to restore wastewater treatment. The island is characterized by a scarcity of water, energy and developable land. Therefore, a multifunctional landscape was designed. An extensive public process supported by the municipal government and major stakeholders generated the design concept. The design analogy referenced the shape of the island and local symbols. The project cost $700,000 (in 2006 dollars). A local contractor, who hired local workers, built the project.[42]

Wastewater pretreatment is done at the residence or business site where free septic tanks and sewer connections were provided. Solar pumps deliver as much as 105,670 gallons per day (400 m³) to three parallel VSF cells with a total area of 0.6

acres (2,300 m^2). The VSF wetlands are 2' 4" (0.70 m) deep, with three layers of gravel (10 mm top, 25 mm middle and 40 mm bottom), and planted with *Canna* and *Heliconia*. Water from the VSF cells flows through three parallel cells of HSF wetland with a total area of 0.2 acres (750 m^2). The HSF wetlands are two-feet (0.6 m) deep, planted with *Canna* in beds composed of 25-mm gravel. The third stage of treatment is three two-feet deep FWS pools. These have an area of 0.2 acres and are planted with *Papyrus*. The treated water flows into a 2' 4" deep, linear polishing pond of 0.05 acres (200 m^2) and then into a closed reservoir for use in irrigation.[42]

The performance of the system was monitored for two years. The average BOD and TSS meet EPA standards. However, performance was better during the first year. The primary cause of declining effluent quality is illegal connections to the sewer system without installing the required septic tanks and grease traps. Nevertheless, the pairing of recreation, aesthetic, social and wastewater functions was demonstrated as viable where a wastewater authority enforces health codes and is held responsible for the small amount of maintenance and adjustment that the biological system requires.

The wetlands establish the visual character of the park. The recreation and opportunities for social gatherings are secondary benefits. The reuse of the treated water to irrigate the park and conserve scarce potable water is another contribution of the wetlands. An unusual secondary benefit is that the lobster claw flowers can be harvested and sold.

Application of treatment wetlands in green infrastructure

Treatment wetlands can be integrated into the municipal landscape when physical planning is done in advance of development to match development density (and massing) with open-space volumes. The wetlands don't require large land areas and can be distributed at various elevations in the watershed, allowing for water reuse in lower portions of the watershed.

In order to illustrate the impact of distributed treatment wetlands, a simple example is provided here for a new residential development (380 dwelling units and a population of 1,000 at the edge of a growing city). The area needed to achieve secondary quality effluent with a VSF wetland is 0.5 acres. For tertiary quality, an additional 1.3 acres of HSF wetland would be required. One to two acres of FWS wetlands would maximize recreation and biodiversity benefits. The total land area of 3.8–4.8 acres is substantially less than the 6.5–10.5 acres of parkland per 1,000 people recommended by the National Recreation and Park Association.[43] The wetland acreage would allow features such as a 0.3-mile circuit path, fishing docks and picnicking areas without consuming more land. Additional acreage is justified for urban habitat and ecological corridors to achieve the 25–30 percent allocation that this book recommends to achieve the urban structure, recreation and biodiversity benefits of green infrastructure.

About 80,000 gallons of treated water would be available daily for irrigation. At 4.2 (US average) and 10 dwelling units per acre, the wetlands would represent less than 5 and 12.6 percent, respectively, of the residential area. If fact, multi-family residences at the edge of the green infrastructure would encourage mixed-density neighborhoods and reward those residents with desirable views and immediate access to public open space.

Conclusion

The purpose of green infrastructure is to systematically integrate anthropomorphic and ecological patterns, functions and values[44] to support healthy ecosystems and provide goods and services that directly or indirectly benefit humans. Treatment wetlands are clear examples of the integration of human and ecological systems since they contribute to provisioning, regulating, cultural and supporting ecosystem services.

The discussion of the advances in the engineering and performance of wastewater treatment wetlands yields conclusions about their effectiveness and potential location. Individual treatment wetlands of either the HSF or VSF type effectively meet secondary treatment standards when 4.5 m^2 (HSF) to 2 m^2 (VSF) of treatment area per person served are provided. A sequence of the two wetland types achieves tertiary water quality. The subsurface treatment wetlands can be distributed throughout the green infrastructure where treated effluent can be fed to FWS habitat wetlands and reused for irrigation. Outside of existing dense urban areas, treatment wetlands are economically viable. The potential ecosystem service value of subsurface and FWS wetlands can be calculated to justify construction or restoration costs to realize a full range of ecosystem services. These benefits are expanded when treatment wetlands are incorporated into a green infrastructure.

The discussion of secondary ecosystem benefits of treatment wetlands within a multifunctional landscape has urban design implications. Simultaneously planning a network of all ecosystem and human landscapes efficiently utilizes public space. Comprehensive physical planning encourages functions to overlap. Compatible

Figure 11.14
Constructed wetlands like this one at a business park in Oregon can be designed to create heterogeneous habitat for wildlife and amenities for people.

adjacent uses enlarge the effective area of the landscape due to spatial overlapping and temporal displacement of functions. Each component of the green infrastructure expresses a primary function and allows many secondary uses or characteristics. These characteristics can contribute significantly to the primary use of adjacent spaces. The example of Koh Phi Phi illustrates this concept. The plants in the treatment wetlands establish the verdant character of the town's central park and contribute to its attractiveness as a social gathering place.

References

1   J. Vymazal, "Removal of Nutrients in Various Types of Constructed Wetlands," *Science of the Total Environment*, vol. 380, pp. 48–65, 2007.

2   D. Spier, "Plummer, Idaho Wastewater Treatment Plant," 2013.

3   H. Brix and C. A. Arias, "The Use of Vertical Flow Constructed Wetlands for On-Site Treatment of Domestic Wastewater: New Danish Guidelines," *Ecological Engineering*, vol. 25, no. 5, pp. 491–500, 2005.

4   S. Wallace, *Small-Scale Constructed Wetland Treatment Systems*, London: Water Environment Research Publishing, 2006.

5   US Environmental Protection Agency (EPA), "National Pollutant Discharge Elimination System (NPDES) Permit Writers' Manual," 2010.

6   J. Vymazal, "Constructed Wetlands for Wastewater Treatment: Five Decades of Experience," *Environmental Science & Technology*, vol. 45, no. 1, pp. 61–69, 2011.

7   J. Vymazal, "Long-Term Performance of Constructed Wetlands with Horizontal Sub-Surface Flow: Ten Case Studies from the Czech Republic," *Ecological Engineering*, vol. 37, no. 1, pp. 54–63, 2011.

8   R. H. Kadlec, *Treatment Wetlands*, Boca Raton, FL: CRC Press, 2009.

9   J. Vymazal, "Horizontal Sub-surface Flow and Hybrid Constructed Wetlands Systems for Wastewater Treatment," *Ecological Engineering*, vol. 25, pp. 478–490, 2005.

10   R. H. Kadlec, "Comparison of Free Water and Horizontal Subsurface Treatment Wetlands," *Ecological Engineering*, vol. 35, no. 2, pp. 159–174, 2009.

11   P. Jenssen, "High Performance Constructed Wetlands for Cold Climates," *Journal of Environmental Science & Health*, vol. 40, no. 6/7, pp. 1343–1353, 2005.

12   P. Cooper, "What Can We Learn from Old Wetlands?" *Desalination*, vol. 246, pp. 11–26, 2009.

13   C. Vohla, M. Kõiv, H. J. Bavor, F. Chazarenc and Ü. Mander, "Filter Materials for Phosphorus Removal from Wastewater in Treatment Wetlands: A Review," *Ecological Engineering*, vol. 37, no. 1, pp. 70–89, 2011.

14   B. Tunçsiper, "Nitrogen Removal in a Combined Vertical and Horizontal Subsurface-Flow Constructed Wetland System," *Desalination*, vol. 247, no. 1–3, pp. 466–475, 2009.

15   K. L. Guenter Langergraber and R. H. Roland Rohrhofer, "High-Rate Nitrogen Removal in a Two-Stage Subsurface Vertical Flow Constructed Wetland," *Desalination*, vol. 246, pp. 55–68, 2009.

16   EPA, "Aquatic Life Ambient Water Quality Criteria for Ammonia Freshwater," 2009.

17   C. Ávila, J. J. Salas, I. Martín, C. Aragón and J. García, "Integrated Treatment of Combined Sewer Wastewater and Stormwater in a Hybrid Constructed Wetland System in Southern Spain and its Further Reuse," *Ecological Engineering*, vol. 50, pp. 13–20, 2013.

18   U. Burka, "A New Community Approach to Waste Treatment with Higher Water Plants," in *Constructed Wetlands in Water Pollution Control*, Oxford: Pergamon Press, 1990.

19 G. K. Gaboutloeloe, S. Chen, M. E. Barber and C. O. Stöckle, "Combinations of Horizontal and Vertical Flow Constructed Wetlands to Improve Nitrogen Removal," *Water, Air, & Soil Pollution: Focus*, vol. 9, no. 3–4, pp. 279–286, 2009.

20 C. Ávila, A. Pedescoll, V. Matamoros, J. M. Bayona and J. García, "Capacity of a Horizontal Subsurface Flow Constructed Wetland System for the Removal of Emerging Pollutants: An Injection Experiment," *Chemosphere*, vol. 81, no. 9, pp. 1137–1142, 2010.

21 V. Matamoros, C. Arias, H. Brix and J. M. Bayona, "Preliminary Screening of Small-Scale Domestic Wastewater Treatment Systems for Removal of Pharmaceutical and Personal Care Products," *Water Research*, vol. 43, no. 1, pp. 55–62, 2009.

22 H. Brix, "Denmark," in *Constructed Wetlands for Wastewater Treatment in Europe*, Leiden, Netherlands: Backhuys Publishers, 1998.

23 J. Vymazal and L. Kröpfelová, "A Three-Stage Experimental Constructed Wetland for Treatment of Domestic Sewage: First 2 Years of Operation," *Ecological Engineering*, vol. 37, no. 1, pp. 90–98, 2011.

24 M. Zapater, A. Gross and M. I. M. Soares, "Capacity of an On-Site Recirculating Vertical Flow Constructed Wetland to Withstand Disturbances and Highly Variable Influent Quality," *Ecological Engineering*, vol. 37, no. 10, pp. 1572–1577, 2011.

25 T. L. C. Moore and W. F. Hunt, "Ecosystem Service Provision by Stormwater Wetlands and Ponds: A Means for Evaluation?," *Water Research*, vol. 46, no. 20, pp. 6811–6823, 2011.

26 S.-X. Zhu, H.-L. Ge, Y. Ge, H.-Q. Cao, D. Liu, J. Chang, C.-B. Zhang, B.-J. Gu and S.-X. Chang, "Effects of Plant Diversity on Biomass Production and Substrate Nitrogen in a Subsurface Vertical Flow Constructed Wetland," *Ecological Engineering*, vol. 36, no. 10, pp. 1307–1313, 2010.

27 A. Feest, I. Merrill and P. Aukett, "Does Botanical Diversity in Sewage Treatment Reed-Bed Sites Enhance Invertebrate Biodiversity?," *International Journal of Ecology*, vol. 2012, pp. 1–9, 2012.

28 C. Mabry and C. Dettman, "Odonata Richness and Abundance in Relation to Vegetation Structure in Restored and Native Wetlands of the Prairie Pothole Region, USA," *Ecological Restoration*, vol. 28, no. 4, pp. 475–484, 2010.

29 P. A. M. Bachand and A. J. Horne, "Denitrification in Constructed Free-Water Surface Wetlands: II. Effects of Vegetation and Temperature," *Ecological Engineering*, vol. 14, no. 1–2, pp. 17–32, 1999.

30 C.-B. Hsu, H.-L. Hsieh, L. Yang, S.-H. Wu, J.-S. Chang, S.-C. Hsiao, H.-C. Su, C.-H. Yeh, Y.-S. Ho and H.-J. Lin, "Biodiversity of Constructed Wetlands for Wastewater Treatment," *Ecological Engineering*, vol. 37, no. 10, pp. 1533–1545, 2011.

31 H. R. Murkin, E. J. Murkin and J. P. Ball, "Avian Habitat Selection and Prairie Wetland Dynamics: A 10-Year Experiment," *Ecological Applications*, vol. 7, no. 4, pp. 1144–1159, 1997.

32 EPA, "The Des Plaines Wetlands Project: Wetlands for River Water Quality Improvement," 1993.

33 S. Hickman, "Improvement of Habitat Quality for Nesting and Migrating Birds at the Des Plaines River Wetlands Demonstration Project," *Ecological Engineering*, vol. 3, no. 4, pp. 485–494, 1994.

34 R. A. McKinney, K. B. Raposa and R. M. Cournoyer, "Wetlands as Habitat in Urbanizing Landscapes: Patterns of Bird Abundance and Occupancy," *Landscape and Urban Planning*, vol. 100, no. 1–2, pp. 144–152, 2011.

35 C. Catterall, "Responses of Faunal Assemblages to Urbanisation," in *Ecology of Cities and Towns: A Comparative Approach*, Cambridge: Cambridge University Press, 2009.

36 G. Thiere, J. Stadmark and S. E. B. Weisner, "Nitrogen Retention Versus Methane Emission: Environmental Benefits and Risks of Large-Scale Wetland Creation," *Ecological Engineering*, vol. 37, no. 1, pp. 6–15, 2011.

37   A. M. Ruiz, J. C. Maerz, A. K. Davis, M. K. Keel, A. R. Ferreira, M. J. Conroy, L. A. Morris and A. T. Fisk, "Patterns of Development and Abnormalities among Tadpoles in a Constructed Wetland Receiving Treated Wastewater," *Environmental Science & Technology*, vol. 44, no. 13, pp. 4862–4868, 2010.

38   R. H. Kadlec, C. Cuvellier and T. Stober, "Performance of the Columbia, Missouri, Treatment Wetland," *Ecological Engineering*, vol. 36, no. 5, pp. 672–684, 2010.

39   J. Vymazal, "Enhancing Ecosystem Services on the Landscape with Created, Constructed and Restored Wetlands," *Ecological Engineering*, vol. 37, no. 1, pp. 1–5, 2011.

40   Blumberg Engineers, "Constructed Wetlands as a Vertical Subsurface Flow Reed Bed Treatment System in Northern China," 2003.

41   C. Tong, R. A. Feagin, J. Lu, X. Zhang, X. Zhu, W. Wang and W. He, "Ecosystem Service Values and Restoration in the Urban Sanyang Wetland of Wenzhou, China," *Ecological Engineering*, vol. 29, no. 3, pp. 249–258, 2007.

42   H. Brix, T. Koottatep, O. Fryd and C. H. Laugesen, "The Flower and the Butterfly Constructed Wetland System at Koh Phi Phi: System Design and Lessons Learned During Implementation and Operation," *Ecological Engineering*, vol. 37, no. 5, pp. 729–735, 2011.

43   R. Lancaster, "Park, Recreation and Open Space Standards and Guidelines," National Recreation and Park Association, 1983.

44   K. Bomans, T. Steenberghen, V. Dewaelheyns, H. Leinfelder and H. Gulinck, "Under-rated Transformations in the Open Space: The Case of an Urbanized and Multifunctional Area," *Landscape and Urban Planning*, vol. 94, no. 3–4, pp. 196–205, 2010.

CHAPTER TWELVE

Stockholm: green infrastructure case study

Context

The city and county of Stockholm demonstrate the planning and implementation of green infrastructure advocated in this book. The city is located approximately at latitude 59° N in southeast Sweden (Figure 12.1) within an astoundingly complex configuration of islands, coastline, freshwater lakes and saltwater estuaries on the Baltic Sea (Figure 12.2).

About half of the County of Stockholm is composed of primarily fertile coniferous forest, but deciduous forests also occur here. Forested land and the amount of protected forest is increasing in the county at the expense of agriculture, but the rate of increase is insufficient to protect biological diversity.[1] Within the city there are eight natural areas, including nature and cultural reserves and an urban national park, with a total area of 5,680 acres (2,299 ha). Of this 828 acres (335 ha) is water and 4,855 acres (1,965 ha) is land.

The built environment

Like many European cities, Stockholm was initially located to be geographically defensible. Constrained by the area of a small island in Lake Mälaren, the city was compactly developed with multistory buildings, narrow streets and little natural open space. As the city expanded, especially after World War II, growth followed the road alignments.

Today, 872,000 people live in the Stockholm city area of 73 square miles (188 km²). Development within the city is compact since nearly 90 percent of residents live in multi-family buildings (Figure 12.3). The resulting population density is 11,944 inhabitants per square mile (4,638 per km²). The region is increasingly polycentric and growing with the addition of 20,000 people per year.[2] The population of the metropolitan area is now 2,050,000.[3] The sections below consider the municipal and regional scale, before focusing on a recently developed urban infill district near the city center.

In a competitive process, Stockholm was designated the first Green Capital of Europe in 2010. The Green Capital competition assesses many factors of sustainability, which is broader than the consideration of green infrastructure, but many factors overlap, of course. Of particular interest here is the regional, municipal and neighborhood green infrastructure that supports multiple uses.

Figure 12.1
Stockholm location
map.

Figure 12.1
Stockholm location
map.

Figure 12.2
Physiography of the
Stockholm region.
Photo 59°19′44.15″ N,
18°3′53.68″ E, 12
September 2007
(accessed 15 April
2013) by Google Earth.

Figure 12.3
Stockholm urban core.
Photo 59°19′21.92″ N
18°04′26.36″ E, 12
September 2007
(accessed 15 April
2013) by Google Earth.

Regional system

Green wedges

The concept of a regional green infrastructure was articulated in the 1930s. Alternating fingers of natural landscape and human habitation with transportation infrastructure was adopted as a general planning principle (Figure 12.4). Traditionally, Swedish farmsteads and villages were constructed on high ground or benches above a river or stream. The floodplain and agricultural fields lay between the watercourse and the settlement. It is often this floodplain and old agricultural fields or pastures that form the spines of the green wedges flanked by the settlements and the roads that connect them.[4] Voluntary comprehensive planning of green wedges and then legally binding detailed development plans for cities and towns were in place by 1998. Stockholm adopted an urban infill plan in 1999 and in 2001 the County of Stockholm adopted a spatial, green wedge regional development plan, which was updated in 2010.[2]

These decisions resulted in a radial regional plan with wedges of continuous green infrastructure that had significant biodiversity value while being close to residential districts. The plan features ten long corridors of agriculture, forest and habitat at least 1,640 feet (500 m) wide (Figure 12.4). These corridors connect huge natural preserves outside the city and are essential to the high biodiversity near the city center. Ecologists in Stockholm found that habitat areas of 740 acres supported the needs of most native species, particularly when the area was more compact, rather than linear in shape. The widths of ecological corridors are variable according to the target species, but a 0.3 mile (0.5 km) width is defined by the regional development plan as the minimum to accommodate both wildlife and recreation uses. There are many existing areas within the green wedges that are less wide than the recommendation,

Figure 12.4
The green wedges are shown as core habitat (dark green), secondary habitat (light green) and large recreation and natural areas (orange) within the urban (white) and aquatic (blue) matrix.[2]

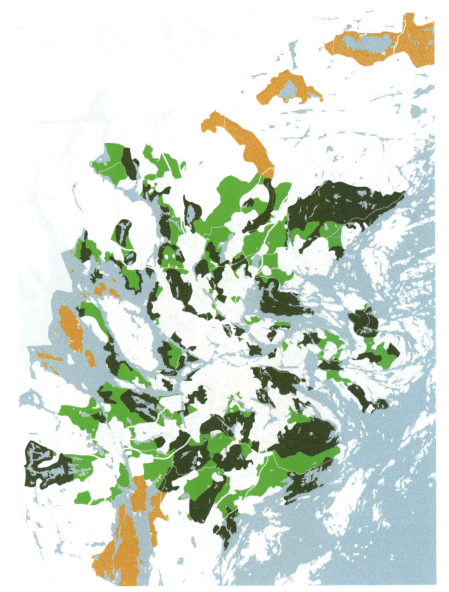

particularly near the city center. These are identified and labeled as one of three categories of weak points where more careful planning is to take place to avoid further erosion and where mitigation measures are to be undertaken. In fact, a detailed study identified all of the corridor breaks and barriers as a first step toward mitigation. Planning documents also stress the almost insurmountable obstacles to dispersal of some species that busy highways present.[5]

Human use of the green wedges (Figure 12.5) is as important as the biodiversity benefits. For example, the National Urban Park in Stockholm receives 15 million visitors each year.[6] To foster public use of this and other green areas, 43 public transit stations

have been designated as green stations. These are transit stops where citizens can walk 984–1640 feet (300–500 m) to reach a green wedge. Major green transit stations feature information about the adjacent natural resource.[5]

The green wedges are being increasingly codified. In 2003 the county made the commitment to add 71 new nature reserves and 28 study areas. By 2012 36 of these were realized. This official protection, rather than planning guidelines, assures that urban growth will follow the existing roads and rail lines rather than sprawling into the landscape infrastructure.

Figure 12.5
Social areas and recreation use are major components of the green infrastructure and this area of the National Urban Park.

The National Urban Park

Stockholm established the world's first urban national park in 1995 (Figure 12.6). The park is part of one of the regional green wedges and the largest park within the city limits. It also extends into two other municipalities. In the European tradition, the 6,670-acre park is a mixture of cultural facilities, such as museums, recreation areas and protected wildlife habitat.

Initially the Parliament defined the area as one of natural interest. The core of the park was inherited from royal hunting grounds of the previous centuries. The municipalities were given planning authority to foster democratic participation but secret negotiations between private construction companies and municipalities regarding development of public land before the initiation of public processes resulted in the development of hundreds of acres within the national interest area boundary. The controversy generated by this practice led to citizen planning efforts and petitions organized by non-governmental organizations and supported by the media. With

Figure 12.6
Plan view of the
Stockholm National
Urban Park. Photo
59°23′34.56″ N,
18°01′28.84″ E, 3 April
2012 (accessed 15 April
2013) by Google Earth.

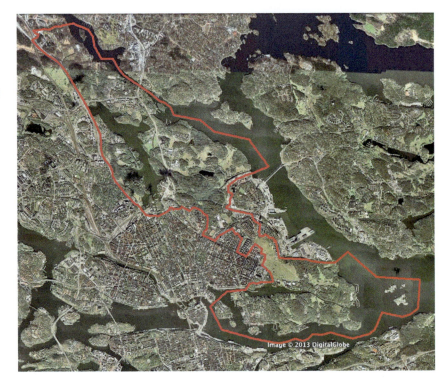

the prospect of a large road infrastructure project that would have damaged the area, the National Parliament voted unanimously in late 1994 to establish the National Urban Park. The act took effect in 1995 and specified more clear boundaries (Figure 12.6), purposes and protections.[7]

Development of new buildings and roads was not prohibited by the act, but development is not permitted if it negatively impacts any of the three purposes of the park – cultural, recreational and environmental. Existing buildings can be expanded if they do not impact the park. In contrast, facilitates in support of park purposes were to be developed and protected within the park boundaries. Figure 12.6 shows that the park boundary encloses two core areas and a corridor through the urban development.[7]

Public agencies are focused on strengthening the ecological connections diminished before the park was created[8] and on the development plans for the industrial and port area to the east of the park.

Ecology and the green wedges

In the initial stages of planning the green wedges, ecologists studied native forest species in need of conservation attention to determine whether the green wedges had the capacity to sustain them. Some species are difficult to sustain in growing urban districts due to large territory requirements, large core area requirements, specialized habitat needs, small or scattered populations or low dispersal rates.

Species with one or more of these characteristics are especially vulnerable to the habitat fragmentation and degradation that accompanies urbanization. Two of the bird species in the study (nutcracker and the honey buzzard) have specialized habitat requirements associated with certain species of shrubs and trees, and both had low and scattered populations. In the study area, forest clearing, removal of mature trees and conversion of deciduous forest to coniferous forest were the most serious threats to the study species.[9]

The six bird species included in the study were honey buzzard (*Pernis apivorus*), goshawk (*Accipiter gentilis*), stock dove (*Columba oenas*), black woodpecker (*Dryocopus martius*), lesser spotted woodpecker (*Dendrocopos minor*) and nutcracker (*Nucifraga caryocatactes*). The study found that the size of the available habitat, and the type and degree of connectivity, determined the presence of breeding pairs of these birds. The study mapped the green wedges and identified 67 sites within and outside the green wedges. Surveys were conducted in 28 of these sites. These defined a gradient from the city center to the rural landscape. Near the city center habitat patches were smaller and more isolated. The forest coverage for the study area was 39 percent. For the area within 6.2 miles (10 km) of the city center, the forest coverage was 25 percent, while the area within 6.2 miles of the city center but outside the green wedges had only 15 percent forested area.

The study discovered a wide range of habitat requirements for the target species. The black woodpecker required territory with mature, mostly coniferous, forest as large as 1,235 acres (500 ha). However, this could be comprised of several habitat patches within an agricultural matrix with only 26 percent forest cover. In contrast, the lesser-spotted woodpecker preferred strips of moist deciduous forest along lake shorelines and required only 49–123 acres (20–50 ha) of good habitat. However, this habitat type is not as extensive as coniferous forest.

The goshawk prefers large forest areas but has adapted to breed in fragmented patches within the urbanizing region. The nutcracker and the honey buzzard required the largest territories, but benefited from good connectivity between habitat patches.

The study outlined above determined that the needs of the bird species in the Stockholm region can be met in the green wedges if large and diverse forest habitats are preserved. It also determined that smaller habitat fragments are valuable if proximity is good.[9] Continuous corridors linking habitat fragments will be more important for terrestrial animals than for the bird species in this study.

Large habitat areas still exist in Stockholm County, but nearer the city center habitat is fragmented into smaller parcels with a few exceptions. However, in this situation groups of fragments may serve as territory for some native species. For birds and mobile terrestrial species, the fragments can simply be close together, but for many species an ecological corridor must connect the habitat fragments. This was demonstrated in a study of a bird, the coal tit (*Parus ater*), in the Stockholm region. This bird was known to be a habitat specialist requiring coniferous forest habitat of 25 to 74 acres (10–30 ha). However, the bird was found in habitat fragments within a network. Patch networks with a total area of 12–25 acres (5–10 ha) but where the fragments were separated by no more that 164 feet (50 m) served as breeding territory. The bird was found in habitat fragments greater than 2.5 acres (1 ha).[10] This finding is important for physical planning in urban and suburban areas where

Figure 12.7
This wetland and forest is in the northern core of the National Urban Park, but adjacent to high-density urban development.

extensive damage to habitat has occurred. As noted earlier, for terrestrial animals it is more likely that the habitat fragments will need to be connected with ecological corridors for the network to serve as breeding habitat.

Wetlands amount to, at most, 4 percent of Stockholm County. About 1.2 square miles (3 km²) of wetlands have been lost and 4.6 square miles (12 km²) remain (Figure 12.7). Wetlands have been lost to roads and other development and 90 percent of the remaining wetlands are impacted by human activity. There are 850 lakes in the county and about 100 of these are impacted by acidification (30 are treated with lime regularly to mitigate the acidity). This is primarily the result of air pollution originating on the European continent. The Stockholm archipelago is impacted by excess nitrogen and phosphorus from sewage plant effluent and stormwater runoff and by heavy metals from urban runoff.[1] The city and county have an ambitious, continuous and cooperative environmental monitoring program. It correctly focuses on habitat and species monitoring to assure sustained biodiversity. However, annual tracking of the populations of target species, such as greater cormorants and other species, is undertaken to monitor endangered species or sudden changes in species numbers.[1]

Urban parks and open space

The green wedges extend from the county into the city. Within the city there are 21,000 acres (8,500 ha) of parkland representing 40 percent of the total land area and resulting in 27 acres (11 ha) of parkland per 1,000 residents.[11] This compares to Los Angeles, with 10 percent of its area dedicated to parkland, and Portland with 15.8 percent.[11] The parkland in Stockholm includes 12 parks that are over 200 acres (81 ha) in size. The dozen parks contain about one-third of the city land area.

The goal of green space near every resident is taken seriously in Stockholm since surveys demonstrate the public demand. Seventy percent of inner-city residents wish to visit green spaces more often and spend more time there. This desire is independent of gender, age and socio-economic status. Distance from a green space and lack of time are the two reasons for less use of green spaces than desired.[5] New planning goals established distance and park size standards. Residents are to be no more than 600 feet (200 m) from a pocket or neighborhood park 2.5–12.5 acres (1–5 ha) in size and no more than 1,500 feet (457 m) from a district park of 12.5–125 acres (5–51 ha). In addition, residents are to be no more than 0.6 miles (1 km) from a nature preserve larger than 125 acres (50 ha) in size.[11]

As demonstrated earlier, the parkland amenity is also an economic value as expressed by rent and property values. When comparing condominiums, those near 27 acres (11 ha) of park land commanded $783 more for each 11 ft^2 of floor area (600 €/m^2) compared to similar units with parks with 17 acres (7 ha) of park environment.[4]

Ecosystem value of the National Urban Park

Deciduous forests dominated by red oak trees are prized in Stockholm. In the National Urban Park one-quarter of all trees are oaks (see Figure 12.9). Oak trees had royal protection beginning in the 1300s and could not be legally cut by private parties until the late 1800s, due in part to their value in shipbuilding. However, much illegal harvesting took place and other oaks were lost when forest was converted to farmland. In 1809 the royal hunting park in Stockholm was formalized and protected the oak forest.[7]

Hundreds of species are associated with old-growth stands of oaks. For example, the oaks are dependent on the Eurasian jays (*Garrulus glandiarius*) to spread their seeds (Figure 12.8). Jays bury a store of acorns in the fall and live on them in the winter. The nearly 100 jays living in the National Urban Park hide about half a million

Figure 12.8
The Eurasian jay is critical for the maintenance of the oak woodland and provides valuable ecosystem services.

Figure 12.9
The National Urban Park provides heterogeneous ecosystems. In this image a wetland and heron rookery are framed by oak and coniferous woodlands.

acorns per year. About 30 percent of these are not recovered from the soil and can grow into new oaks. An estimated 85 percent of the park's oaks are the result of the jay's natural seed dispersal. In order to estimate the economic value of birds' work, the cost of humans planting oaks can be calculated. Depending on the planting method (seeds or seedlings) each pair of jays does a job that corresponds to $880–3,920 per acre. Jays are limited to oak forests and unwilling to cross open areas. Therefore, it is important that large areas of oak forest or corridors connecting smaller patches are preserved to maintain the population of both birds and oaks.[4]

The National Urban Park contains a great diversity of habitats including deciduous and coniferous forests, meadows and pastures, wetlands, lakes and rivers, a long coastline and numerous islands. There are 880 species of flowering plants, 40 fish species, 1,000 species of butterflies and about 100 species of birds that breed in the park. Nine of the 14 species of bats in Sweden are found in the park, including two threatened species (whiskered and Natterer's bat). Of course, many exotic, invasive species exist here too. One is the American mink.

The most important habitat type in the park is the deciduous forest, since most of the country is dominated by coniferous forest. In this forest, the oaks are associated with elm, ash, linden and maple. Man has managed all habitat types in the park, including the deciduous forest, for centuries through mowing, grazing and tree planting. Groves of 200–300-year-old trees create a unique ecological environment, which is increasingly rare in Sweden and Europe. As limbs or entire oak trees die, they remain standing and become a long-lasting resource for hole-nesting birds, mammals and a host of beetles and other insects. There are actually about 1,500 species of insects, wood fungi and lichens linked to oaks, especially the ancient ones.

The 1,200 species of beetles, which are involved in the decomposition of the bark and decaying wood, make up the majority of the species linked to the oak trees. Ninety percent of the beetle species prefer standing trunks in sunlight. Many endangered invertebrates, such as the broad-banded beetle (*Plagionotus detritus*) are members of the old-growth oak groves. In addition, oak and beech acorns support birds and mammals.[12]

The large size of the park supports core habitat areas, although the species most sensitive to human activity or needing the largest territories may be compromised. Keys to the dispersal of offspring are corridor connections between the north and south core areas of the park and more regionally to the deciduous forest stands south of Stockholm (Figure 12.4). The corridors between the core areas are vulnerable to development and habitat loss. The city is working carefully to develop the royal port, on the eastern edge of the city, to strengthen the corridor within the National Urban Park and reduce the hostility of the matrix. Extending an ecological corridor south of the park will be difficult and require local and regional coordination and public support. Since deciduous forest is not the dominant forest type and because the National Urban Park is more isolated by urban development than in the past, there is a concern that the deciduous woodland in the park is a relic landscape that will slowly decline. Reduction of the original oak ecosystem below 25 percent of its original size is a threshold that threatens the viability of the ecosystem. The long life span of the oaks creates some uncertainty about the long-term prospects of the forest.

City center

The green infrastructure of the city center primarily expresses human values. Vibrant streets, public squares, urban parks, historic districts and sustainable transportation serve the citizens in the cultural, government and financial old town. These spaces are also part of the green infrastructure of the city, even if they don't focus on the non-human aspects of the environment. They are volumes that make high-density, mixed-use districts vibrant and desirable places to live, work and shop. Stockholm offers a full range of urban spaces from the largely paved plazas that can host thousands of people for celebrations (Figure 12.10) to green oases that provide a respite from the bustle of the city. There are promenades (Figure 12.11) along the water and through the old town that connect a variety of spaces and use areas, such as transportation centers, government complexes and the urban waterfront.

The combination of high population density and high percentage of open space is unusual. In San Francisco, the population density is higher than in Stockholm, but this is at the expense of parkland and especially biodiversity. Only 14 percent of the land area in San Francisco is park and open space and the park acreage per person is very low (Table 12.1). In contrast, the city of Austin covers more than three times the area of Stockholm but has only one-quarter of the density. The percentage of land dedicated to open space is much lower in Austin than in Stockholm, although acres per 1,000 people are quite high. Austin manages two Texas state parks within the city limits. In summary, Austin is a sprawling low-density city with a great open-space system, while San Francisco is a very urban, high-density environment without the balance of habitat and open space amenities of Stockholm.[14]

Figure 12.10
Outstanding
architecture frames a
series of urban plazas
and parks large enough
to host civic
celebrations, fairs and
street performers.

Figure 12.11
Pedestrian streets,
anchored by
transportation hubs and
the government center,
teem with tourists and
locals for shopping and
entertainment.

Table 12.1 Comparison of area occupied, density, percentage of green space and park acreage per 1,000 people

City	Area sq. mi/km²	Population	Density sq. mi/km²	Green space percent	Parks ac/1,000 persons
Stockholm	188/73	872,000	4,600/12,000	40	27
Austin	704/272	820,000	1,259/3,262	16.6	36.8
San Francisco	122/47	805,000	6,633/17,179	14	5.5

New Urbanism proponents in the US worry that green infrastructure is a recipe for the ruralization of American towns and cities. Stockholm demonstrates that cities can have it all – vibrant urban environments and rich biodiversity. Providing 25 percent or less open space in a city stresses the remaining ecosystems and is too low to accommodate both recreation and urban biodiversity without conflict. Population densities need to increase in most American cities in order to preserve land for recreation, scenery, stormwater treatment, habitat and other ecosystem functions and services.

The high population density in Stockholm has substantial secondary benefits since it precludes the loss of natural landscape to suburban sprawl. This regional city is clearly the center of civic life and remains the focus of smaller cities connected to it by roads and rail lines.

Green transportation infrastructure

Stockholm will not expand its street infrastructure for automobiles in the future. Instead the emphasis will be on public transportation, bicycle and pedestrian infrastructure. Those who commute by bicycle in the city of Stockholm has nearly doubled since 1982.[3] Currently 15 percent of commuters within the city travel by bicycle and the city's goal is to increase this to 30 percent by 2030. The improvement can be attributed to several factors, including more bike lanes, fewer automobiles on the roads, improved traffic controls and opportunities to carry bicycles on buses, light rail trains and ferries. The number of bicycle lanes, air stations, storage facilities and winter maintenance of bicycle routes is increasing steadily.[13] The routing of bicycle and pedestrian paths encourages recreational use as well as transportation to workplaces.

Hammarby Sjöstad

Introduction

Stockholm addresses green infrastructure at the regional scale with a hierarchical public transportation network, the green wedges and habitat for native species. The National Urban Park and other large parks offer urban biodiversity and recreation benefits. The city center and an inner ring of mixed-use districts focus on green spaces to satisfy social, aesthetic, stormwater management and urban habitat. This is best implemented at Hammarby Sjöstad.

Figure 12.12
The city provides a fleet of bicycles for rent in the city center. These are popular with visitors and locals who need to move about the city for meetings.

Planning context

Hammarby Sjöstad was originally a wooded area with meadows and a farm on the southern shore of Hammarby Lake, and was used as a picnic ground by the residents of the neighborhood (Södermalm) just north of the lake. Purchased by the city in 1917, the area was made available for shipping and industrial use to take advantage of the canal constructed in 1914 to connect Hammarby Lake to the Baltic Sea. As Stockholm grew the industrial area became attractive as an opportunity to build residences near the center of the city, rather than as suburban sprawl, and to address the poor appearance, noise and pollution created by the industrial and port activities. However, industrial users had not abandoned the land as they did in so many other cities.

The industrial brownfield site was planned for redevelopment as an Olympic Village during Stockholm's 1996 bid for the 2004 Olympic Games. When Athens, Greece was chosen instead, the private sector's interest in financing the redevelopment evaporated. However, since a great deal of planning work had been done already, the city continued the development process. The initial planning for the Olympics inspired high sustainability goals consistent with previous housing projects associated with the international games.[15]

The initial sustainability plan for the property was developed when a government composed of liberal parties and its environmental partners were in control of the city council. When this changed in 1998, the new conservative government weakened the sustainability goals of the project and favored privately owned and more expensive housing, as well as fewer requirements for environmental measures.[16]

For example, special toilets allowing separate collection and treatment of urine from other wastewater were eliminated from the development requirements. This shifted wastewater treatment costs from the developers to subsequent city operations.[16] Later, wastewater treatment in an experimental plant in the district demonstrated that source separation significantly reduces the energy required for treatment of wastewater.[17]

Development process and costs

Large-scale development in Sweden is generally initiated by the municipality, which often exercises eminent domain (compulsory purchase). Although most of the land for this redevelopment was already owned by the City of Stockholm, approximately $83 million was required to purchase private land to assemble all of the required parcels. Ultimately, the city invested $0.65 billion in the project, while the private sector invested $3.8 billion.[3] The high land cost resulted from paying more than market value for some parcels to avoid eminent domain appeals that would slow the development process.[2] The industrial uses of the site were automobile repair, an asphalt company, varnish manufacturing and metal processing. The soil contamination was moderate and cost about $17 million for remediation or capping.[3]

Hammarby Sjöstad is 494 acres (almost 100 acres of which is water); there are 49 apartment units per gross acre (122.5 per hectare) and a population density of 108 residents per gross acre (270 per hectare) in residential or mixed-use buildings of 4–13 stories (seven-story average). Ultimately there will be 11,500 apartments, of which 46 percent will be rentals and 54 percent owner occupied. At completion there will be 26,000 residents with an additional 10,000 jobs in the project area.

Figure 12.13
The lake and canal are central features of Hammarby Sjöstad. Note the oval vegetated parcel on the right – this is the oak woodland with its ecoduct connection to the regional landscape. Photo 59°18′19.96″ N, 18°05′59.86″ E, 12 September 2007 (accessed 15 April 2013) by Google Earth.

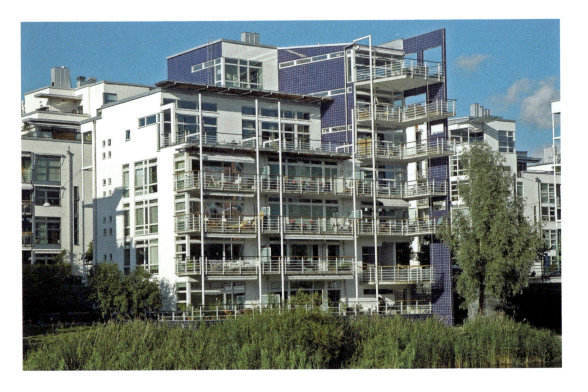

Figure 12.14
The beautiful high-quality housing is expensive due to unit size, good design and central location.

These workers occupy over three million square feet of office, retail and light industrial space.[5] A criticism of the development is that the initial goal of providing low-cost housing has not been realized. Most of the development parcels were sold to private developers, resulting in rents and purchase prices well beyond the middle and lower economic strata (Figure 12.14). Therefore, from a social standpoint Hammarby Sjöstad is not an example of a socially sustainable project.[18] Without rent or price controls, the attractive environment, access to public transportation and central location caused the market rates for the housing to rise rapidly.

Open-space system

High-density urban districts can be the counterpoint to green infrastructure. At Hammarby Sjöstad there are 74 acres (30 ha) dedicated to public green space and an additional 160 square feet (15 m^2) of courtyard space per dwelling unit.[19] The space dedicated to the residential courtyards (see Figure 12.18) is quite high and supports the goal of at least 15 percent of the courtyard space receiving four hours of sunlight on the spring and autumn equinox.[20] Roughly 40 percent of the land area is available for recreation, open space, urban plazas, residential courtyards, wildlife habitat and corridors and stormwater management. The substantial area of water increases the ecological value of the green infrastructure, especially where the aquatic and terrestrial systems meet. If the water area is included, then more than 50 percent of the project area is dedicated to the green infrastructure.

Figure 12.15
The pergola and wood deck serve picnickers, joggers and a yoga class on this sunny afternoon.

There are a number of public and semi-public spaces in the development. A favorite is the wooden deck at the north end of the project (Figure 12.15). At a street end, the space is prominent and accessible by residents and the public. It has a varied program including two stormwater treatment facilities (see Figure 12.23), public art, a pergola, a perennial garden, board walks (Figure 12.16) and the stepped deck which serves both groups and individuals. These are high-quality, flexible and informal urban places that engender a sense of place.

There is also a more formal urban plaza (see Figure 12.19) connected to the central park that serves the neighborhood's civic celebrations. Other public spaces match their character to their context. The expensive and engaging fountain, plaza and garden shown in Figure 12.17 are at the intersection of retail and residential buildings. The fountain is set back slightly but visible from Lugnet Alle and the light rail cars, while the perennial gardens make the transition to the residential structures arrayed along one of the canals.

Closer to home, every building with a complex shape has a partially enclosed courtyard. These are multiple-use spaces offering access to sunlight, improved privacy, turf play areas, lush plantings and the community recycling system.

Sustainable transportation

Recreational paths serve the 27 percent of the residents who walk or bicycle to work, in addition to those using the system for pleasure or exercise. The opportunity to

Figure 12.16
The boardwalk and dock encourage families and pets to enjoy social time and the terrific view of the activities on the lake and the wetlands bordering the Hammarby Sjöstad neighborhood.

Figure 12.17
This beautiful and interactive fountain is at the interface of a retail and residential section. Its water display changes, offering endless mystery to children and a varied scene for the resident.

provide the miles of separated paths and neighborhood parks is due, in part, to the low number of automobiles. In Hammarby, only 62 percent of households own a car and these seem not to be used on a daily basis. In fact, 52 percent of the residents travel via public transportation (Figure 12.19), while only 21 percent commute by private automobile.

Largely due to this use of public transportation (Figure 12.20) and walking or bicycling, the decrease in CO_2 emissions per residential unit is 52 percent below the levels of the early 1990s.[21] A car-sharing program in the district attracts 6 percent of the population (910 people) and 100 companies who subscribe. The system employs 46 energy-efficient cars. Fewer cars in the neighborhood means less land dedicated to parking. There are 0.55 parking spaces per dwelling (totaling 4,000 spaces within underground garages) and 0.15 spaces per unit of street and surface parking (totaling 3,000 spaces).[21] Although exceptionally low by American standards, where 1.25 spaces of on-site parking are typically required, the original plan set the standard at 0.4 spaces per unit to accommodate residents, workplace and guest parking. This limit was to encourage public transit ridership but was nearly doubled in 1998 due to pressure from developers.[22] The clean and efficient light rail service connects residents to the city center and suburban areas (Figure 12.20).

Figure 12.18
Residential courtyards are large and heavily planted, offering privacy between units and places for play and entertainment.

Figure 12.19
Sewage sludge is processed in the wastewater treatment plant to generate biogas (methane), which is used to power the city's fleet of efficient buses.

Figure 12.20
A light rail train (left) passes through the center of Hammarby and its central park and plaza. One of the schools helps frame this plaza with its multistory façade.

Stormwater treatment

Stormwater treatment is an important part of the green infrastructure and is well developed and diverse, especially considering that the project planning was done 15 years ago. Hammarby Sjöstad uses eight different treatment pathways for stormwater, including filters, infiltration, swales, oil/grit separators, open channels, ponds, infiltration through engineered soil, treatment at the wastewater plant and direct discharge to receiving water. In general, stormwater is managed in three different ways. Some of the stormwater is treated in the wastewater treatment plant, although it is treated separately from wastewater. In other catchments stormwater is treated locally in a variety of landscape features or below ground. Residential streets with fewer than 800 cars per day comprise the third catchment type. In this case the water is discharged directly into the lake without treatment. Unfortunately, calculations estimate that this untreated stormwater adds 3,774 pounds (1,712 kg) of suspended solids to the lake each year, while the landscape and vault treatment methods add 564–1,406 pounds (256–638 kg) per year depending on the removal efficiency of the different treatment systems. Furthermore, the no-treatment scenario delivers over 44 pounds (20 kg) of zinc and over 55 pounds (25 kg) of cadmium to the receiving waters.[15] Unfortunately, Hammarby Lake remains polluted from high levels of heavy metals, even after a few decades of improvement.

An infiltration trench was constructed and tested at Hammarby Sjöstad. Located in the street median (Figure 12.21), the infiltration trench is 15 feet (4.5 m) wide and 2–2.5 feet deep, wrapped in a filter fabric and covered with 16 inches of topsoil. It treats water from the street (8,000 vehicles per day) and parking. Fed by catch

Figure 12.21
The trees in this rail and auto corridor are offset in their parkways because infiltration beds below the turf collect stormwater from the street for water quality treatment before discharge into the lake.

Figure 12.22
The mass of common reeds is a striking landscape feature that frame recreation areas and also improves water quality.

basins, the trench holds a two-year water quality storm easily and contains the ten-year storm up to a 27-minute duration before overflow. Studies cited in the chapter on stormwater indicate the high water quality performance of infiltration trenches in reducing many contaminants. The test in Hammarby concentrated on the hydraulic performance of the system and the impact on trees. Trees planted in the median were surrounded by a soil buffer and were healthier than street trees in tree wells in the sidewalk that received only rainfall and runoff from the sidewalk. Greater availability of water and oxygen from the infiltration trench are assumed to account for the enhanced tree growth.[23]

A water quality feature of the previous industrial site was retained. There is a shallow bench at the lake edge along its eastern border that fosters a dense stand of common reed (*Phragmites*) (Figure 12.22). This wetland intercepts runoff from the new development. Sedimentation of suspended solids, heavy metals and bacterial degradation occur here, as does removal of excess nutrients.

A significant stormwater treatment system is at the northern end of the lake (Figure 12.23). It receives runoff from three acres of urban streets. Storm runoff is pretreated in an oil/water separator where large particles are also captured. The water then flows into a sedimentation pond bound on all sides by a gabion planted with common reed. Once the smaller particulates settle to the bottom of the basin, the water flows slowly through a free-water surface constructed wetland. Here, water is directed along the length of four stepped wetlands (Figure 12.24) to maximize the distance and time that the water is in contact with the substrate, soil and

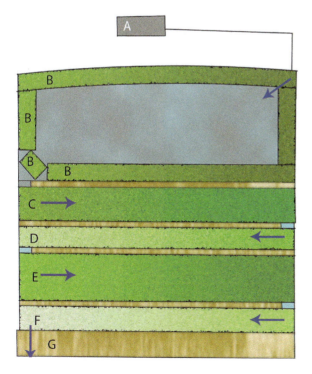

Figure 12.23
Stormwater runoff from streets flows through this stepped wetland for water quality improvement. The channels should be completely vegetated for optimum performance.

Figure 12.24
Stormwater treatment wetland. A, oil/water/grit separator; B, sedimentation basin with wetland plants suspended over a wire cage; C–F, vegetated wetlands; G, boardwalk and outlet to the lake. Based on Alm 2005.[24]

Figure 12.25
This major pedestrian space collects stormwater from roofs, terraces and landscapes. The canal walk connects to the Luma civic park.

vegetation.[24] This constructed wetland sequesters heavy metals and suspended solids, and removes hydrocarbons, pathogenic bacteria and nitrates. Nitrogen and phosphorous removal by the plants is probably limited, but adsorption of phosphorus to the sand and gravel in the substrate would be effective if materials high in calcium or magnesium are used.

For stormwater treatment the effectiveness of the design at Hammarby Sjöstad is mixed. No treatment of runoff from the minor streets is a performance gap. The canal shown in Figure 12.25 collects water from roofs, terraces, walks and lawns. With the exception of the lawn areas, these surfaces don't generate runoff that is significantly contaminated. The water shown in the image isn't stormwater at all, but flow from a canal and lake to the east. With the exception of some sedimentation, there is little here to provide water quality improvement or delay of storm flows. The incidental wetland vegetation along the landscaped side of the canal is too narrow to be effective. Nevertheless, the canal is beautiful (drained and cleaned twice a year), continues the waterfront theme of the neighborhood and provides space for a promenade and space between the high-rise buildings offering solar access and privacy.

Biodiversity

The building density precludes much biodiversity, with two significant exceptions. The *Pharagmites* vegetation along the lake edge was preserved (Figure 12.22).

Figure 12.26
Two ecoducts connect Hammarby Sjöstad and the undeveloped land across the highway. Photo 59°18′19.96″ N, 18°05′59.86″ E, 12 September 2007 (accessed 15 April 2013) by Google Earth.

It provides habitat for juvenile fish and other aquatic organisms. The biodiversity gem of the project is the 14-acre preserved oak woodland (see Figure 12.27) at the northeast corner of the site. This natural area was retained at the insistence of the public for its scenic character and the iconic oaks that Stockholmers identify with.

Figure 12.27
The woodland within Hammarby Sjöstad preserved 150 old-growth oak trees.

Figure 12.28
The Hammarby ecoduct connects an urban canal green space and oak woodland to the more natural riparian corridor to the east. This landscape offers diverse habitat and water quality improvement functions.

Too small to function as an ecosystem, this habitat fragment is still home to species well adapted to human activity, as well as being a gorgeous place to stroll. The wildlife bridge across the highway on the southeast corner of the oak woodland (Figure 12.26) allows wildlife to move from the woodland to the riparian vegetation along the eastern canal (see Figure 12.28). A second wildlife crossing (these are called ecoducts in Sweden) is a connection for people, and perhaps wildlife, to the large undeveloped tract to the east.

Ecoducts are constructed to make links between green wedges or within them to mitigate a barrier to movement along a corridor. These are usually crossings over major highways. The Swedish transportation administration recommends a minimum ecoduct width of 120 feet (40 m). In addition, human use is to be limited and preferably allowed only during daylight hours, limited to one side of the structure and buffered with shrub planting, and with low or no lighting.[4]

Conclusion

Stockholm is a model for other cities. It integrates environmental and human systems at a variety of scales. The city is even willing to pursue the issue of climate change mitigation and adaptation, as few in the world have. The ridership on public transit and the level of pedestrian and bicycle use have resulted in significant reductions in

greenhouse gas emissions. These reductions have been extended significantly with efficient district heating and alternate energy technology. The per capita CO_2 emission in Stockholm is 3.7 metric tons, which is very low compared to New York City (7.1 tons), Washington, DC (19.7 tons) and London (5.3 tons). The city's goal is to achieve three metric tons by the end of 2015.

The regional plan for green wedges simultaneously locates future urban development in compact centers and tracts of habitat large enough to support species with large territory needs. The public transit links to satellite towns limits the impact of commuting to the regional city.

Stockholm is equally successful at the local scale, in part because of the regional structure. The excellent network of open space in Stockholm links a series of urban plazas with a waterfront promenade and trails through the National Urban Park. The extensive system balances ample recreation and social spaces (Figure 12.29) with preserved ecosystems that support rare native species. Hammarby Sjöstad illustrated the emerging use of stormwater management landscapes integrated into the urban context in numerous and attractive ways. The continuous green infrastructure supports human health with easily accessible opportunities for vigorous physical activity and for stress-reducing immersion into natural settings. The very large percentage of open space is possible due to excellent planning, the commitment of the government and citizens and the high-density residential and commercial development.

Figure 12.29
The scale and detail of open space is related to the context. This public residential garden in Hammarby Sjöstad has the character of a herb or community garden.

References

1   S. Fjord, "Regionalt miljöövervakningsprogram för Stockholms län 2009–2014," Environmental Department, County Administrative Board of Stockholm, Stockholm, Sweden, 2009.

2   E. Langby, "Regional Development Plan 2010 for the Stockholm Region," Stockholm Regional Planning Board, Stockholm, Sweden, 2010.

3   "Stockholm City Plan Summary," City Planning Administration, Stockholm, Sweden, May 2009.

4   B. Malmros, "När, vad och hur? Svaga Samband i StockholmS regioNeNS gröNa kilar," TMR (Growth, Environment and Regional Planning), Stockholm County Council, Stockholm, Sweden, 2012.

5   S.-I. Nylund, *Grönstruktur och landskap i regional utvecklingsplanering.* Stockholm: Regionplane-och trafikkontoret, Stockholms läns landsting, 2008.

6   J. Colding, "Stockholm Urban Assessment," *Millennium Ecosystem Assessment*, 2005. [Online]. Available: www.millenniumassessment.org/en/SGA.SwedenStockholm.html.

7   P. Schantz, "The Formation of National Urban Parks: A Nordic Contribution to Sustainable Development," in *The European City and Green Space: London, Stockholm, Helsinki and St Petersburg, 1850–2000*, Aldershot: Ashgate, 2006.

8   K. Lofvenhaft, M. Ihse and C. Bjorn, "Biotope Patterns in Urban Areas: A Conceptual Model Integrating Biodiversity Issues in Spatial Planning," *Journal of Planning Literature*, vol. 58, pp. 223–240, 2002.

9   U. Mörtberg and H.-G. Wallentinus, "Red-listed Forest Bird Species in an Urban Environment: Assessment of Green Space Corridors," *Landscape and Urban Planning*, vol. 50, no. 4, pp. 215–226, 2000.

10 E. Andersson and Ö. Bodin, "Practical Tool for Landscape Planning? An Empirical Investigation of Network Based Models of Habitat Fragmentation," *Ecography*, vol. 32, no. 1, pp. 123–132, 2009.

11 A. Nelson, "Stockholm, Sweden: City of Water," University of Washington, Case Study, 2006. [Online]. Available: http://depts.washington.edu/open2100/Resources/1_Open SpaceSystems/Open_Space_Systems/Stockholm_Case_Study.pdf (accessed 6 November 2012).

12 U. Mörtberg and Länsstyrelsen i Stockholms län, *Landskapsekologisk analys av Nationalstadsparken: underlag till Länsstyrelsens program för Nationalstadsparken.* Stockholm: Länsstyrelsen i Stockholms län, 2006.

13 M. Erman, "The Walkable City: The Concept of Stockholm," City Planning Administration, Stockholm, Sweden, May 2012. [Online]. Available: www.corp.at/archive/ppt/CORP2012_SLIDES24.pdf (accessed 15 January 2013).

14 A. Loukaitou-Sideris, "Urban Parks, UCLA Institute of the Environment and Sustainability." [Online]. Available: www.environment.ucla.edu/reportcard/article.asp?parentid=1455 (accessed 6 November 2012).

15 D. Vestbro, "Conflicting Perspectives on the Development of Hammarby Sjöstad, Stockholm." [Online]. Available: www.infra.kth.se/bba/HamSjo«stad.pdf (accessed 15 January 2013).

16 A. S. Maleitzke, "Sustainable Development in the Case of Hammarby Sjöstad, Stockholm," 2005. [Online]. Available: www.adammaleitzke.com/SPAN_Thesis_01.12.2007.pdf (accessed 15 January 2013).

17 J. Paques, "A New Wastewater Treatment Plant for Hammarby Sjöstad: A Comparative Study Between Four Alternatives," 2003. [Online]. Available: www.stockholmvatten.se/commondata/rapporter/avlopp/Sjostadsverket/R25_2004_Joost_Paques.pdf (accessed 15 January 2013).

18 J. Rutherford, "Unbundling Stockholm: The Networks, Planning and Social Welfare Nexus Beyond the Unitary City," *Geoforum*, vol. 39, no. 6, pp. 1871–1883, 2008.

19 City of Stockholm, "Hammarby Sjöstad: A New City District with Emphasis on Water and Ecology," Real Estate and Traffic Administration, Stockholm, Sweden, 2011.

20 L. Fränne, "Hammarby Sjöstad: A Unique Environmental Project in Stockholm," GlashusEtt, Stockholm, Sweden, 2007. [Online]. Available: www.hammarbysjostad.se (accessed 1 February 2013).

21 City of Stockholm, "Facts and Figures," City of Stockholm, 2010.

22 K. Brick, "Follow Up of Environmental Impact in Hammarby Sjöstad, Report Summary," Grontmij, Environmental Impact, 2008. [Online]. Available: www.hammarbysjostad.se/inenglish/pdf/Grontmij%20Report%20eng.pdf (accessed 1 February 2013).

23 K. Karlsson, M. Viklander, L. Scholes and M. Revitt, "Heavy Metal Concentrations and Toxicity in Water and Sediment from Stormwater Ponds and Sedimentation Tanks," *Journal of Hazardous Materials*, vol. 178, no. 1–3, pp. 612–618, 2010.

24 H. Alm, "Skelettjord: att hantera trafikdagvatten i stadsmiljö (Managing Traffic Water in Urban Areas)," Stockholm Vatten, Stockholm, Sweden, 2005.

CHAPTER THIRTEEN

Green infrastructure in context

Introduction

This book is based on the premise that the purpose of green infrastructure is to systematically integrate anthropomorphic and ecological patterns, functions and values[1] to support healthy ecosystems and provide goods and services that directly or indirectly benefit humans. The corridors and spaces that comprise a green infrastructure vary in their purpose and character. They reflect the great diversity of human and ecosystem needs. The corridors and spaces are best conceived as having multiple functions. Perhaps one purpose dominates others in some portions of the system, but the design for multiple functions will make virtually every place more sustainable economically, socially and environmentally. A multifunctional orientation will also break the cycle of achieving one purpose while creating other deficits that must be reconciled in the future.

It will be least expensive and result in better outcomes if green infrastructure is planned decades in advance of suburban or urban development. This is not to say that green infrastructure is a suburban or rural concept, although it should be applied to those contexts as well. Instead, it should be the organizing structure for the densest new urban development. In fact, population densities in excess of 20–30 units per acre is the context where green infrastructure will offer the greatest human and economic benefit.

Green infrastructure in existing cities

What is the role of green infrastructure in existing and densely developed urban centers where the opportunity for a network of corridors and spaces was squandered decades ago? Green infrastructure is restorative in these settings, and although expensive it is less costly than alternative approaches. The cases of Philadelphia and Milwaukee validate this claim. The old, failing combined sanitary and stormwater sewer system in Philadelphia incurs huge economic burdens for the treatment of wastewater, not to mention the environmental damage. Therefore, the city is converting 4,000 acres of impervious surfaces to pervious ones. The $1.6 billion dollar plan to replace and treat the stormwater flows from the roofs and impervious surfaces through the use of green roofs, permeable paving, bioretention basins and similar measures in the city is a bargain compared to other infrastructure or treatment alternatives.[2] This positive economic outcome is in addition to the many recreation, aesthetic, human health and biodiversity benefits that this book has documented.

The story of the Menomonee River Valley in Milwaukee is somewhat different. Originally a wild rice wetland, the valley was drained and filled in the 1800s to serve industry. Expansion of development included stockyards, railroad switching yards, heavy industry, an interstate highway and eventually the storage of coal, salt and other substances when the city began to deindustrialize. By the 1980s it was difficult to imagine a more hopelessly polluted and benighted place than this. Nevertheless, a plan emerged for the removal of the industrial infrastructure and pollution (300 contaminated acres have been restored). However, the plan included sites for new light industry and the jobs they bring (4,200 jobs have been created).[3]

In contrast to the first generation of industrial land use, the new vision integrated industry into a landscape that provided stormwater treatment, recreation, open space and habitat. Urban stormwater was collected in landscape fingers that extended between the buildings and conducted it to treatment wetlands (Figure 13.1). A 70-acre industrial park benefited since no storm sewers were needed, while the river ecosystem was significantly enhanced. The stormwater was contained and treated within the new 45-acre landscape filled with native plantings and wildlife habitat.[4] Flooding risks were reduced through riverbank restoration, while the public benefited from open space, miles of walking and bicycling trails and from new sports fields and a canoe ramp. In fact, the trail, the Hank Aaron State Trail, now has a "friends of" group (http://hankaaronstatetrail.org) dedicated to its continued maintenance, programming and expansion. The trail is 12 miles long and now connects to the 100-mile-long Oak Leaf Trail. Of course, there are awkward connections and less than optimal spaces and adjacent land-uses that one would expect

Figure 13.1
Menomonee River Valley stormwater park.

Figure 13.2
The green infrastructure is expanding by reconnecting the linear spaces and providing bridges to cross the river. Each new connection increases the population with access to facilities and restored natural areas.

from a retrofitted industrial district, but the green infrastructure here is continually improving (Figure 13.2). The land values and the tax revenue in the project area have increased at amazing rates. The cleaner river and the native plant habitat have improved the biological diversity. The site is used by schools for science education and by the community for an annual foot race and celebrations. In each of these categories, economics, environment and social, the green infrastructure is benefiting the community and ecosystem.

Slightly farther west the green infrastructure expands to include a regional park group (the 55-acre Milwaukee County Grounds, 51-acre Hanson Park, 20-acre Hoyt Park and 35-acre Gravel Sholes Park) with many attractions. This serves to illustrate the myriad components that can be assembled to form a green infrastructure plan. The design of the individual elements is beyond the scope of this book, but consideration of them as contributors to a systematic plan is germane. Using Figure 13.3 as a beginning, notice that the elements are linked by the Oak Leaf Trail that follows the riparian corridor of the river. At upper left a golf course is visible. In addition to their recreation purpose, golf courses can be designed to support birds and other wildlife, provide open space for the public and valuable residential development sites. The course route would better achieve its multifunctional goal if it were organized as a buffer between human settlement and wildlife habitat and ecological corridor. Specific species can be targeted for conservation within golf courses. For example, amphibians are a particularly vulnerable group. Research shows that habitat can be

Figure 13.3
The Menomonee Valley green infrastructure expresses the connectivity and variety of spaces of a well-developed system. The element that is absent is a corridor network through the residential and commercial districts. Another conspicuously missing relationship is high-density housing or mixed-use development adjacent to urban or natural open space.
43°3′6.95″ N, 88°1′46.50″ W.

created or preserved around the water features to successfully sustain viable amphibian populations in golf courses. For bird habitat development, golf course designers have clear planning and development guidelines through the Audubon Society Sanctuary Certification Program.

At the far left of Figure 13.3 a stream that was once in a culvert has been restored. However, other visible reaches flow in concrete channels. Nearby is a large community garden that, strangely, has extensive automobile access. This suggests that the location is wrong. It ought to be near high-density residential housing where there is little private open space for gardening.

A forest fragment is near a county flood control basin that forms an extensive wetland. The wooded area (about 45 acres/18 ha), the riparian corridor, a small amount of meadow and the extensive wetland represent a diversity of habitat types connected to each other. This heterogeneity supports a rich variety of species. The turquoise dot in the image is a popular swimming pool run by a non-profit organization on land leased from the county. Historically, the site of a swimming hole, the modern pool is not well located. It should be at the edge of the residential district where its extensive parking lot would be less intrusive.

Similarly, highways, many smaller streets and a railroad line compromise the parkland and represent barriers within the corridor for wildlife and cause high mortality due to collisions with automobiles. Furthermore, development is encroaching. A substantial portion of what seems to be parkland has been re-zoned for development by businesses and institutions. The protection of existing parkland is a matter for constant vigilance by the public. Transportation planners often regard parkland to be the solution to their problems. Even the public owners of the land

Figure 13.4
This development in Copenhagen maximizes mixed-use density, light rail transit and green infrastructure.

find development of parkland simple and inexpensive, rather than a resource to husband. In Figure 13.3, one of the encroaching buildings is the county park headquarters itself. Like other developers, the government should tackle the issues of brownfield redevelopment instead of the simpler and more profitable clearing of greenfields or forestland.

Despite these shortcomings, the green infrastructure here along the Menomonee River is a terrifically positive resource for the community. Milwaukee elected to focus its redevelopment and landscape restoration on the creation of jobs and sites for light industry, but many communities elect instead to create high-density, mixed-use developments. However a mixed-use development plan could have used the same concept of a central, open-space corridor with fingers of landscape extending into the development (Figure 13.1). In this case the fingers of landscape would serve as stormwater catchment, but also as urban plazas and urban parks for multistory buildings on the perimeter. Figure 13.4 demonstrates this model, as do portions of the Hammarby Sjöstad and Stapleton developments.

Higher-density development allows a greater percentage of the site to provide green infrastructure support and benefits. At somewhat lower density (Figure 13.5) a positive balance of 30 percent green infrastructure and 20–30 units per acre for housing creates a sustainable ecosystem and human environment.

The examples above from the Menomonee Valley stormwater park and green infrastructure illustrate several elements linked by the riparian corridor. While an

Figure 13.5
Capitol gateway photo by US Housing and Urban Development.

exhaustive list of potential elements may not be helpful, some categories and examples illustrate a heartening richness of opportunity. Beginning with water-related elements, the river and stream corridor provide ribbons to attach stormwater and wastewater treatment wetlands, but these can be augmented with fishing lakes, aquaculture ponds, reservoirs, irrigation canals, fish hatcheries, wharfs and docks. Swimming pools, spray pools for children and ornamental water gardens are small-scale elements appropriate to residential areas in contrast to wildlife refuges that often contain large water bodies and wetlands. However, to continue in the more urban context, many land uses or facility types can contribute to the green infrastructure. For example, schools, campuses, cemeteries, community gardens (allotments), memorials, botanic gardens and arboreta obviously offer symbiotic opportunities. Perhaps less obvious, but clearly benefiting with the proper site design, are hospitals, assisted care facilities, seniors' centers, recreation centers, zoos and sculpture gardens. While not all can be placed adjacent to riparian corridors, all of the facilities noted should be linked by pedestrian and bicycle routes separated from the motorized vehicular system where possible. At the highest urban density, boulevards and pedestrian promenades and boardwalks with more formally designed pools, canals and tree rows can link civic centers, residential and commercial plazas framed by multistory buildings.

In the context of the larger parcel, industrial, business and technology parks can be transformed from their traditions as temporary, speculative and destructive uses in the metropolis to contributors in more than the economic sense. Surely, the public is weary of paying for cleaning the toxic waste left behind when companies have exhausted the profits that can be extracted from their enterprises. Since this group of facilities consumes large tracts of land, it is especially important to plan for integration of habitat, ecological corridors and sustainable stormwater, waste treatment and transportation (Figure 13.6). Green roofs and permeable paving are especially appealing reinforcements for vegetated corridors and use areas in these

Figure 13.6
This stormwater
wetland is important
for the treatment of
stormwater from the
large buildings and
parking lots associated
with the suburban
business park.

districts. It should be noted that most light industrial and technology businesses would serve the community better if they were integrated into mixed-use neighborhoods rather than segregated in districts better reserved for companies that generate noxious substances, noise or large volumes of traffic.

Other facilities that can be reimagined as contributors to green infrastructure systems are military bases, sports fields, power line transmission corridors, irrigation canals and parking lots. These elements consume large amounts of land and can contribute significantly to habitat, connectivity and visual quality. To do so their development must be guided by a multifunctional orientation codified by ordinances, since the inertia of single-use thinking is well established for these uses. Underground utilities including potable water, stormwater, sewage, electricity and data can be included within corridors that separate the rear property lines of newly platted land. Maintenance and material costs over the long term could be much lower than when these are located below streets. A strip adjacent to paved pedestrian and bike paths would serve these utilities. The size of storm and sanitary sewers can be much reduced or eliminated by using landscape treatment techniques illustrated in this book.

For decades ecologists have advocated vegetated corridors separating residential housing in order to increase biological diversity.[5] Located where alleys were in traditional neighborhood design, these corridors could perform stormwater, community agriculture, recreation, path and habitat functions, as they do in Village Homes, [6] but at a municipal scale. The concept is applicable to higher-density commercial and residential development. The great benefit of this approach requires amendments to subdivision development ordinances.

Finally, the reestablishment of hedgerows or ecological corridors through land used for commodity agriculture to connect ecosystem preserves to each other is the large-scale companion to the municipal green infrastructure. It is important that these systems are linked to achieve maximum human and ecosystem benefits. Commercial forestry, oil and gas exploration and production, mining and other resource extraction activities join commodity agriculture in the need for modern design and management to produce the full range of ecosystem services.

Demonstration plan

The plan offered in Figure 13.7 is a physical plan drawn to scale to illustrate green infrastructure integration into new mixed-use development. The plan demonstrates the population and dwelling unit density of a compact neighborhood and includes a full range of land uses. The total area of the development is 427 acres. There are three general categories of residential development shown on the plan. A variety of housing types would be present in each category, but a minimum average is specified. In Figure 13.7, item C, high-density residential use (30 dwelling units per acre, du/ac), frames the central open space and the commercial district. Thirty units per acre are possible without the need for below-grade or structured parking. Therefore, this plan does not assume high-income residents in any housing category, although a proportion of residential buildings at 50 units or more per acre (with below-grade parking) would be desirable around the park. When open space is adjacent, then increasing density does not represent a decline in the quality of life of the residents.

Item L is mixed-density residential use with an average density of 20 units per acre, such as town houses and row houses. Item M is low-density residential, but with the continued expectation that the density varies within the district to meet a minimum average of nine units per acre. To achieve this, the lots would be small (4,800 ft^2) or include some two-, three- or four-family buildings.

The green infrastructure would provide the residents with a number of benefits. A school (item K) site (7.5 acres) is included that efficiently shares a public park space (11 acres). Two community gardens (2.8 acres) (item E) are included to serve residents without much private open space. A 60-feet-wide corridor (item B), over one mile long, circles the central open space. The width allows for bicycles, pedestrians, trees and space for exercise equipment and picnicking facilities along the path. This corridor buffers a habitat area (21 acres). The actual habitat area really includes the wastewater and stormwater treatment areas. The vertical subsurface flow and horizontal subsurface flow wetlands occupy two locations. One serves the residential area and the other serves the commercial district. The wetlands total is 17 acres. The free-water surface wetland (3 acres) is an amenity and habitat feature. The total area of the central open space is 61 acres.

The ecological corridors are 4.4 miles long and generally 60 feet wide. They serve both as wildlife corridors and stormwater swale and treatment areas. The corridors entering and exiting the site at the top and bottom of the image are 120 feet wide since they would connect to the larger municipal network. The wildlife/stormwater corridors comprise 31 acres.

The plan achieves 3,393 units and a total population of 8,483. There are 7.95 dwelling units per gross acre and a population density of 19.8 people per gross acre. Of course, the population density is much higher along the roads. The density of

Figure 13.7
A, community agriculture; B, ecological corridor; C, residential 30 du/ac average; D, wooded habitat; E, community garden; F, buildings; G, road and parking; H, vertical and horizontal flow wetlands; I, free-water surface wetland; J, bioretention basins; K, school and parkland; L, residential 20 du/ac average; M, residential 9 du/ac average; N, plaza planting area.

jobs generated was not estimated. Nevertheless, the plan meets the minimum standard of 19 for a total of residents and jobs needed to support light rail transit systems, even when considering density per gross acre and without the jobs estimate. The plan is based on three-story buildings, maximum, for the multi-family residential and mixed-use buildings. Therefore, density of population, dwellings units and jobs could be increased using the same footprint by adding building stories.

The open space, including habitat, corridors, wetlands, school grounds, park, community gardens, stormwater retention basins and a 4.5-acre urban agriculture plot, represents 27 percent (117 acres) of the development site. This is just slightly less than the 30 percent recommendation for provision of excellent access to recreation, positive views and good biodiversity with connections to regional habitat reserves.

Conclusion

The issues of human health and quality of life and the health of ecosystems are linked through an understanding of green infrastructure and the ecosystem services it offers. An understanding of these issues fosters collaborative solutions to multifaceted problems by planners, designers, health care professionals, government agencies and developers. Agreement on goals and standards can improve the widespread adoption of early comprehensive planning. The implementation of multifunctional components of a green infrastructure network will lead to a future of economic, environmental and social health.

References

1   K. Bomans, T. Steenberghen, V. Dewaelheyns, H. Leinfelder and H. Gulinck, "Underrated Transformations in the Open Space: The Case of an Urbanized and Multifunctional Area," *Landscape and Urban Planning*, vol. 94, no. 3–4, pp. 196–205, 2010.
2   J. Green, "Philadelphia's Cutting-edge Green Infrastructure Plan," *Uniting the Built and Natural Environments*, 10 May 2010. [Online]. Available: http://dirt.asla.org/2010/05/10/philadelphias-cutting-edge-green-infrastructure-plan (accessed 3 May 2013).
3   C. De Sousa, "Milwaukee's Menomonee Valley: A Sustainable Re-Industrialization Best Practice," Sustainable Brownfields Consortium, University of Illinois, Chicago, 2012.
4   D. Misky and C. Nemke, "Centralized Stormwater Management Key to Redevelopment Success," *Water World*, vol. 3, no. 4, n.p., 2009.
5   W. E. Dramstad, *Landscape Ecology Principles in Landscape Architecture and Land-use Planning*, Cambridge, MA: Harvard University Graduate School of Design, 1996.
6   M. Francis, "Village Homes: A Case Study in Community Design," *Landscape Journal*, vol. 21, no. 1–2, pp. 23–41, 2002.

Illustration credits

1.1   Google Earth © Google 2013, © TerraMetrics 2013.
1.2   Author, 2011.
1.4   Adapted from Tzoulas, 2007.
1.7   Author, 2008.
1.8   Dmadeo under license, GFDL or CC-BY-SA 3.0, 2.5, 2.0, 1.0.
1.9   Author, 2010.
1.10   Author, 2012.
2.1   Dawn Aroltta, Center for Disease Control. Government Work license.
2.2   Amanda Mills, CDC, Government Work license.
2.3   Haze. License CC-BY-SA-2.0.
2.4   Amanda Mills, CDC, Government Work license.
2.5   Mikael Häggström. License CC-BY-SA-3.0.
2.6   US Navy, Sean Evans. License – public domain.
2.7   David Iliff. License CC-BY-SA 3.0.
2.8   David Iliff. License CC-BY-SA 3.0.
2.10   David Iliff. License CC-BY-SA 3.0.
2.11   Daniel Hughes. License CC-BY-SA 3.0.
2.12   Nicholas A. Tonelli. License CC-BY-2.0.
3.1   Medocino National Forest, USFS, Government Work license.
3.2   USGS: Robert Morton, Jeremy Bracone, and Brian Cooke.
        http://pubs.usgs.gov/of/2007/1388/start.html.
3.3   Miguel Vieira. License CC-BY-2.0.
3.4   Daniel Schwen, License CC-BY-SA-3.0.
3.5   Google Earth, © Google 2013, © TerraMetrics.
3.6   US Fish and Wildlife Service, National Wetland Inventory,
        www.fws.gov/wetlands/Wetlands-Mapper.html.
3.7   Neal Herbert, US National Park Service, license Government Work.
3.8   Charles Young, USFWS.
3.9   USFWS, Joel Trick, Government Work license.
3.10   G. Brändle, Agroscope Reckenholz-Tänikon. License CC-BY-3.0.
3.11   John and Karen Hollingsworth, USFS Region 5.
3.12   D. Gordon E. Robertson. License CC BY-SA 3.0.
        http://commons.wikimedia.org/wiki/File:Hermit_Thrush_in_winter.jpg.
3.13   Eric Neitzel USFS Apache Sitgreaves National Forest.

3.14   Mike Goehle USFWS, Government Work license.
        RemovingWaterChestnutMikeGoehleUSFWS.jpg
4.1   Presse03. License CC-BY-SA-3.0.
4.2   Author, 2012.
4.3   Google Earth © Google 2013, GeoBasis-DE/BKG, 2009.
4.4   Garry Tucker USFWS.
4.5   Author, 2012.
4.6   USFS Northern Region, Government Work license.
4.7   Google Earth © Google 2013, © TerraMetrics 2013, Data SIO, NOAA, US
        Navy, NGA, GEBCO.
4.8   US Army Corps of Engineers, Government Work license.
4.9   Image from US Geological Survey, Government Work license.
4.10   Teresa Pratt, US EPA, Government Work license.
4.11   Austin, 2011.
4.12   Austin, 2011.
4.13   US Department of Energy, Argonne National Laboratory, Government
        Work license.
4.14   Walter Siegmund. License CC-BY-SA 3.0.
4.15   Garry Tucker, US Fish and Wildlife Service, Government Work license.
4.16   Author.
4.17   Dtobias. License CC-BY-SA 3.0.
4.18   NOAA, Government Work license.
4.19   Author, 2012.
5.1   Author, 2012.
5.2   Forest City, reprinted with permission.
5.3   Author, 2012.
5.4   Binh Giang, 2008. License, public domain.
5.5   Google Earth © Google 2013, © Gray Buildings, 2008 ZENRIN.
5.6   Google Earth © Google 2013, © Gray Buildings, 2008 ZENRIN.
5.7   Alastair Rae. License CC Share Alike 3.0 Unported.
5.8   NASA and the Visible Earth team. Government Work license.
5.9   LandsatEMT+NASA_USGS2000. Government Work license.
5.10   USGS, Robert Morton, Jeremy Bracone, and Brian Cooke, Government
        Work license.
6.1   Author, 2010.
6.2   Noah Elhardt. License CC-SA-2.0.
6.3   Author, 2011.
6.4   Google Earth, © Google 2013, © TerraMetrics.
6.5   David Iliff. License CC-BY-SA 3.0.
6.6   Author, 2011.
6.7   Google Earth, © Google 2013, © TerraMetrics
6.8   Google Earth, © Google 2013, Image © DigitalGlobe, 2013, Image ©
        TerraMetrics 2013.
6.10   Hawk: Dominic Sherony. License CC-SA 2.0. Capercaillie: David Palmer.
        License CC-SA-2.0. Marmot: Davefo. License CC-SA-3.0.
6.11   Author, 2011.

6.12   Graphic by Author.
6.13   Graphic by Author.
6.14   KlausFoehl, 2010. License CC-SA-3.0.
6.15   US Housing and Urban Development. Government Work license.
6.16   Author, 2011.
7.1   Author, 2012.
7.2   Author, 2009.
7.3   Author, 2012.
7.4   Author, 2012.
7.5   Author, 2010.
7.6   Author, 2010.
7.7   Google Earth. © Infoterra Ltd & Bluesky, 2013.
7.8   Google Earth. Image © Getmapping plc, © Infoterra Ltd & Bluesky, 2013.
7.9   Author, 2012.
7.10   Author, 2012.
7.11   Author, 2012.
7.12   Google Earth © Google 2013, © TerraMetrics 2013.
7.13   Author, 2012.
7.14   Slaunger. License CC-SA-3.0.
7.15   Author, 2012.
7.16   Author, 2012.
7.17   Author, 2012.
7.18   Author, 2012.
8.1   Author, 2012.
8.2   Author, 2011.
8.3   Author, 2013.
8.4   Author, 2012.
8.5   Author, 2013.
8.6   Mark Secrist, USFWS. License CC-SA-2.0.
8.7   Google Earth © Google 2013, © TerraMetrics 2013.
8.8   Author, 2011.
8.9   Google Earth © Google 2013, © TerraMetrics 2013, with overlay by
       Author.
8.10   Author, 2011.
8.11   Author, 2010.
8.12   Author, 2010.
8.13   Author, 2011.
8.14   Google Earth © Google 2013, © TerraMetrics 2013.
8.15   Leonard Rosen, city of Lenexa.
8.16   Author, 2011.
9.1   Author, 2009.
9.2   Author, 2012.
9.3   Author, 2009.
9.4   Author, 2009.
9.5   Author, 2009.
9.6   Bouba. License CC-SA-3.0.

9.7   H. Zell. License CC-SA-3.0.
9.8   Evaswrectmw. License CC-SA-3.0.
10.1 Author, 2011.
10.3 Author, 2011.
10.5 Google Earth, © Google 2013, © TerraMetrics, 2013.
10.6 Author, 2011.
10.7 Dwight Burdette. License CC-3.0.
10.8 Author, 2011.
10.9 Photo courtesy of University of British Columbia, 2010.
11.2 Author, 2011.
11.3 Graphic by Author, 2009.
11.4 Graphic by Author, 2009.
11.5 Jan Vymazal.
11.8 Blumberg Engineering. www.blumberg-engineers.com.
11.9 Author, 2012.
11.10 Author, 2007.
11.11 Dori. License CC-SA-3.0
11.12 Author, 2012.
11.13 Hans Brix, Aarhus University, Denmark.
11.14 Author, 2010.
12.1 Adapted from US Central Intelligence Agency, Government Work license, public domain.
12.2 Google Earth, © Google 2007, © Cnes Spot Image, 2013.
12.3 Google Earth, © Google 2013, © Cnes Spot Image, 2013.
12.4 Author, adapted from Regional Growth, Environment and Planning, Stockholm County Council: www.tmr.sll.se/english/RUFS-2010/Maps.
12.5 Author, 2012.
12.6 Google Earth, © Google 2013, © DigitalGlobe, 2013.
12.7 Author, 2012.
12.8 Shay Golan.
12.9 Author, 2012.
12.10 Author, 2012.
12.11 Author, 2012.
12.12 Author, 2012.
12.13 Google Earth © Google 2013, © Cnes Spot Image, 2013.
12.14 Author, 2012.
12.15 Author, 2012.
12.16 Author, 2012.
12.17 Author, 2012.
12.18 Author, 2012.
12.19 Author, 2012.
12.20 Author, 2012.
12.21 Author, 2012.
12.22 Author, 2012.
12.23 Author, 2012.
12.24 Author, 2012, based on Alm 2005.

12.25   Author, 2012.

12.26   Google Earth, © Google 2013, © Cnes Spot Image, 2013.

12.27   Author, 2012.

12.28   Author, 2012.

12.29   Author, 2012.

13.1   Aaron Volkening. License CC-BY-2.0.

13.2   Edgar Mendez, Milwaukee Neighborhood News Service. License CC-BY-3.0.

13.3   Google Earth, 2007, Data SIO, NOAA, US Navy, NGA, GEBCO.

13.4   Author, 2012.

13.5   Government Work license.

13.6   Author, 2009.

13.7   Author, 2013.

Index